The Road to Rome

Travel and travellers between England and Italy
in the Anglo-Saxon centuries

Stephen Matthews

BAR International Series 1680
2007

This title published by

Archaeopress
Publishers of British Archaeological Reports
Gordon House
276 Banbury Road
Oxford OX2 7ED
England
bar@archaeopress.com
www.archaeopress.com

Archaeopress
10 years

BAR S1680

The Road to Rome: Travel and travellers between England and Italy in the Anglo-Saxon centuries

ISBN 978 1 4073 0118 1

Printed in England by CMP (UK)l

Cover image: S. Maurice and the Alps

All BAR titles are available from:

Hadrian Books Ltd
122 Banbury Road
Oxford
OX2 7BP
England
bar@hadrianbooks.co.uk

The current BAR catalogue with details of all titles in print, prices and means of payment is available
free from Hadrian Books or may be downloaded from www.archaeopress.com

CONTENTS

Acknowledgements

Many people have helped me along the way: but most I would like to thank Sheila Sharp and John McSween who read and commented upon earlier drafts, Jane Jordan and Dr Alex Rumble who provided translations and above all Dr David Hill whose Anglo-Saxon course was the origin of my study and whose support and encouragement have been unfailing ever since. The faults that remain are mine, not theirs. David Davison and especially Wendy Logue at Archaeopress, and most patient of all has been my wife, Jill, who must at times have been bored beyond reason. In spite of all, she helped right to the end, with the index, for which much thanks.

I am grateful too, to the various publishers and authors who have allowed me to cite from their publications. Most are acknowledged in the Documentary Appendix but I would like to thank the following particularly for their generosity in giving me permission to reproduce the longest of my extracts:

Stephen Allott, for extracts from his *Alcuin of York* (1974).

Columbia University Press, for
E. Emerton, (edited and translated), *The Letters of Boniface* (1940).
S. Lopez and I.W. Raymond, *Medieval Trade in the Mediterranean World* (1990).
J. Tschan (trans.), *Adam of Bremen, the history of the bishops of Hamburg and Bremen* (1959),

Continuum International Publishing Group for extracts from
C.H. Talbot, *The Anglo-Saxon Missionaries in Germany* (1954)
F.G. Sitwell, *St Odo of Cluny, being the life of St Odo of Cluny by John of Salerno and the Life of St Gerald of Aurillac by St Odo* (1958).

Edward Arnold (Publishers) Ltd., for (eds) H.R. Loyn and J. Percival, *The reign of Charlemagne* (London 1975). © H.R. Loyn and John Percival 1975.

Jane Jordan, for extracts from her unpublished translation of *De Raris Fabulis*.

Liverpool University Press for *Gregory of Tours, The Glory of the Martyrs*, Translated by Raymond van Dam (1988)

Penguin Books Ltd for
Gregory of Tours, The History of the Franks, translated by Lewis Thorpe (1974). Copyright © Lewis Thorpe 1974.
Bede's Ecclesiastical History of the English People, trans. Leo Sherley-Price (1990). Copyright © Leo Sherley-Price 1968.
Bede's Lives of the Abbots from D.H. Farmer (ed.), *The Age of Bede* (1983). Translation copyright © J.F. Webb 1965.
Notker's Life of Charlemagne, Translated by Lewis Thorpe (1969). Copyright © Lewis Thorpe 1969.

Springer Science and Business Media for Graydon W. Regenos (trans.), *The letters of Lupus of Ferrieres* (1996), originally published by Martinus Nijhoff.

Weidenfeld and Nicholson, for *The Anglo-Saxon Chronicles*, translated and edited by Michael Swanton (2000).

N.D. Wykes, for extracts from B. Colgrave, *The Life of Wilfrid, by Eddius Stephanus* (1985).

The age of some of the translations has made it hard to find copyright holders: if any have been missed or remain unacknowledged, I beg their forgiveness and a suitable entry will be made should this book ever be reprinted.

LIST OF ILLUSTRATIONS

Apart from numbers 1, 6 and 9, the illustrations are intended to illustrate the topography and thus the physical difficulties of the route.

ABBREVIATIONS

Allott	S. Allott, *Alcuin of York*
Asser	Alfred P. Smyth, *The Medieval Life of Alfred the Great* (Palgrave 2002)
BHE	Bede's *Ecclesiastical History of the English People* (1990)
Birch	Birch W. de Grey, *Cartularium Saxonicum* (1885-99)
BLA	Bede's *Lives of the Abbots of Wearmouth and Jarrow* (1983)
Chronicle	M. Swanton (trans.), *The Anglo-Saxon Chronicles* (2000)
Eddius	B. Colgrave (ed. and trans.), *The Life of Wilfrid by Eddius Stephanus* (1985)
EHD	D. Whitelock, English Historical Documents, I (1979)
GP	William of Malmesbury, *Gesta Pontificum Anglorum*, N.E.S.A. Hamilton (ed.) (1870)
GR	*Gesta Regum Anglorum,* trans. Mynors et al., (1998), Vol. 1. (1998)
H&S	Haddon A.W. and Stubbs W., *Councils and Ecclesiastical documents relating to Great Britain and Ireland* (3 vols 1869-71)
Jaffe	P. Jaffe, *Regesta Pontificum Romanorum* (Leipzig 1885-8)
JW	John of Worcester, *Chronicon ex Chronicis,* R. R. Darlington and P. McGurk (eds) (1995)
OEC	V. Ortenberg, *England and the Continent in the tenth and eleventh centuries* (Oxford 1992)
LP8	R. Davis, *The Lives of the Eighth century Popes* [Liber Pontificalis], (Liverpool 1992)
LP9	R. Davis, *The Lives of the Ninth century Popes* [Liber Pontificalis], (Liverpool 1995)
Moore	W.J. Moore, *The Saxon Pilgrims to Rome and the Schola Saxonum* (Friburg 1937)
RFA	B.W. Scholz, *Carolingian Chronicles* (Michigan UP 1970)
Talbot	C.H. Talbot, *Anglo Saxon Missionaries in Germany* (1954)
Tyler	J.E. Tyler, *The Alpine Passes* (1939)
VER	*Vita Edwardi Regis* (The life of King Edward), F. Barlow (ed. and trans.) (1962)
WBB	Whitelock D., Brett M., and Brooke C.N.L., *Councils and Synods with other documents relating to the English church* (1981)

NOTE: In the text I have avoided tiresome repetition by referring to the *Anglo-Saxon Chronicle* simply as the *Chronicle*. Other annals containing the same word are given in full.

For brevity, many footnotes give short titles only: full publication details are given in the bibliography.

CHAPTER 1

INTRODUCTION

This book started its life as a study of people travelling between England and Rome from the Augustinian Mission until the close of the Anglo-Saxon period but that proved to be too limiting a subject, for two reasons. One was that so much of the evidence about how people travelled around lay in continental sources and it seemed foolish to ignore it simply as a matter of principle. The second is that the means by which people travelled proved to be so exhaustive a study that it led into all kinds of by-ways: accommodation, money carrying and changing, safety, language and a whole range of human problems that still exist in modern travel but are more easily solved for the traveller, usually by other people. It was not enough to catalogue the travellers, even in the painstaking detail that Wilfrid Moore had done seventy years ago (albeit only up to AD 800): the question turned to, how did they manage to do it before the days of organised mass travel in the high middle ages? The later centuries have been better studied, but the earlier ones have not.

The result is thus something of a hybrid: more than a study of English sources alone, but less than a study of the whole of European travel. The theme is primarily the north-south routes that converged on the Alps and joined the north of Europe to Italy. Where appropriate, I have confined my evidence to material from England, that is, to those people who made the journey and their motives, the timing and duration of their journeys, and the routes that they followed. Elsewhere, in sections which address the mechanics of travel, I have widened the range of sources, to include material from all Anglo-Saxon sources irrespective of where the journey was made, provided that it was compatible with a journey to Rome. I have also adopted some contemporary foreign parallels where Continental experience would match English. Thus I have included material ranging from Gregory of Tours at the beginning of our period, and Albert of Stade, some time after the end. In including these additional sources I have tried to throw light on the problems of travellers to and from England rather than provide what would be an inadequate description of the whole of continental travel. Apart from a few references I have excluded the generality of Welsh, Irish and Scottish travellers because their travels introduce a range of different issues.

The north-south routes were essentially land journeys and the sources give us few glimpses of real life at sea. Most references to sea travel are stock description, whether written by the travellers themselves, like the report from the

Papal envoys of 786, or from those who were probably land based commentators. A few narrators give the impression of having been to sea, but others use stock descriptions. Aidan's advice to Utta [D17.8] sounds as if it came from a man who had crossed the North Sea, whilst the author of the *Encomium Emmae* must have been familiar with boats and anchorages [D71].[1] Alcuin's picture of the sailors at York must also be a memory of boats moored by long tow-ropes, perhaps in tidal waters [D71.6]. The author of the enigmatic poem *The Seafarer* similarly seems to have had actual experience at sea, for the opening passage has a reality unlikely to arise from a third party [D71.5]. In contrast, the advice given by the exiled husband to his wife that she should set off across the sea to join him as soon as 'you hear the cuckoo singing sad amid the grove' is no more than generalisation and poetic colour.[2]

My reason for limiting the time span of the evidence so severely is that it is easy to fall into the trap of treating the medieval period of a thousand years as one with little change between AD 500 and 1500. The European economies were totally transformed during that millennium and we must not assume that the travel industry was as well developed the whole way through with no change. Lodging and shipping arrangements changed dramatically as did the numbers of people on the move and a study of as basic a provision as the siting and fortunes of hostels would give illuminating insights into the changing flow and volume of traffic. War and political alliances played their part in determining the route, as we shall see. There was a great deal of change even within the five hundred years included within this survey both in the routes and in the facilities available, and that makes it worthy of study in its own right.

Secondary Works

Anglo-Saxon travel has received little interest as a subject of its own. There are references in more general works (listed in the bibliography) such as those by Ohler or Leighton but these cover a wider canvas and they do not point the changes and developments in our period. There are illuminating passages by Levison and more recently Ortenberg but these are concerned more with the fact and the consequences of the contacts between nations than with the journey in its own right. The classic study of

---

[1] Passages in the documentary appendix are identified in the commentary by the prefix letter D followed by a number.

[2] R. Hamer, *A Choice of Anglo-Saxon Verse*, pp. 79.

the early part of the period is by Moore but he included Englishmen who went to Rome from all Continental sites not just from England. He, too, was primarily interested in who made the journey and said little about how it was made. There are valuable studies of Archbishop Sigeric's visit to Rome in 990 but these concentrate upon the route taken and not its difficulties: they throw only an incidental light upon other travellers and their ways. The route was often determined by politics. Commercial, diplomatic and similar traffic could easily be interrupted, and despite the theoretically neutral status accorded to a pilgrim, warring states and greedy officials posed difficulties for them too and this aspect, generally little considered, has been illuminated by Christie's study of the Lombards. Whilst not directly concerned with pilgrim traffic his exploration of the power politics of northern Italy does much to explain why it is likely that the Alpine route did not emerge as the preferred way until after the Carolingian destruction of the Lombard kingdom. Diana Webb's *Pilgrims and Pilgrimage in the Medieval West* has a few references to the early centuries but she too concentrates upon motive rather than method.

Tyler examined the trade routes through the Alpine passes from the mid-tenth century onwards and his book is a mine of information on travellers of all nationalities. He did address the technical difficulties of travel and although his graphic accounts of the hazards of the journey were drawn in the main from after our period they still provide useful parallels.

Levison demonstrated the influence of England upon the Continent in the eighth century and Ortenberg has followed him by exploring the innumerable cultural exchanges in the last two centuries even when we did not always know the people involved. I have considered a more limited group for I have confined my study to people whom we know went, whether or not we know their names, and those whose journeys can reasonably be inferred. I do not claim to have provided an exhaustive list of everyone who made the journey and leaving aside error or oversight there can often be room for debate about whether a particular individual existed and should be included. Some references may simply be fictional, such as the rich Thegn who went to Rome vainly seeking a cure before coming home and being cured by St Swithun.[3] He may have existed or he may have been invented only to illustrate the power of the Saint. Another possibly fictitious traveller is an English priest, Volmarus, who reached Rome seeking a cure for

blindness. There, he was advised to go to the shrine of St Adalbert at Egmond, on the Dutch coast near Haarlem, where the necessary miracle occurred.[4] Even seemingly unimpeachable evidence can be misleading. Although at first sight Gervase of Canterbury seems reliable in his record of the Archbishops of Canterbury, his accounts must be treated with caution. He gives fair detail, for example, of Plegmund's first journey to Rome, to receive the pallium from Pope Formosus, although it almost certainly did not take place.[5] On the other hand Sigeric, who undoubtedly did go, merits no more than a variant of a stereotyped formula which by itself would suggest that he received the pallium by messenger.

Much more recently, and while I was assembling material for this book, McCormick's comprehensive work opened up a whole range of new ideas, centring upon trade.[6] I cannot emulate his scholarship and his book is essential reading for an understanding of the economic background to my travellers. There are important differences of approach from this work. For a start, our periods overlap, for he started at AD 300 and finished at 900, while I start in the sixth and continue until the eleventh century. This book is centred more on travel to and from the north of Europe and across the continent, rather than within the Mediterranean basin, as is apparent in a comparison of our lists of known travellers. Finally, I have included a lengthy appendix of texts which illustrate the mechanics of travel, instead of simply mentioning and referencing the events. That said, I, like everyone else, stand in his shadow.

The documents in the appendix are all translated. Most of these have been taken from published versions and I am grateful to the various authors and publishers whose consent has been acknowledged above. I am aware of the dangers involved in using translations and on a few occasions I have included the original text where either I do not feel that the translation accurately reflects the original author's meaning, or there is room for ambiguity. In the overwhelming number of cases, the meaning is perfectly clear.

Inevitably much of what follows overlaps what others have written. We are all using the same material though for different purposes. What I have sought to do is to sketch the *who*, the *why* and above all, the *how* of Anglo-Saxon travel to Rome, using sources which as far as possible spring from that period.

---

[3] Ælfric's 'Life of St Dunstan'; Migne, PL cxxxiii 933ff; D. Dales, *St Dunstan*, p. 53.

[4] Cited in Michael Hare, 'Abbot Leofsige of Mettlach: an English monk in Flanders and Upper Lotharingia in the late tenth century', *Anglo-Saxon England* 33, pp. 109-144. The episode is recorded in the *Vita S. Adalberti*, written 977 x 993.

[5] See, S. Matthews, 'Archbishop Plegmund and the Court of King Alfred', *Journal of the Chester Archaeological Society* 74 (1999).

[6] M. McCormick, *Origins of the European economy. Communications and commerce, AD 300-900.*

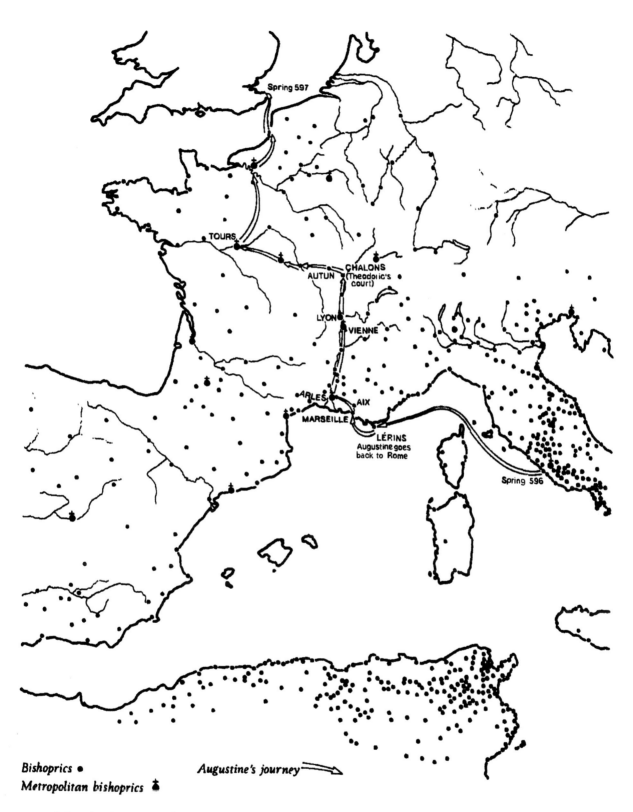

Spring 597

TOURS

CHALONS
(Theodoric's
court)

AUTUN

LYON

VIENNE

ARLES

AIX

MARSEILLE

LÉRINS
Augustine goes
back to Rome

Spring 596

Bishoprics ●
Metropolitan bishoprics ♦

Augustine's journey ⟶

MAP 1. AUGUSTINE'S ROUTE IN 597. FROM D. HILL, *AN ATLAS OF ANGLO-SAXON ENGLAND*

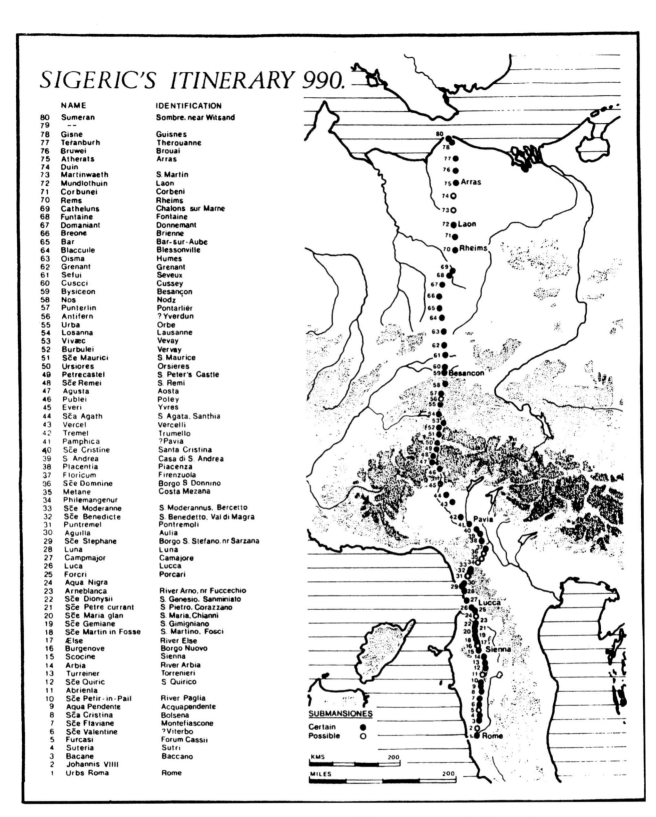

MAP 2. ARCHBISHOP SIGERIC'S ROUTE IN 990, COURTESY OF DR DAVID HILL.

CHAPTER 2

THE SOURCES

In drafting this book, I became aware that the various passages that illustrate travel were being used several times in different contexts, which led to frequent repetition and a sense of having read it all before. I also used extracts from longer texts in different places and this caused them to lose much of the impact that they had when read as a whole. I therefore decided to divide the book into two parts, starting with argument and narrative, followed by a second half, which is an appendix of documents in roughly chronological order. Although the reader may find that reference to the appendix breaks the flow, I believe that the result enables the longer passages to stand as narrative much better. I have not carried this to extreme, for I have kept some shorter passages in the main text where it reads better to do so, as well as putting them in the appendix.

The sources

With few exceptions references to travel itself are incidental. Usually, the last thing that the narrators were interested in was how the travellers reached their destination. It is unfortunate that we have no record for the journey to Rome as detailed as the Guide for the pilgrim to Santiago, which was written in the twelfth century but incorporated older material. Two continental texts from the late tenth century do provide an unusual wealth of information; the *Life of St Gerald of Aurillac* and a chapter in Richer's *History of France* in which Richer himself vividly described his journey from Rheims to Chartres. Richer's story is rare in coming straight from the mouth of the traveller; for most others were written by a biographer or like Willibald's journeys, a listener. Eddius probably accompanied Wilfrid on most of his travels, but kept his own feelings well in the background. By contrast, some accounts did manage to display a remarkable degree of feeling, for few people could read the story of Ceolfrid's departure for Rome without appreciating the real sense of loss and impending tragedy felt by the narrator.

Most specific references to people and places are found in records such as the *Anglo-Saxon Chronicle* and Bede's *Ecclesiastical History* together with the later Anglo-Norman writers. They are supplemented by continental sources such as the *Royal Frankish Annals* and Flodoard's *History*. There is much detail in individual Lives such as Bede's *Lives of the Abbots*, Eddius' *Life of Wilfrid* and Asser's *Life of Alfred*. The *Lives* of the missionary

Saints, Willibald, Boniface and others add detail, though disappointingly little considering their journeys and adventures. In this genre one exception is the *Life* of the Norican, St Sturm, where we do receive an immediate picture of life on the road. Gregory of Tours is a mine of incidental information for the beginning of the period and the circumstances he described must still have been familiar to later travellers. There are interesting but generally unspecific references in Wills and Charters. The importance of the account of Archbishop Sigeric's return journey from Rome is witnessed by the amount that has been written about it and the scrutiny it has received. It is our only English detailed and specific record of the potential stopping places along the way, but as we shall see it closely matches another detailed continental route.

The two colloquies *De Raris Fabulis* and its later variant *De Raris Fabulis Retractata* contain in their jumbled elements the record of a journey to Rome, either actual or idealised.[7] It has been cut about and merged with other material to produce a schoolroom text of gradually increasing complexity but in its original form, which I have tried to reconstruct in part, it must have given the prospective traveller useful general information about the journey. One particular passage echoes the bilingual travel aids in Old High German and Latin available on the Continent, and these are also considered. The Colloquies contain several elements and it is now hard to establish the exact order and internal division so that there can be no absolute certainty about where some particular passages belong. For our purpose that may not matter for there may well be little difference between conditions of travel at home and abroad. Both texts borrow from a common original; they overlap but the shorter, *Retractata*, adds substantially more of the travel text. Although *Fabulis* is generally treated as a Welsh or Cornish text because of its glosses, it is not at all certain that all its elements originate from either place nor is there is any reason to suppose that the underlying travel text did so. Whatever its exact form, the text gives us much useful information upon how a party of travellers actually operated and matches shorter references in the record of known journeys, such as Willibald's. The present manuscripts date from the tenth and early eleventh centuries but although the underlying originals are obviously older, it is not possible to put a date to them.

---

[7] W.H. Stevenson, *Early Scholastic Colloquies*.

One of a group of little used documents is the *Liber Vitae* of the monastery of S. Salvatore in Brescia on the pilgrim route southwards from the Alps.[8] As a source this presents as many problems as opportunities. At first sight the entry of an Anglo-Saxon name in the list suggests that the person passed through the monastery and this is borne out by otherwise well attested visitors like King Æthelwulf. Unfortunately that is not necessarily the case, for an entry can mean no more than that the named individual wished (or was wished) to be remembered by the community in their prayers. Professor Keynes raised that question in connection with Æthelbald, Æthelwulf's second son, for whom there is no other evidence that he went to Rome and indeed the best existing record, the Papal letter, suggests that Alfred went on his own. The most likely interpretation is that the entry of his name was an act of remembrance. A similar question hangs over Æthelswyth, the West Saxon wife of the Mercian King Burgred, who fled to Rome after his defeat by the Vikings in 874. Her journeys are discussed below and it is best to conclude by echoing Keynes' observation that in the case of any particular individual the judgement may reflect wishful thinking rather than solid evidence. The undoubted value of the entries lies in the supposition that either the named individual took that route across the Alps or that someone else who wished his name to be remembered did so. Thus, in the case of a well-attested traveller like Æthelwulf, we may conclude with reasonable certainty that he took a more easterly route rather than over the direct St Bernard. The association of Marcoardus with him in the *Liber Vitae* supports this, for as Keynes observed, it is an open question whether the latter stayed at Prum after his retirement. If he did, the easterly route becomes more probable. However, even this supposition needs modification, for entries could be copied from one *Liber Vitae* to another and if that happened even the route cannot be established with certainty. The source must therefore be used with caution both as a means of identifying actual travellers, and their route.[9] This is especially so if there is no other sure evidence of their journey.

Scattered and sometimes fragmentary though these sources are, put together they paint a clear picture of the considerations and problems that faced the Anglo-Saxon traveller to Rome, as well as the satisfaction that many obtained from completing the journey.

---

[8] Simon Keynes, 'Anglo-Saxon entries in the Liber Vitae of Brescia', in (eds) J. Roberts and J.L. Nelson, *Alfred the wise. Studies in honour of Janet Bately*, pp. 99-119.

[9] Keynes, *Liber Vitae*, pp. 89-90, 92-94.

Chapter 3

The Timing, Planning and Duration of Journeys

The sources do not tell us much about how long it took to get to Rome or the time of year when the journey was best made. Two questions can be posed at the start. First, how did people know when to start the journey and did they have any real choice in the matter? Second, were people aware of and prepared for the physical hazards of the journey? The evidence is patchy but it is worth reviewing what exists to see whether there is any pattern of when journeys were made. Appendix 3 catalogues some journeys where there is sufficient evidence, taking the starting date where known, or otherwise working backwards from an arrival time. Some of them also illustrate the problems of the journey.

We have little direct evidence as to the thought processes that determined a departure time and generally we have to infer the reasons from the few facts that we have. There is also little evidence to show whether travellers were aware of or concerned by the dangers or whether they took hazards as they came. The dangers were physical, which could be anticipated, and those stemming from human behaviour, from politics or lawlessness, which could not. Even though it was hard to plan journeys so as to avoid trouble, it is remarkable how few instances of human interference are recorded. Flodoard reported a number of occasions when the Alpine Saracens interfered with travellers [D51]. Ealdwulf was captured by pirates in the Channel in 809 [D39.8] and in 1061 Tostig was ambushed and robbed on his return, probably only a day out of Rome [D74.1]. Gerald of Aurillac had two of his horses stolen, but managed to recover them easily [D62.12]. Odo of Cluny had a similar experience, with one horse, and was attacked by a yokel, who was restrained by bystanders.[10] Generally, too much has been made of these and other episodes, for in truth they represent the occasions when the normal expectation of safe passage failed and are exceptions rather than the norm. Two examples may be given to demonstrate the seeming normality of travel even in apparently dangerous times. The *Chronicle* records the journeys of Æthelhelm and Abbot Beornhelm to Rome, in 887 and 890 respectively. In both years the Vikings were active in northern France:

> [886-7] Here the raiding-army went up through the bridge at Paris, and then up along the Seine as far as the Marne, and then up the Marne as far as Chezy; and then settled there [and] on the Yonne, two winters in those

two places...And in the same year in which the raiding-army went out up over the bridge at Paris, Ealdorman Æthelhelm took the alms of the West Saxons and of King Alfred to Rome.

> [890] Here Abbot Beornhelm took the alms of the West Saxons and of King Alfred to Rome ... And the same year [889] the raiding-army went from the Seine to St Lo which is between the Bretons and the Franks; and [890] the Bretons fought against them and had the victory, and drove them out into a river and drowned many.

These passages serve to remind us of the small scale of early medieval warfare and the ability of a small party to pass undetected at sea, simply because of the short range of visibility. In their paper on William the Conqueror's crossing of the Channel, the Grainges demonstrated the difficulties of mounting an effective coastal watch and the constraints that they listed applied not only throughout our period, but long after.[11] It also raises the question of how much travellers knew of events further along the road. Good forward intelligence was useful and we will see examples of questions that could be and were asked to avoid trouble.

The physical dangers were the effort required and the two extremes of cold and heat, coupled with the illnesses that arose from them. Unless a sea route was taken, the Alps had to be crossed by either a western pass, such as the Mont Cenis or the Great St Bernard, with the option of a central one if the traveller had followed the Rhine. The Mont Cenis does not feature in the English record of known routes, though it may have been used without record. Such evidence as we have indicates that for Englishmen the usual route became that over the higher Great St Bernard, the saving in distance presumably outweighing the harder double crossing not only of that but of the Jura to the north.[12] Was it better to cross the passes in the summer when the conditions were better? If travellers were able to plan the departure date, that might have seemed the obvious choice, especially for the aged or infirm, or those travelling on their own or in small parties. Nevertheless, a summer crossing presented a major hazard once the passes had been cleared, for the southbound traveller had next to suffer the intense heat and malarial fevers of the Po valley.

---

[10] Sitwell, *Life of St Odo of Cluny*, bk. II, chs 9 and 10.

[11] C. and G. Grainge, 'The Pevensey Expedition: Brilliantly executed plan or near disaster?', S. Morillo (ed), *The Battle of Hastings*.

[12] Tyler, p. 21.

One wonders whether the people who died in or around Pavia did so from frostbite or fever. Was fever the cause of the disaster that overtook King Lothar and his companions at Piacenza in 869? It seems likely also that Carloman's army brought it back to Germany on its return from Italy in 877 [D42].

If the traveller was going north a late crossing led onto the north European winter with all its difficulties. Was it better after all to risk the snows, which might well be familiar to the northern traveller, with a harder crossing of the Alps, in order to have an easier run from then on? There is no direct statement from our period of how English people felt but it is worth quoting from one of three crossings cited by Tyler for later periods. From just after the end of the Anglo-Saxon period we have the record of Henry IV's crossing of the Mt Cenis in 1076-7, which Tyler remarked was a particularly severe winter [D81]. Despite the difficulties, they crossed. There is no indication in the narrative that the journey could not have been deferred until better weather, rather the implication is that such hazards were an accepted if difficult part of travel which had to be endured. This tone is echoed elsewhere as when John of Worcester recorded the death of Archbishop Ælfsige from frostbite. He did not suggest that the Archbishop was doing anything courageous, exceptional or even foolish in making what was presumably a winter crossing. It is simply a bald statement. Although it was given more colour and detail by William of Malmesbury [D56.3] there is still no hint of exceptional or heroic behaviour. Although I have no record of any other Anglo-Saxon who was defeated, people might nevertheless have been deterred by the snows. One who did delay his crossing was Isaac the Jew who stayed in Vercelli for the winter of 801-2 on his way back to Charlemagne's court [D39.4 and 5]. He had a reasonable excuse for he was bringing back a prized elephant and could not take the risk of losing it.

We have occasional glimpses of the organisation required to launch a party of travellers on its way. It may be that individuals set out on their own, clutching a few possessions, but their chances of reaching a distant destination were probably slim. The odds probably improved over the centuries but the age of the lone traveller soon passed – if it ever existed – for it was replaced in the high middle ages by a variety of mass tourism, of the kind described by Mitchell in her account of the mid-fifteenth century journey to Jerusalem.[13] Larger parties needed to be organised and we return elsewhere referred to the likelihood of some degree of internal structure. The visits of senior figures, whether lay or clerical, must have been meticulously planned in advance, starting with a decision on the route to be taken and the obtaining of consent from the relevant authorities. The 839 entry in the *Royal Frankish Annals* is significant in pointing to the need for the kind of planning as also are the many references to the obtaining of passports and letters of introduction. Two well-documented arrangements are

[13] R.J. Mitchell, *The Spring Voyage.*

those for the visits of Archbishop Æthelheard to Rome in 801, and that of Lupus of Ferrières in 849. The former appears first to have written to Alcuin asking for help. Alcuin replied, sending him a saddle and arranging for him to be met by a courier of Alcuin's at S Josse [D38.9]. By implication the 'boy' was to see the party across Europe and back again. Alcuin next wrote to Charlemagne asking the king to ensure that proper hospitality was offered, as the Archbishop had requested. Finally, when the journey was over Alcuin wrote to both archbishops, of Canterbury and York, expressing his pleasure that the journey had been safely completed, a fact which he must have learned either from his 'boy' or from an archiepiscopal letter which has not survived. Similar advance arrangements can be seen in Lupus of Ferrières' business trip to Rome, in his successive letters asking for assistance, money and accommodation along the way [D46].

A few journeys are well documented and a notable early one was that of Abbot Ceolfrid who left Northumbria in June 716 and died in Langres the following September [D29]. He did not make good progress, especially bearing in mind that the early part of his journey was by sea and it may be that his infirmity slowed the party. The fact that it was a large group, over eighty people, may well have contributed to this. One wonders whether, had he lived a few months longer, he would have found the strength to cross the Alps in October or November, or whether he would have deferred the crossing until the following spring. Neither Bede's nor the 'Anonymous' narrative is explicit but they suggest that the start had been delayed until there was good weather for departure. It is not clear, therefore, whether Ceolfrid had thought about the consequential Alpine crossing before he left. Had he moved faster and been in better health he could have crossed before the worst of winter. We simply do not know what governed his movements. Although we do not know Ceolfrid's thoughts the next examples show that others might have made better plans.

In his *Life of Boniface*, Willibald tells us that the Saint began to plan his departure to Rome as soon as the winter was over but that he was delayed by the need to appoint a successor. When that was done he diverted to London to take ship for Quentovic. It is not clear why he did so for a more obvious route would have been from Nursling to Southampton and then across the Channel. He had sailed from London to Frisia before, which is a logical route, and it may be that he preferred a familiar departure point. Possibly he had some business in London on the way. Having arrived at Quentovic and waited for the rest of his party he then set out straightaway for Rome, because he was aware of 'the passing of the days (and) the threat of winter.' [D20.2]. A little later, Willibald himself followed the same timetable [D24.2]. Passages such as these suggest some awareness of the time scale involved, the critical points to be passed and perhaps most significantly, a willingness to cross the Alps at a time other than mid-summer. There is no suggestion of their planning a summer crossing nor of their waiting for the snows to clear next spring and one can only wonder what were the criteria for a 'suitable time' in the summer?

By contrast, Wilfrid, in his leisurely journey in 678 left Frisia 'at the first sign of spring'. That would give him an early summer crossing followed by a long walk down Italy in the summer heat. This may have been a deliberate plan or it may have arisen through ignorance. Wilfrid had been to Rome before, with Benedict Biscop, but he had taken a different route, south through the Rhone valley and probably by sea to Rome. Likewise, Cadwalla must have made a slow crossing in 688-9, for, according to the *Chronicle*, he left England before May 687 and died in Rome in April 689 shortly after arrival. Assuming a normal rate of progress, he should have arrived before then and it may be that he was entertained at the Lombard Court for some considerable time on the way. Although he was not returning to England but crossing to Bavaria, Alcuin must have intended a spring crossing in 781 for he met Charlemagne in Parma on the way in the middle of March. One person who must have made a summer crossing and succumbed to the heat or exhaustion was Æthelmod who died on 15 August 962, by implication shortly after his arrival. The *Chronicle* recorded that 'In this same year, Æthelmod the priest went to Rome, and there passed away on 15 August.'

At the other end of our period we have a very rapid visit by Archbishop Robert who was elected in probably March 1051 and 'in that same spring' set off for Rome to obtain his Pallium. If we believe the *Chronicle* he was back in England by June, after a remarkably quick journey. The determining factor in his departure was the need to establish his authority after election by obtaining the Pallium and returning to England as soon as possible. That consideration would not only dictate his starting time but would over-ride other questions of weather or convenience. The same urgency dominated his second visit to Rome in 1052-3, for fleeing as an exile he had no choice but to leave in September. He sailed from the nearest place, the Naze, and we may assume that he probably then took the quickest and most direct route for he was back in Normandy the next year where he died at Jumièges. We cannot infer a route back to England from that for he was undoubtedly seeking shelter in his old abbey rather than intending to cross the Channel [D45.15].

Sometimes plans had to be altered. In 1061 Tostig was clearly planning an early summer crossing of the Alps, going north, for he sent his wife and most of the attendants on in advance. He and the rest were then delayed and did not leave Rome until some time between early April or mid-June. Barlow preferred the later date but that need not be so.[14] They were probably still in Rome to receive the Papal Bull dated 3 May; that still leaves time for a departure before June. At the latest they left before Pope Nicholas died on 27 July. Whichever date applies, they would have

crossed the passes well before the end of summer but some weeks later than planned, and are unlikely to have been back in England before the winter [D74].

Although we do not know of many Anglo-Saxons who made the Alpine crossing more than once or twice, some people of other nationalities did so, such as Carolingian agents or those on Church business. Tyler cites Bruno of Toul, later Leo IX, who crossed at least eight times, four over the Great St Bernard.[15] If a crossing were viewed as such an exceptional ordeal, especially in the winter, would it not have attracted more comment and better description? One of the features of the narratives is the conventional language in which the snowy peaks of the Alps are described. The repetition from one author to another suggests literary effect rather than real terror. Consider the wording of the Lives of Wilfrid, Boniface and Willibald [D12.13, D20.2 and D24.2]. Surely the stylised formality of these passages indicates that either there were no major difficulties, or if there were any, they were not worthy of record. They stand in contrast to the more graphic detail of Henry IV's crossing or to the gory attempt to save the life of Archbishop Ælfsige. Apart from those recording death or other dangers, there are few personal entries in the English records. As we have seen, the topographical descriptions are formal and literary and even Sigeric's record, though detailed, tells us nothing of the route or what he thought of it. There are a few human touches which may be mentioned. About 972, Germanus was returning to England with Oswald but decided to stay at Fleury. One reason was that he was attracted by the beauty of the place and the other was the discipline of the House.[16] Later, the Ramsey Chronicler records that Abbot Ælfwine's health was so damaged by the rigours of his journey to Rome in 1062 and the cares of office that he had to retire.[17] At second-hand, Einhard commented upon the strain upon Charlemagne:

> At this point I really should explain how difficult Charlemagne found the crossing of the Alps when he came to enter Italy, and after what effort on the part of the Franks the pathless ridges of the mountains were traversed, and the rocks which reared themselves up to the sky and the abrupt abysses…[18]

A human touch is provided by the story of St Odo's crossing of the Alps, not so much in his saintly conduct in helping the feeble old man but in the reminder of the poor man's diet, and the travellers trudging up the mountain pass [D62.1]. Apart from the timing of the journey, there was considerable variation in its duration. Several considerations determined peoples' movements for they were rarely free agents. Some like Robert had to hurry through circumstances that they could not control. Some

---

[14] VER, p. 37, n. 3.

[15] Tyler, p. 68.

[16] *Ramsey Chronicle*, pp. 24-5.

[17] *Ramsey Chronicle*, p. 177.

[18] Einhard, *Life of Charlemagne*, ch. 6.

were in a hurry to reach Rome before old age or infirmity overtook them. Some enjoyed a journey akin to the grand tour of later centuries. Much depended upon why they made the journey and whether they intended or expected to return.

In marked contrast to Archbishop Robert's rapid movements is the state visit made by Æthelwulf and Alfred in 855-856. Although we can only guess at their departure time, we do know that they took more than twelve months to complete the trip, a delay which nearly cost the king his throne. We may assume that on his return he waited for the passes to clear in the late spring for he was betrothed to Judith in July before marrying her at Verberie-sur-Oise in October. His route was presumably the direct one across eastern France.[19] It is unfortunate that we do not know how long Cnut took over his state visit in 1027 but there is no indication that he hurried. Another pair who were not in a hurry were Wulfred and Wigberht in 814-15 who were recorded in the *Chronicle* as going south one year and returning the next. Unfortunately we do not know their departure times but presumably they wanted time to stay in Rome and also have an easy crossing, both of which required a lengthy stay, possibly approaching a year [D45.2, 45.3].

Political factors could be dominant. King Eardwulf of Northumbria was expelled from his kingdom in 808. He reached Nijmegen in the spring of that year and went from there to Rome, passing through again on his return the same year. He moved quickly because he had to obtain assistance and recover his position. We can speculatively reconstruct a timetable by which he had lost his kingdom and left England in the winter of 807-8, passed through Nijmegen in the spring, as we are told, and in order to return by the end of the year made two Alpine crossings in the same season, one in early summer and the other in autumn or early winter [D39.7, 39.8].

Clerics were often in a hurry, especially Archbishops of Canterbury and later of York who had to secure their authority by receipt of the Pallium in person from the Pope. Quite apart from gaining authority, they had much to do and their visits were completed as soon as they could be. If we read the text in the obvious way, Sigeric was only in Rome for a few days in 990 [D59] and like Eardwulf, probably made both crossings in the summer months. Robert, too, can only have spent at most a few days in Rome.

English sources give us only a limited impression of the anticipated daily mileage. Probably the nearest calculation is that of Landon, who reckoned that in the time of Richard I, 'the ordinary traveller or pilgrim' could maintain an average of thirty miles a day, with perhaps a maximum

of thirty-eight for an express rider.[20] This does not help a great deal as much depends upon what is meant by an ordinary traveller or pilgrim and whether he even had a horse, quite apart from the hazards of interruption through poor weather, adverse wind and obstructive officials. Although I want to avoid comparison with or evidence from later periods it is worth remarking upon the speed with which clerics or those engaged upon Church business could move. For the fourteenth century, on the papacy at Avignon, Yves Renouard wrote 'Also the fastest couriers took five days to reach Paris or Metz, eight days to reach Brussels, ten days for Valencia, twelve days to reach John or London, and thirteen for Venice, Rome and sometimes Naples'.[21] Since technology would have changed little – though comforts provided *en route* might have done – the comparison is probably still valid.

There are some references to the speed of the Alpine crossing itself but not from Anglo-Saxon sources. A Deacon called Magnoald was sent by St Gall to establish the facts of St Columban's death in November 615. He brought back the news from Bobbio to Steinach 'for he was able to undertake the journey by day and by night'.[22] Not only does this testify to determination and speed but it also suggests the ability of a determined traveller, who possibly knew the route, to travel by night, or at least for some of the hours of darkness. Papal sources give us some details. We can follow the progress of Pope Stephen's flight from Rome in 753. He left Pavia on 15 November and after crossing the Great St Bernard and passing through St Maurice, reached Ponthion on 6 January 754.[23] Both the Pope and Magnoald were in a hurry for different reasons, and no doubt others would take longer than they did, but none would want to linger on the passes. Later, in 867, the Annals of St Bertin give us precise information about an exchange of letters. Hincmar of Rheims wrote to the Pope in July using clerics disguised as pilgrims 'to avoid the snares of his enemies'. That pretence may well have slowed their progress for they could not use official facilities to travel quickly. They arrived in August but as the Pope was ill could not get a reply until October. They set out then and Hincmar had his reply on the 13 December, between six and ten weeks later.[24] Some journeys were completed with remarkable speed and we have already noted Archbishop Robert's in 1051. For the moment, one more example will serve although it was not to Rome but to Jerusalem. In 1020 Abbot Wythman resigned his office and left Ramsey for the Holy Land. He visited the sacred places and returned to England the next year, 1021.[25] We do not know his route.

[19] ASC. For the supposed meeting between Alfred and Grimbald, see P. Grierson, 'Grimbald of St Bertin', *English Historical Review* 55.

[20] L. Landon, *Itinerary of Richard I*. Pipe Roll Society, NS. 13, p. 186.

[21] Y. Renouard, *La Papauté à Avignon*, p. 28.

[22] 'et ille coepit iter agere die noctuque' Gougaud, *Routes*, pp. 253-71 n. 1.

[23] *LP*, under Stephen II, chs. 24-5.

[24] *The Annals of St Bertin*, Janet L. Nelson (ed. and trans.), sa 867, pp. 140-42. The date in October was not given.

[25] W.D. Macray, *Chronicon Abbatiae Ramesiensis*, p. 124.

Many of the travellers were working to a fixed timetable with little room for choice. We know too little to be certain of Mellitus' movements in 609-10 but he had to be in Rome for the Synod held there in February 610. If he took the route used by Augustine and his peers he probably made the sea crossing from Marseilles in the winter despite the discomfort that might cause. Ulf in 1050 had to be in Vercelli by September and he must have worked back from that, probably making a summer crossing of the Alps. That simple fact by itself indicates a considerable sophistication in the travel arrangements, at least in the later Anglo-Saxon centuries. It could be no hit or miss process if a deadline were to be met. We can see a little of the planning of a journey which had to be made to a timetable in the correspondence of Lupus of Ferrières, who in 849 was sent to Rome on an urgent royal mission. He wrote three letters in the summer; one asked for hospitality and money, another for hospitality and the third for gifts that would ease the wheels of Italian bureaucracy as well as a good trotting horse (*equo tolutario*) to help him on his way [D46.5]. He told both of his anticipated hosts to expect him at the end of summer or early autumn, which would presume crossing the Alps about that season

The conclusion from what evidence we have must be that even at an early period people travelling in an official context had sufficient knowledge of the duration and dangers of the journey to be able to plan departure times if they could and I return to the mechanics of travel later. They did not shrink from a winter crossing if it were necessary or more convenient. There are some indications that there was a preferred time to cross: going north, at the earliest clearing of the snows in Spring when the traveller would benefit from the northern summer, or just before the worst of winter when the southbound traveller would not suffer from the heat of the Italian summer. This seems the logical reading of Boniface's story and was quite possibly what Ceolfrid intended. More independent travellers might have had less idea, for Æthelmod must have risked

the high summer and crossed in mid-year for he died in Rome on the 15 August, by implication shortly after arrival. Despite his example, English preference does not seem to match the assertion by Albert of Stade, recording his journey of 1236, that the best month for the crossing was August.[26] Albert, however, explicitly based his preference upon local factors – food, the condition of the road and so forth – rather than as a part of an overall plan. Some English may well have shared his view, though some of them may also be among those who died in Italy. Whilst those with a free choice chose the best time, others with other imperatives did what was necessary and risked the consequences. There is no evidence that important journeys were delayed simply to gain an easier crossing of the Alps, rather that even from an early time, people had an understanding of the requirements of the journey as a whole. How they found out is another matter.

There is evidence from the fifteenth century, when more specific information is available, although it is important to remember that what held then need not have done so earlier, for many material reasons. Nevertheless, and with that caveat, we find that George Hay noted that of the Englishmen going to Rome in the later fifteenth century

> most travelled in winter, the Hospice being fullest from December to June, and the Alpine passes would have been full of snow. The travellers seem to have preferred to risk the snows rather than the heat of Italy in the summer, when plague and disease spread easily. Moreover, many wished to be in Rome for Easter, and this would mean leaving England in January or February …[27]

According to Hay, the preferred routes were then over either the Mont Cenis or through Germany via the Reschen Pass, leading on to Venice. That route would have helped pilgrims going on to Palestine, but it does not seem to have been used in our period.

---

[26] Tyler, p. 27.

[27] George Hay, 'Pilgrims and the Hospice', *The English Hospice in Rome*, p. 103.

CHAPTER 4

WHO WENT AND WHY

Many commentators start with Bede's observation that 'At this period, [*c.* 680] many English people vied with one another in following this custom, both noble and simple, lay folk and clergy, men and women alike'.[28] 'Many' is a relative word and how many went can never be established. We must remember that Bede was making a point to emphasise the piety of his race. We can be certain that after the first recorded journeys of Wilfrid, Benedict Biscop and Cadwalla, in the context of whose journey Bede made the remark, the number of people who went to Rome almost certainly increased steadily, despite political, military and climatic difficulties. Most secondary commentators have concentrated upon the motive of pilgrimage and consequentially view the journey in that context but the analysis in Appendix 2 of those whom we know to have made the journey indicates that pilgrimage was only one motive amongst many. It may even not have been the most common reason for going. The motives may well have been mixed so that any particular individual, like Archbishop Sigeric, may have gone primarily for one reason, in his case to obtain the Pallium, but whilst there also visited the shrines and other sights in a mood of genuine piety. Motives could be even more mixed where there was a large group, such as Earl Tostig's in 1061, and the Council of Chalons-sur-Saone in 813 noted that 'many people, both clerics and laity went on pilgrimage to Tours and to Rome, through superstitious motives, which were not pure'.[29] Tostig himself went at least in part for political reasons, perhaps to further the cause of the house of Godwin with the Papacy and justify their support for Stigand as Archbishop of Canterbury. Archbishop Aldred went to regularise his own position. Tostig's wife may have gone as an act of piety but perhaps also for the journey itself. Those in the escorting party, such as the knight Gospatric whom we will meet again later, may have gone in part because it was their duty to defend their lord in his travels. In addition to these primary motives, all must have shared in the experience of pilgrimage and veneration at the Holy sites. Some travellers' motives will never be known. Were there any precursors of Bartholomew of Burghersh who in 1337 petitioned to go to Santiago rather than go on military campaign for his lord?[30] In this volume we can only account for those whose existence was known and the groupings that

follow are drawn from them alone. The individuals are listed in Appendix 2 but some general comments upon them are given below.

The nature of pilgrimage

Pilgrims fell into three broad groups. Some went to Rome as part of a lifelong wandering, a true *peregrinatio*, a withdrawal from the earthly life and its ties in favour of the spiritual. Others went to Rome but intended to return to England and home. Finally, some went intending to stay in Rome till they died. There were very few Englishmen recorded amongst the first group, which was more of an Irish habit, more among the second, and it is they who tended to go from mixed motive. A number, too, fall in the last group, both rich and poor among them. Whilst we can only comment upon those we know about, the sources hint at many others. We do not know how many attempted the journey. Of those whose passage has left no record, many will have been pilgrims but many also will have been merchants and those travelling on business. Brief comments like that of Flodoard's for 923 give us only limited help: 'A great number of the English who were travelling to the threshold of St Peter for the sake of prayer were killed by the Saracens in the Alps'. [D51.2]. How many is a great number? Was Flodoard correct in suggesting that they were all pilgrims, for it is clear that many people travelled together along the same routes, forming the largest party compatible with the needs of food and accommodation.

Church Business

As time passed it became necessary for Archbishops of Canterbury and after a time those of York to have to go to Rome and receive the Pallium in person. There are so many of these that it will be enough to mention here only the best documented, Archbishop Sigeric in 990. Many were elderly and some died on the way, as we shall see. For all of them it must have been an unwelcome distraction from their archiepiscopal duties. At times it was thought prudent for Bishops to visit as well, as for example in the time of Stigand when Herman and Walter had to go to have their appointments confirmed. Wilfrid referred to Rome in all his successive disputes with kings, Archbishops and others. During the period, not only were such important matters referred to Rome, but, increasingly, lesser matters like confirmation of land grants and of liberties were taken there too, as in

---

[28] BHE, V.7.

[29] Hefele, *Conciles*, III, ii., p. 1145.

[30] Webb, *Pilgrims*, p. 176 (j).

965 when Glastonbury was involved.[31] The negotiation for the transfer of the See from Crediton to Exeter in 1049 was another.[32] Sometimes letters concerning these matters were taken to Rome by people going for some other purpose but many must have been conveyed by couriers of whom we otherwise know nothing. A journey has to be inferred simply because business was transacted. Some people went for disciplinary reasons, such as Ulf who narrowly escaped censure at the Synod in Vercelli in 1050. At a lower level we must not forget all the practical advice obtained from Rome on choral, liturgical and other matters, particularly in the century or so following conversion. Benedict Biscop imported French builders to build Jarrow after the Roman fashion[33] and Wilfrid built his church at Hexham from Roman memories:

> Without a doubt it was the spirit of God who taught our Bishop to plan the construction of such a place, for we had never heard of its like this side of the Alps.[34]

When Abbot John returned with Benedict he not only had the duty of reporting upon English orthodoxy but was made choirmaster at Jarrow to teach singing and chanting after the Roman fashion.[35]

State Business

This was only finely divided from Church Business. As we have seen, King Eardwulf was expelled from his Kingdom of Northumbria and after visiting Charlemagne and obtaining his support, went on to Rome. In 855, according to the *Chronicle*, Æthelwulf 'proceeded to Rome and stayed there for twelve months.' Since the visit followed an earlier one by his young son Alfred, was made when there was both a Viking threat and pressure from his eldest son who opposed his return and limited his power when it occurred, politics must have played as important a part as piety in the motive. It is hard to disentangle the truth of what happened but the record makes it clear that it was more than a simple act of piety, especially since we learn that he made a political marriage on the way home. It is most likely that the king either intended to retire but was persuaded to return by the promise of imperial support, or went to Rome to obtain support against the growing threat posed by his son Æthelbald, almost copying King Eardwulf's situation.

An involuntary traveller was Alfred who was sent to Rome in 935 to answer a charge of treason against Athelstan [D49.1].

Other officials were the couriers who took the Romescot or Peter's Pence to Rome. They were noted in the *Chronicle* for a few years from 882 and probably continued to go, unrecorded, for there is a strong suggestion that in 1061 Tostig threatened to stop payment, as a return both for the attack upon him on the homeward journey and the refusal to confirm Archbishop Aldred of York in plurality with Worcester [D74]. Unless there were some other high level contact, such money would be taken by these often anonymous couriers.

Political Sanctuary

This was a variation of state business. In 874, Burgred King of Mercia was driven from his kingdom by the Danes – after warnings from the Papacy about his and his people's moral standards – but fled to Rome where he eventually died. He seems to have preferred to do that rather than take refuge in his Queen's home kingdom of Wessex, where he might have been a political embarrassment. It is not clear whether Queen Æthelswith accompanied him in 875, which is suggested by the *Liber Vitae*, or whether she did not leave for Italy until 888, dying at Pavia probably on the way out to Rome [D45.8]. This is an example of an ambiguity arising from an entry in the *Liber Vitae* and is discussed further below. It was not only English kings who sought sanctuary in Rome for in 1064 the Irish King Donnchad did the same, retiring to Rome after he had lost his kingdom.[36]

Political summitry

We next have what we would today call meetings of heads of state. I referred above to the mixed motives which probably underlay Æthelwulf's visit in 855 but Cnut went in 1027 in great splendour at the time of an Imperial coronation.[37] The *Chronicle* merely noted his journey but John of Worcester recorded that it was made 'with great state'. It is clear from his letter to England that he did travel with all ceremony and the provision of an Imperial escort must have emphasised this. Whilst piety played its part, the main motive behind Cnut's journey must have been its political importance for a major player upon the European stage. Not long after, in 1050, Macbeth, the Scottish King, in similar fashion 'distributed (or rather scattered) money at Rome, some at least to the poor' [D73]. The motive is obscure but he may well have taken advantage of the Synods held at Rome and Vercelli that year to make a political impression and for that reason I include his journey here.

[31] William of Malmesbury, *The Early History of the Church of Glastonbury,* John Scott (ed.), ch. 61, p. 129.

[32] H & S, I.691.

[33] BLA ch. 5.

[34] Eddius, ch. 22.

[35] BLA ch. 6.

[36] Donnchad's journey is mentioned in the Irish Annals. See A. Gwynn, 'Ireland and the Continent in the eleventh century', *Irish Historical Studies,* VIII no. 31, pp. 196-7. Gwynn noted that Donnchad's was the last such pilgrimage.

[37] ASC has the journey under 1031 which is clearly incorrect. See the discussion in M.K. Lawson, *Cnut,* most particularly from p. 102.

Legal reasons

Wilfrid took his legal case to Rome when he lost his See in 678.[38] And later, according to the *Chronicle* entry for 1052, Archbishop Robert appealed to Rome against his sentence of outlawry. In between and at a lower level we have the unnamed Earl who appealed to Rome against Dunstan's condemnation of a prohibited marriage, only to have the Archbishop ignore the Papal ruling.[39] We do not have an example of the law being applied but Edgar's law codes provided for defaulters of Peter's Pence to take themselves off to Rome and not come back until they had a receipt from the Pope [D14.6]. Again, Englishmen were not the only people to do this for in 928 Howel, King of Wales, led a delegation of three bishops and a senior layman to Rome 'to consult the wise in what manner to improve the laws of Wales'. He returned in 930 for a second opinion.[40]

Medical needs

Illness may have caused some to go, although the evidence is slight and suspect. We have the story of the dumb man in the reign of Edward the Confessor who spent three years in Rome looking for a cure.[41] Earlier there was the rich thegn who about 850 travelled to Rome seeking unsuccessfully a cure for blindness, returned and was cured by St Swithin.[42] Whilst such trips may have happened, one suspects that unsubstantiated stories were probably created to demonstrate the effectiveness of the home grown miracle cure over the continental.

Traders

Although many traders must have made the journey we have no record of an actual individual who did so. We must not forget the story of St Gregory and the English slaves. It is far from clear that St Gregory actually saw them in Rome, but he instructed the priest Candidus to buy them when the latter reached Gaul. He obviously knew of slaves as an available commodity and that must suggest an organised long distance trade even by the sixth century. Slaves are perishable goods and any trader's object must have been to pass them as quickly as possible along an organised route. Benedict Biscop went to Rome to purchase relics, books and other treasures and there is no reason why others should not have taken or brought back more ordinary goods.[43] As early as 755 there must have been enough travellers of different kinds for Pepin to enact that tolls should not be levied on pilgrims, as opposed to

merchants or others.[44] This was echoed in 796 by treaty arrangements between Offa of Mercia and Charlemagne to ensure that traders and true pilgrims who might well be travelling together, were each given their proper treatment. One group had to pay tolls and the other was exempt. In the letter from Charlemagne to Offa the distinction is clear [D34.3]. One of Charlemagne's regulations makes the interesting point that the purpose of tolls was not simply to raise money, though that can never have been far from any royal mind, but to recoup the expense of providing assistance to travellers, through bridges and ferries. It is expressed negatively by ordering that no toll is to be levied if no assistance is given and one must maintain some scepticism over motive, but nevertheless the stated logic is interesting [D34.4]. It is clear that by the ninth century at the latest English goods were passing along the northern part of the route and although the references which show this do not relate to individual traders or journeys, they are worth reproducing to illustrate the volume of movement that must have passed unrecorded. Evidence of commercial activity by Englishmen living in or visiting Rome is provided by the regulations of Pavia, which refer explicitly to the treatment of English traders arriving at the city [D65]. The exemption of the *Schola Saxonum* from toll by Pope Marinus supports this for, generally, only traders foreign to a market were to pay toll [D45.5]. Although this must indicate commercial activity, it tells us little about what was traded. We can learn more from a decree quoted by Tyler, issued by Giso, Bishop of Aosta in 960 [D63]. In this are stated his claims to tolls on goods either brought into, or passing through this city which stood, of course, just south of the Great St Bernard. A charge was apparently levied in money or kind on all goods passing through the city. In Tyler's summary: '… amongst the goods actually mentioned are the following; arms, such as swords and lances, shields and armour; reins, spurs and horses; salt; metals, for example, lead, tin and copper; scribes' ink (*atramentum*) hawks and even apes.' The source of the lead and tin must surely be western Britain[45] which would accord with the Exeter Guild statutes dating from the first half of the tenth century which stipulated that: 'At a pilgrimage south, each man (is to contribute) five pence.' Although it has been generally accepted as relating to journeys to Rome, the passage causes problems. The Anglo-Saxon has *aet suthfore*, translated as 'pilgrimage'. It must cover more than that to include all journeys south and it is hard to envisage that pilgrimage would be the only motive. Does it mean no more than that any member would be supported or does it indicate some sort of joint stock trading? Given the hazards, that would not be surprising. It must betray another example of mixed motive.

Our last example is the letter which Cnut sent back to England from Rome in 1027 when he reported that he had successfully negotiated free passage [D69]. Note the fact

[38] Eddius, ch. 29.
[39] Stubbs, *Memorials*, p. 200.
[40] H & S, 1, p. 210.
[41] The dumb man, if he existed at all, is in the *Evesham Chronicle*, W.D. Macray (ed.) (Rolls Series) p. 47.
[42] The blind man is in Ælfric's 'Life of St Swithun', W.W. Skeat (ed.), *Ælfric's Lives of the Saints*.
[43] BLA, chs. 4, 5, 6.
[44] Tyler, p. 33.
[45] See J.R. Maddicott, 'Trade, industry and the wealth of King Alfred', *Past and Present*, pp. 19-21.

that although there are so many references to Englishmen being freed from tolls, that was not strictly true. As the Pavian regulations make clear, individual liability to toll was compounded into an annual sum, paid by the English kings to secure free passage.

It is a reasonable conclusion that through our period an unknown but probably increasing number of traders went to Italy, if not to Rome itself, and that it is the nature of the records and the particular interests of those who created them that has led to their names being lost. Alcuin mentions one such un-named merchant in a letter to Bishop Remigius of Chur. Alcuin's reference to him as 'our' merchant need not imply that he was English, in context, rather the contrary [D38.16]. Merchants were an invisible element and we will return to them when we consider the routes that people took.

Messengers and letters

Guides and messengers were common. The former are considered later on, but messengers form an allied group that may be considered as a type on their own. It is clear from surviving papers that a large number of letters passed between England and Rome even though we do not always have any knowledge of who took them. There were probably two groups of carriers; those who were making the journey anyway for another purpose, and professionals whose sole purpose was to carry a message. This was so from the earliest period of the Augustinian mission. Bede tells us in the *Ecclesiastical History* that Mellitus brought back letters from Rome in 610, but he was not a professional courier.[46] Letters were brought by anonymous messengers in 624 when the Pope authorised the consecration of Romanus.[47] In that letter the Pope referred to earlier ones he had received from Æthelwald. Again shortly after 624 Pope Boniface sent a letter to Edwin.[48] Sometimes there is a reasonable inference that letters or messages were carried by other travellers as Mellitus had done. For example, in a letter dated between 891 and 896 Pope Formosus wrote to the Bishops of England, clearly replying to an earlier message that he had received 'but because, as our esteemed brother Plegmund has told us ...'[49] Plegmund did not go to Rome in person on that occasion, despite Gervase of Canterbury's assertion, but we know from the *Chronicle* that in 890 Abbot Beornhelm 'took the Alms of the West Saxons and King Alfred to Rome' and we may suppose that he took with him the letter to which the Pope was replying. We do not know who brought back the reply; it was possibly the Abbot himself on his return journey. It is unlikely to have been entrusted to another later traveller for we do not know of any of substance at the right time. It could have been brought by one of his party who had stayed behind for the purpose.

Messages could be either written or verbal or written with further verbal explanation. We have certain letters from the Papacy which were clearly written in response to information received in Rome about events in England but for which there is no known visitor who could have taken that information there. Sometimes the subject is general and of a nature where the source could be verbal comment by unrecorded travellers. One of this kind is the letter from Pope John VIII to King Burgred of Mercia between 872 and 874.[50] It warned him of the consequences of his evil doing and began simply '*sicut audivimus* [according to what we have heard]' We have no record of an individual going to Rome who could have informed the Pope. Clearly someone had done so, but whoever it was might not have taken specific letters of complaint but simply made allegations. By contrast other Papal letters were replies to specific issues. Of one, written 877x878, Whitelock commented 'this letter has obviously been written in response to one from the Archbishop which has not survived.'[51] The subject matter is too specific to be a response to anecdotal information. In 956 there was an exchange of letters about the privileges of Canterbury, another subject too specific to be entrusted entirely to word of mouth.[52] On neither of these occasions do we know of any visitors of rank. Although it is possible that correspondence was entrusted to more humble folk, and we know that in extremis this was done as when the Papacy used a pilgrim to smuggle a letter through the Lombard blockade, it would nevertheless be an unsuitable method for legitimate and important administrative matters and I suggest the existence of a more reliable one. There is enough evidence to indicate the existence of a body of professional messengers who knew the way and the techniques and perhaps made several round trips, taking messages out and bringing back the replies, mirroring the common use of imperial *missi* in the Carolingian empire. They may have travelled on their own or in small groups (as in 889), for speed, or they may have acted as long distance guides to those who had never made the journey before but whose names were recorded. The surviving correspondence of Boniface and Alcuin alone indicates that it was quite normal for significant figures to correspond over long distances, using regular and named messengers. These, like more official couriers, may well have guided others along the way: people could coalesce into bigger groups not only for added security but simply to benefit from having someone who knew the way.

The evidence is slight but I suggest that it is sufficient to indicate the growth of a corps of professional couriers, equivalent to but perhaps of lower status than the Carolingian *missi*, who took these letters at times when there was no significant visitor. The letter from Pope Honorius to King Edwin makes clear that as early as 634 there were messengers who had successfully completed the journey both ways [D17.6]. We know the name of

[46] BHE, II.4.
[47] BHE, II.8.
[48] BHE, II.10.
[49] WBB, p. 37.

[50] WBB, p. 1.
[51] WBB, p. 3.
[52] Wilkins, *Concilia* I.223; Jaffé 3678 & 3679.

one later courier for when King Eardwulf of Northumbria was driven into exile, he was sent back in the care of an Anglo-Saxon Deacon, Ealdwulf, who was already in Rome and returned there after a traumatic trip [D39.8]. He must have been one such professional. The *Chronicle* entry for 889 tells us that 'In this year no journey was made to Rome except by two couriers whom King Alfred sent with letters.' The entry is quite matter of fact and suggests nothing unusual in either the existence of couriers or their role. There may be a slight clue in the wording of the account of Sigeric's return journey from Rome for the word used is *Adventus*, more often indicating a coming than a going. Could the narrative indicate the perspective of somebody until then living in Rome but who returned to England with the Archbishop? If so, was he a professional and does this also explain why the narrative lists the route in reverse order, going north? [D59]

In a letter of 801 to Charlemagne, Alcuin asked for his protection for Archbishop Æthelheard and his party on their journey to Rome and gave a mutual obligation as one of the reasons: 'They have all been most loyal to me, helping me on my journey and protecting my boys as they travel about' [D38.13]. We shall see that one of his 'boys' met the party at St Josse with letters for the Archbishop. Messengers did not only accompany travellers, for sometimes they simply carried letters or messages. In 721 Boniface wrote to the Pope telling him of the progress of his mission. The letter was taken by a messenger called Bynan who returned immediately with the Pope's reply. In Willibald's *Life of Boniface* he is described as 'an experienced and trustworthy messenger, Bynan by name'.[53] The same role was played by Witto. In 798, Alcuin asked Arno of Salzburg to send Witto to him with news.[54] There was no purpose in the journey other than the carrying of messages. Witto had already been to France and back twice, had gone to Rome with Arno and was to go again in 800/1. Although he must have been a seasoned traveller he was probably not, in my terms, a professional messenger but a reliable traveller between friends, who could be also trusted with giving less formal, verbal, accounts.

The system could be remarkably sophisticated as is shown by a letter of 801 from Alcuin, complaining to contacts in Rome that he had not received a letter from them. His wording makes clear that the postal route had two stages, from Rome to Troyes, by the hands of Saxons, presumably English, returning to England, and then by 'our people' from Troyes to Tours [D38.12]. The implications of this short passage are enormous. There was first in normal times a sufficient number of Saxons on the route to ensure that a letter could be taken. Second, those parties contained someone reliable enough to deliver letters to the right place. Third, there must have been regular 'in house' contact between Tours and Troyes to guarantee the other leg of the journey. Fourth, this must have been a well known part of travel arrangements, at least for organised parties. Finally, it tells us that English, if indeed that is what they were, regularly passed through Troyes. There need be no conflict between the proposition that mail, including business mail, was carried in this way and the assertion by Barlow that before 1049 business was done when the successive English Archbishops visited Rome.[55] This may be true of face to face negotiations, except on the very rare occasions when a legate was sent to England, but the content and dating of various letters make it clear that a whole range of matters was covered by a mail service.

The system was not foolproof for there was always the danger of illness or robbery but there seems to be little complaint about the honesty of couriers. Lupus of Ferrières, who was invariably anxious, did warn about their competence, when he asked for an explanation in writing rather than by word of mouth 'because messages relayed by couriers are not reliable for they are often noticeably marred by falsehoods' [D46.11]. There are few complaints of deceit but error could easily arise from poor memory or understanding. It is, however, surely unlikely that messages of importance, length or subtlety were sent by word of mouth instead of by letter, and any communications so secret that they could not be trusted to writing would surely be entrusted to someone who knew what they were about and would get the message right.

True Pilgrims

Finally, we return to those whose only motive for making the journey was piety; the true pilgrims. We can never know how many there were or how many succeeded in reaching their destination. Some references are undated and I have included these among the miscellaneous entries in Appendix 5. I have referred to the numerical vagueness of entries like Flodoard's but although some people perished along the way, it is clear that many completed the journey and either stayed on to live in Rome or returned safely. The English residents in Rome formed a sizeable body which was large or courageous enough to be specifically mentioned as having suffered in the Saracen raid upon Rome in 846. In 864 they saved the True Cross from destruction during a riot in Rome and between 873 and 875 Pope John VIII referred to them in a letter to the two English Archbishops, in terms that implied both their number and status [D35.5]. English residents in Rome tended to live in an area close to St Peter's (Illustration 8) which became known variously as the Saxon Burgh or the *Schola Saxonum*. It was never a formal 'school', rather an enclave in which fellow nationals could live with mutual support. It did seem to

---

[53] Talbot, *Missionaries*, p. 43.
[54] Dümmler, *Alcuini Epist.* No. 156, p. 253; Moore, p. 77 n. 3.

[55] F. Barlow, *The English Church 1000-1066*, p. 300; D. Sturdy, *Alfred the Great*, pp. 48-9 (though his assertion that parties contained around 30 to 80 warriors seems to originate from the size of Ceolfrid's group. There is little other evidence).

have a rudimentary organisation as there are references to its 'leading men'.

Some of the travellers were royalty. These have been considered by Stancliff,[56] and unlike Burgred who fled to Rome because he had lost his kingdom, Cadwalla, King of Wessex (688), Cenred King of Mercia and Offa of East Anglia (709), and Ine of Wessex (726) seem to have had no reason to leave their homeland save the salvation of their souls. English Kings were not alone in this for Cyngen, King of Powis who left in 854[57] and Dunwallon, King of Strathclyde, who left in 975,[58] both abandoned their kingdoms, the latter taking the tonsure. Ordinary folk followed suit. Before 912 Werthryth, wife of Cered, 'disposed of all her property to a kinsman Culthwulf', with the intention of going to Rome.[59] In 972, Æthelmod, a priest, 'went to Rome and there passed away on 15 August'.[60] About 1050, Askyll, 'a Danish nobleman, gave all his property to Peterborough and retired to Rome.'[61] For one reason or another, these left their mark but from the many references to those going for the sake of prayer, one must conclude that the greater number of people who went left no individual record and we have no means of estimating their number.

---

[56] C. Stancliff, 'Kings Who Opted Out', P. Wormald (ed.), *Ideal & Reality in Frankish & Anglo-Saxon Society.*

[57] For Cyngen: J Williams ab Ithell (ed.), *Annales Cambriae* (Rolls 1860), p. 13; H. & S., I, p. 206.

[58] For Dunwallon: Thomas Jones (ed.), *Brut y Tywysogyon or the Chronicle of the Princes* [Peniarth MS 20 version], p. 41.

[59] For Werthryth, see W. de G. Birch; *Cart. Sax.* no. 537; H.P.R.Finberg, *Early Charters of the West Midlands*, no. 270.

[60] ASC.

[61] Kemble, *Codex Diplomaticus Aevi Saxonici* (1639-48), IV p. 140.

CHAPTER 5

THE MECHANICS OF TRAVEL

The sources give us a quantity of incidental information about the way in which people travelled, though there is nothing as detailed as the Guide for the pilgrim to Santiago, which dates from the twelfth century though incorporating earlier material. We are fortunate in having the record of a journey to Rome incorporated into the two Colloquies, *De Raris Fabulis* and *Retractata*. The generalities in them can be tested by matching against evidence contained in records of actual journeys and as this indicates general reliability I have drawn upon them. I have reproduced what I believe to be the most probable 'travel' sections in the Documentary Appendix [D52.2 and 53].

Transport

Did people walk or ride? The true pilgrim should walk and we have examples of this. Wilfrid walked. The passage is a little uncertain and it may be that Wilfrid only completed the journey on foot. He certainly had a horse available on the return journey, so the completion on foot may be symbolic. Even if so, it demonstrates what a pilgrim ought to do.[62] According to John of Salerno, St Odo walked over the Alpine pass but only after having given his horse to a 'feeble old man'. John himself seems to have walked [D62.1]. In legend, though possibly not in truth, St Egwyn was said not only to have walked but to have done so in chains having thrown the key in the Avon before he left. Miraculously it was restored to him in Rome, which must have assisted his return journey after absolution.[63] There were as many variations as there were in later times for whilst the poor pilgrim might have walked with his few possessions upon his back, a richer one could have had them carried by a horse or donkey, even if he himself did not ride. Riding on a donkey or an ass was a sign of humility and we are told for example in the *Life of Herluin*, the founder of Bec, that

> The man who had been highly regarded by everyone went on business to other courts, mounted on an ass, the subject of sorrow or scorn to other people for his method of transport and his humility of manner, for he was afraid of being mixed up in the world and did not

wish to ride horses any more, serving on the back of an ass the Lord ...[64]

Ceolfrid rode on a horse both southwards in England and then on the continent until he was too weak and had to be carried in a horse litter.[65] Wilfrid too, in 705 fell ill on the return journey and after first riding on a horse, had to be carried in a litter to safety at Meaux.[66] We are not told whether it was carried by man or horse but if we take the passage literally it was probably the former as he was carried 'by his friends'. There are innumerable references to the use of horses by people other than pilgrims. One illustration of their use and of the complications that could arise comes from the story of the man in danger of being sold himself unless he could raise the money to pay for a horse. We return to this below, in the passage concerning Money.

Some who were in a hurry must have ridden: surely Archbishop Robert must have gone on horseback to complete his rapid journey in 1051 [D45.13].[67] It is probable that there were horses with the party which included Archbishop Ælfsige in 959 for before he died of frostbite in the Alps the remedy to try to save him was to put his feet in the warm entrails of a horse [D56]. Whilst we cannot be certain that the animal was from his party, the likelihood is that it was, rather than one chanced upon in the neighbourhood or bought. The matter of fact narration is a slight hint that it belonged to them, for it does not mention the good fortune of finding a horse or the need to buy one. We have already seen that a century later the Royal party containing Henry IV had horses for we are told how they were moved across the snows [D82]. There is no reason to doubt the obvious fact that, from early in our period, they were used by travellers who had the funds. Towards the end of it, the more secular party of Earl Tostig in 1061 clearly had horses, for at their head rode a knight called Gospatric who tricked the robbers into thinking that he was the Earl [D74]. On his last fatal trip, the chests used to hold St Boniface's Bible and other impedimenta were carried by boat, but that would not always be possible [D20.4] and although we know nothing of how traders managed,

---

[62] Eddius, chs. 50 and 56.

[63] The life of St Egwyn and this particular miracle are summarised in D. H. Farmer, *The Oxford Dictionary of Saints*. For his Life, see W.D. Macray, *Chronicon Abbatiae de Evesham* (Rolls Series).

[64] Gilbert Crispin, 'Life of Herluin', ch. 62. Quoted in R.A. Brown, *The Norman Conquest of England*, p. 44.

[65] BLA, ch. 22.

[66] Eddius, ch. 56.

[67] ASC (C, D & E). See F. Barlow, *Edward the Confessor*, pp. 104-6.

they must have had pack transport when they could not use rivers.

The use of horses in the Alps must predate the Anglo-Saxon travellers for in Gregory of Tours' *Glory of the Martyrs* we read of their use, presumably in winter, by St Victor of Milan [D2.1]. Once more the tone is matter of fact and even if the story is not historically true, at least it reveals that Gregory saw nothing unusual in such a journey over probably the Mont Cenis rather than the Great St Bernard. Horses were not the only animal available. St Sturm rode an ass through the 'pathless wilderness' but there are far fewer references to them than to horses [D26.1].[68] About 960 Egelwin was riding a mule through Lombardy on his way north after visiting Jerusalem and Rome when the Emperor's camp followers stole not only it but also its valuable load including a pallium for St Dunstan. Fortunately Egelwin's prayers to the distant Archbishop made the mule go mad so that it shook off its captors and all was restored to its rightful owner.[69] If William of Malmesbury is to be believed, we have one reference to a camel. On his return from Rome, Aldhelm brought back a marble altar which was broken when the camel carrying it slipped and fell on a steep path. Fortunately, the marble was restored to its original state and the party resumed its journey with everyone reaching the French coast safely [D16.3]. Earlier in our period, Brunhilda was humiliated by being displayed on a camel before being torn to pieces by wild horses.[70]

The answer to the question of transport depended, as so often, upon who you were, how wealthy you were, why you were going and related to that, how rapidly you wanted to make the journey.

Roads and Rivers

Much has been written about the state of medieval roads – though less about the earlier centuries – but for our period at least there is very little firm evidence. Later stories might be representative of what might have happened earlier but how typical were they of the generality? I refer below to the complaints of Peter of Blois but how much did he write for dramatic effect [D84]? The story in the *Life of St Odo of Cluny* of the poor man expecting to reach a shepherd's encampment before nightfall suggests that his account was largely true [D62.2]. A few facts are certain and must not be overlooked. People travelled and often did so in large numbers with a substantial baggage train; heavy and valuable goods were transported by road; some effort was put into the construction of bridges; the maintenance of bridges was one of the three major obligations of a landowner; there are few comments in the sources about the state of the roads.

People travelled. Anglo-Saxon Kings were as constantly on the move as later medieval ones, and like King Harold racing north to Stamford Bridge and south again in 1066, could move quickly if they had to. They might have to move with a substantial administrative retinue. Like them, more ordinary people moved building materials over long distances, not only by water but by land in wagons which must presume serviceable roads with adequate fords or bridges. Some vehicles were designed with deep fords in mind: Charlemagne was concerned that his army's supplies should not be damaged [D34.4]. Others may have taken the same care. Where there was no bridge or ferry there might well be a ford and these are mentioned in estate boundaries among others. The numerous place names indicating the existence of a ford, make it unnecessary to mention more than one. A charter of King Cynewulf granting land to the Church of Wells set out the bounds of the property. The boundary runs

… on the same stream as far as the River Wellow, then along the bank of the river as far as the ford at the Wellow, and then along the public way as far as the elder which they call 'Elder-tree', and from there back along the muddy torrent to the east ford, thence … [71]

Blair noted the existence of an early major ford crossing the Thames near St Frideswide's church at Oxford which had a critical influence upon the development of the town.[72]

Bridges were built in fair number not only for their utility for road transport but because of the facility they provided to control and tax traffic passing along the rivers. Since a bridge is as much a blockade as a passageway they also played a major military role, as defences against the Vikings on rivers like the Thames and the Seine. If we believe the *Vita Genovefae*, Clovis' attack on Paris failed because he could not control the Seine and prevent supplies getting through.[73] One major undertaking was the wooden bridge, 500 yards long, that Charlemagne built across the Rhine at Mainz. Since it was later burned to water level the implication must be that even its piles were wooden, rather than a wooden superstructure on stone [D34.2]. We not only have bridges of the usual kind with piers, but pontoons, one of which is mentioned in a miraculous event recorded by Gregory of Tours. The bridge collapsed on a Saint's day festival, but fortunately, through the Saint's intervention the people were all blown to the river bank and no one was drowned [D2.6]. Some pontoons were designed with temporary military needs in mind; like that mentioned in the *Royal Frankish Annals* which was designed to be taken apart and re-assembled [D39.2] The particular river is not stated but we will meet the method of construction again. Later, under 808, we have another military bridge across the Elbe [D39.7]. We cannot tell whether such constructions remained for civilian use or whether each

[68] Talbot, p. 186.

[69] Egelwin's mule is in Stubbs, *Memorials* p. 245.

[70] E. Peters, *Monks, Bishops and Pagans*, p. 111; for other references to the use of camels, see McCormick, *Origins*, pp. 76-7.

[71] Sawyer 262; also translated in EHD, no. 70.

[72] John Blair, *Anglo-Saxon Oxfordshire*, p. 87.

[73] *Vita Genovefae*, B Krusch (ed.), chs. 35 & 39 (MG SSRM 3).

would be dismantled in the fortunes of war but practice probably varied. Even if dismantled, the expertise was there to be adopted for a busy trade or pilgrim route. It is remarkable how few references there were to dangerous or badly maintained bridges. The near disaster on the Rhone is an early one but another account comes from a much later date (991) in Richer's account of his journey from Rheims to Chartres. Given the language of the rest of the story the crossing of the bridge was possibly much exaggerated for dramatic effect but it cannot have been a total fabrication [D61].[74] Since Richer was enjoying the telling of a good tale and the crossing was made at night after they had lost their way, the terrors might be more romantic than real.

There is a remarkable dearth of complaint or even comment of any kind about the state of the roads. What is a road? Many, if not most, would not correspond with our idea of a defined ribbon. The track must have been wider and less defined on flatter and softer ground as people tried to avoid eroded stretches, but in hilly terrain, especially narrow passes, the way must have been far more confined. We must remember that apart from well-engineered modern roads, it is the topography rather than the traveller that dictates the nature of the path. We do not know the extent to which travellers did follow Roman-engineered roads but it is clear that they recognised distinct types of them. The *Life of St Sturm* points to the difference for as the Saint was riding along a *viam* he came to a *semita* [D26.3]. Talbot translated these respectively as a *road* and a *path* but we do not know what precisely was the difference between them. The two passages are not far apart in the printed text, only some dozen lines, and the contexts must mean that the differing words are used deliberately. There are obvious implications. What is the difference between a *via* and a *semita*? Was the distinction one of function or of construction? Was one a throughway suitable for heavier vehicles such as wheeled carts as opposed to merely people on foot or animal? Whatever it is, the passages make clear that not all early medieval roads were the same or perceived as being so. A *semita* occurs again in William of Malmesbury's account of Aldhelm's return over the Alps [D16] where there would have been the remaining worn system of Roman roads. Is there any significance in the fact that the main road had no name but had to be described whilst the minor path had a name, albeit an archaic one? Both were presumably different from the contested right of way referred to in the next paragraph.

There were disputes then as now between travellers and landowners, for their interests might well clash. In the Life of Willibrord we read of one such dispute, again over a *semita* which crossed between two cornfields. In trying to prevent the Saint from following the path the 'keeper'

ultimately lost his life – such are the dangers of insulting a Saint [D25.2]. Before leaving roads it is worth noting that although there are frequent references to the harshness of a particular winter, it is rare to find that bad weather was blamed as the reason for a failure to make a journey. I have already referred to Isaac who over-wintered in Vercelli in 801-2 rather than cross the Alps but he had a valuable elephant with him [D39.4 and 5]. It was not surprising that he waited till the next summer. That exceptional test offers little guidance as to the normal expectation. That is given in later entries in the *Frankish Annals*. These give references to the winter weather and its effect, both at the time and later when the snows melted. These bear examination for some suggest that a hard winter was not seen as a hindrance to movement, rather the reverse.

> 811 The peace announced between the Emperor and Hemming, the king of the Danes, was only sworn on arms because of the severity of the winter, which closed the road for travelling between the parties. Only with the return of spring and the opening of the roads, which had been closed because of harsh frost, did twelve magnates of each party … meet.

> 815 But since the weather suddenly turned warm and made the ice on the river melt, the campaign was held up.

> 821 a winter so long and cold that not only brooks and rivers of medium size were covered with thick ice but even the biggest and most important streams such as the Rhine, the Danube, … For more than thirty days heavy wagons crossed over the rivers as if they were bridges.

There may have been a balance between a usual hard winter, which actually eased movement, a mild one which left the roads too soggy and an extremely hard season which made movement too difficult. There is some support for this in English records, in for example the entry in the *Life of King Edward* for 1065:

> Edward stirred up the whole population of the rest of England by a royal edict and decided to crush (the rebels) impudent contumacy by force. But because changeable weather was already setting in from hard winter, and because it was not easy to raise a sufficient number of troops, [others] … urged that the attack should not be mounted.[75]

It may be that for some people the weather made very little difference. We read in the *Chronicle of San Juan de la Pena* that on campaign in the Pyrenees in the tenth century, King Sancho decided to attack, for his men were so hardened to the weather that it made no difference to them [D54]. If this was typical, it makes sense of the apparent willingness to undertake the rigours of an Alpine crossing even in winter. It is safer to admit that we know very little and that anecdotal evidence may be misleading.

---

[74] Richer in R. Latouche (ed.), *Histoire de France* (Paris 1937) pp. 225-231. The text is incompletely quoted in R. Lopez, *The Tenth Century* (New York, 1959), p 42. For a fuller treatment see, J.S. Matthews, 'Life on the road in Tenth Century France', *Medieval Life*, Issue 10, 1998, pp. 3-6.

[75] VER, ch. VII.

The quality of the roads must have varied with the degree of economic development of a particular area, so that St Sturm may have met more difficulties than a traveller in the Po valley, but that apart, a frozen lane which might seem tricky to us in a car might be a welcome alternative to slippery mud for a man on foot or on horseback. We must not impose our own standards on them.

This is not to say that there were no complaints. Simeon of Durham tells us of the woman who was so inconvenienced by the deep puddles on the road that she took the short cut through the churchyard of St Cuthbert's church. The result was disastrous:

> One of these [women … as she was one night returning home from an entertainment, was continually complaining to her husband that there was no clean piece of road to be found, in consequence of the deep puddles with which it was everywhere studded. So at last they determined that they would go through the churchyard of this church (that is, of Durham) and that they would afterwards atone for this sin by almsgiving. As they were going on together, she was seized with some sort of indefinite horror, and cried out that she was gradually losing her senses. ... as soon as she set foot outside the hedge which surrounds the cemetery of the church, she immediately fell down; and being carried home, she that very night ended her life.[76]

This was a foolish course for the churchyard was forbidden territory for women, and the punishment for breaking the Saint's rules was death.

Some travellers deliberately took the journey more gently; Bede tells us that Theodore and Hadrian rested for the winter on their way north through France. No doubt the Archbishop's age dictated the more leisurely pace [D17.9]. Despite these occasional glimpses of frail humanity, the inescapable fact is that people made the journey if they had or wanted to, and complained little.

Rivers were both a corridor and an obstacle. Sometimes there was no bridge and the crossing had to be by ferry. These must have existed but the evidence is scarce. Gregory of Tours tells us of one which replaced a pontoon bridge over the Loire. The ferry consisted of two linked boats, one of which sank, but its passengers were able to scramble aboard the other [D1.1]. Another explicit description of a ferry comes from after our period in the pilgrim route to Santiago. The boat was a primitive dug-out unsafe for horses which had best swim across, and the ferrymen charged too much and overloaded the boat [D82.1]. There is nothing to suggest that other commercial ferries were any better but there were non-commercial arrangements also. When Ceolfrid left for Rome in 716 he started on the north bank of the river but took a boat to the other shore in what was presumably a local boat [D29.1]. We have another example of a hostile crossing in

the travels of Gerald of Aurillac [D62.4]. Then it was the controller rather than the ferryman who was the problem but a bribe ensured that all was well.

We must not forget river and coastal traffic. The former was particularly a feature of continental travel especially along the major arteries of the Rhine and the Loire. After a close examination Holland argued that they were not always the preferred choice:

> Downstream traffic is easy on any of these [French] rivers… but in the Dark Ages upstream traffic must have been very difficult on the Loire and next to impossible on the Rhone. Strabo himself says that merchandise was often carried to the upper waters of the Loire by carts rather than up the Rhone, though the latter lies only a short distance away. …[Towing from the bank] is indicated by a charter of the year 558, requiring that a footpath be left along the Seine for boatmen.[77]

Later:

> All this indicates that up until the thirteenth century the waterways of France did not constitute through traffic routes from one end of the country to another but served chiefly to carry local provisions to the cities built upon their banks; and further that these provisions usually came downstream, the barges or rafts which bore them being towed back empty or lightly laden, or in the case of the Rhone being probably sold for lumber.
>
> It seems therefore, then, that land traffic was much more important than water traffic in developing the cities of France.[78]

Even if some rivers, like the Rhone, ran too fast for easy use upstream others could still give access to the heart of continental Europe. Alcuin's poem, *Carmina* IV [D37][79] describes such a journey as far as Spier clearly enough for us to envisage him making it himself. The German Emperors regularly used the Rhine and the Main and among other years the Annals record the latter's use:

790	Upstream to the palace at Salz
790	Downstream to Worms
793	By ship on the River Renitz into the River Main
806	From the palace of Thionville down the Moselle and the Rhine to Nijmegan
819	From Bingen down the Rhine to Koblenz

---

[76] J. Stevenson (trans.), Simeon, *History of the Church of Durham*, ch. 23.

[77] L.B. Holland, *Traffic Ways through France in the Dark Ages, 500-1150*, p. 6.

[78] Holland, *Traffic*, pp. 16, 25.

[79] Alcuin, *Carmina* IV E. Duemmler (ed.), MGH Poetae Latini Medii Aevii I, p. 220.

St Boniface used the Rhine on several occasions. On hearing of the death of Ratbod, King of Frisia 'he joyfully took ship and sailed up the river'. He took ship again when he sailed down the Rhine on his last fatal journey [D20.4]. St Sturm did the same for when searching for his site he took to the water and set off upstream [D26.1]. After failing to find the place they wanted, they returned the same way. The description of St Columbanus' enforced trip down the Loire to Nantes under guard gives us a vivid and perhaps the best picture of life on the river. Several small boats were involved, carrying not only the Saint but his guards and the necessary oarsmen. They carried the food they needed, and tents for their overnight camps on the riverbank during the journey, which took several days [D6]. We will return later to the subject of tents.

Not only were the larger continental rivers regularly used, but free passage on them was a valuable economic right, as it could also be on roads. From an early period, the abbey of St Martin of Tours enjoyed exemption on a number of rivers and in the later eighth century this was extended to cover other market goods.[80] Exemption from river tolls or the right to benefit from them must indicate value and thus a volume of traffic. This traffic could be of both freight and humans, as is instanced by the many references to activity on the Rhine and other rivers. River and lake travel was no novelty for Gregory of Tours and in the *Glory of the Martyrs* he described a miracle set in Lake Leman on the Rhone. A gale nearly swamped the boat carrying the relics of the saints from St Maurice back to King Guntramn, but the priest called upon the saints and the waves subsided [D2.10]. Since this was on one of the routes to England, some of our earlier travellers may have experienced similar storms, if not the miracle. A similar miracle preserved the relics being brought from Ostia to Tours when the ship was in danger of running onto a rock in a gale [D2.11].

Until the Saracens became too much of a menace there was regular sea contact between Italy and the south of France. This was the classic route used by Augustine and his immediate followers and despite difficulties it was used when needed until well into the eighth century. However, by 911 the Bishop of Narbonne was unable to return to his See from Rome because they had blocked the passes.[81] By implication the sea route was also too dangerous.

There is little evidence that coastal routes were used around England although it is hard to believe that they were not. Ceolfrid left the Tyne and travelled south by land before taking ship for the continent. As soon as Hwaetberht had been elected he hastened after and caught up with him when he was waiting for a ship on the Humber. Since we know he took the direct route on the Continent, he must have followed the coast south from the Humber, before taking the short Channel crossing.[82] For what it's worth, in later fiction if not fact, Kari, in Njal's Saga, sailed round the British coast rather than go north by land.[83]

Accommodation and the size of parties

Having started upon the journey, where did people sleep? The answer must be the same as to other questions: it depended upon their circumstances. The popular image of hospitality offered by hospices *en route* may well be false at least in the early years of Anglo-Saxon travel though there is some evidence that they became more numerous as time passed. Monastic and Episcopal hospitality certainly existed but it is important to draw a distinction between the provision of accommodation along a route and provision at the journey's end. All the evidence indicates that the traveller was much better provided for at his destination than he was in getting there. The *Xenodochia* in Rome and the accommodation at St Gall were provided essentially to look after pilgrims at their destination.[84] The same was true of Santiago [D82.3]. There was some accommodation provided along the way, more so as the years passed and travel became a bigger volume business, but the repeated mention of a relatively few famous hostels emphasises that there could still be substantial gaps in between them. Along the central route the common mention of St Josse, Auxerre, (and later) the Great St Bernard and Fiesole, merely indicate how big were the distances in between. Further, many of them were very small, that at Fiesole only providing for a few people, perhaps literally the two or three of the donation [D40]. To make matters worse, the evidence indicates that very often the founder's original charitable purpose was soon forgotten and that the money and facilities were easily appropriated to other uses. At the Council of Meaux, in June 824, there were complaints that over time the funds of some of these hospices were appropriated to other uses so that they were unable to function. Canon 40 declared that 'hospices, and especially those founded by the Scots (Irish), ought to be re-established.' Even if that abuse were corrected, the problems of accommodation were not immediately solved, for at the Council of Paris, in February 845, Canon 25 decreed that 'the residence of the Bishop ought to be situated close to the church and to be available for the reception of strangers and the poor'. That would not have been necessary had the rule been kept. Canon 40 went on to address a particular national problem, 'Hospices, in particular those which have been founded by the Irish, ought to be re-established'.[85]

Neglect of the needy traveller was constantly criticised in church Councils and other edicts, apparently with little

---

[80] Boehmer-Mulbacher; Regesta Imperii I.611.

[81] Catel, *Memoires de l'histoire du Languedoc*, p. 775, quoted in Reinaud, *Invasions des Sarrazins en France, et de France en Savoie, en Piemont et en Suisse.* (I have used the English translation of Reinaud's work by H.K. Sherwani, *Muslim Colonies in Frnce, northern Italy and Switzerland*, p. 134.

[82] *Anonymous Life*, chs.31, 32. See EHD, no. 155.

[83] Otto Springer, 'Medieval Pilgrim Routes from Scandinavia to Rome', *Medieval Studies* no. 12, 1950.

[84] J.M. Clark: *Abbey of St Gall.*

[85] Hefele, *Conciles*, IV, I, pp.121-2.

success. Adam of Bremen probably painted a fair picture in his praise of Bishop Anger [D76.3, 76.4 and 76.5]. Some hospices did function as they were intended, at least for a time, such as that at St. Judo's at Saint-Josse-sur-Mer at the start of the direct continental route. This had been given to Alcuin by Charlemagne specifically to aid travellers and served as a meeting point for them, as for example Æthelheard. Alcuin sent his 'boy' there to ensure that the Archbishop's party was well received.[86] We have seen that some eminent travellers were accommodated by bishops as in 668 when Abbot Hadrian and Archbishop Theodore respectively visited the Bishops of Sens and Meaux, and Paris on their way north and were no doubt well entertained in those places but we do not know how they fared in between.[87]

Similarly, Richer was hospitably entertained in two religious houses along his way, though his (lay) guide fared less well [D61]. Against this, the existence of word lists in foreign languages which incorporate quite mundane commands tells us that many travellers were obliged to stay in and pay for secular accommodation [D55]. Even monasteries appreciated generous gifts from wealthy clerics or kings [D72], which might put them beyond the reach of the humble traveller, unless they had special facilities for them. Common sense suggests that these were more likely to be available along established pilgrim routes. It is most likely that for the traveller with money, hospitality could be obtained at religious houses but that there were gaps which had to be filled either with secular and commercial accommodation, or self-sufficiency. The inadequacy of early commercial accommodation is demonstrated by the minimum provision that Charlemagne enacted [D34.4]. The pilgrim was to be given shelter, fire and water, but not apparently food, unless the host felt generous enough to offer it. The fact, once again, that this minimum had to be prescribed, underlines the difficulties faced by the humble traveller. Even his own *missi* were not to seek help from royal estates but from the public, as a form of tax upon the unlucky [D34.4].

Most famously, accommodation was provided in Rome and the *Xenodochia* there have been studied by Krautheimer.[88] Accommodation was provided elsewhere as well; in Pavia there was Sta Maria Brittonum, founded in 886[89] and there was provision too in Lucca where four churches provided for pilgrims. What exactly was the role of these hostels is obscure; whether they provided accommodation for all, or only for the sick; whether they provided food alone and for how long. References to hospitality given in the chronicles of particular houses suggest that assistance was unstructured and that the motive was to relieve distress rather than to provide routine help for the traveller.

Frequently the account is coloured by a desire to glorify the motives of the benefactor, as in the early twelfth century Evesham Chronicle [D80]. Some houses were dedicated to the pilgrim traffic, like Auxerre, and in Rome accommodation was available from the early centuries, but generally it came slowly elsewhere. The distribution and development of hostels deserves study as a reaction to and promoter of the growth of pilgrim and transport routes and although this paper does not attempt to address so vast a subject, we may note in passing several questions worth exploration. To what degree did facilities exist at the start of our period and how rapidly did they develop: to what extent were hostel facilities provided outside the main towns and especially the main centres of pilgrimage; to what extent were facilities provided by lay as well as secular bodies and finally, even when there were formal arrangements, as there appear to have been at St Gall, how many travellers could be accommodated; was some sort of contribution required, or required if one had the means, and did they cater mainly for the sick and infirm?

Monastic reluctance

The evidence suggests that apart from a few specialised sites, like St Judoc's (above), St Omer and later at the Great St Bernard, a general monastic preference for seclusion as well as fear of the expense tended to discourage the entertainment of visitors and large numbers of passers-by, unless there was a clear commercial advantage to the house in providing for them. The English charters testify to monasteries' willingness to purchase exemptions from the obligation to receive royal servants on their travels. In 844 Bishop Ceolred purchased exemption from entertaining *principes* (ealdermen?) and 'men who bear hawks or falcons, or lead dogs or horses'. In 855 King Burgred of Mercia sold a similar exemption to Alhwine, Bishop of Worcester in respect of the monastery at Blockley. In an unreliable charter of 848 Breedon on the Hill purchased relief from feeding 'ambassadors from over the sea or messengers from the West Saxons or Northumbria.' A little later, in 854, King Æthelwulf found it convenient to pay Bishop Swithun of Winchester with the grant of land at Brightwell 'for the expenses of hospitality to distinguished foreign visitors, or, in the interval of these, for the relief of paupers.' Exactly fifty years later King Edward granted various lands to Bishop Denewulf of Winchester in exchange for the 'escort of travellers from other regions to the next royal manor (*villam*) on their way'.[90] This reluctance to provide assistance unless paid to do so contradicts the popular image of a welcoming monastic hospitality. Although that could be available for some as we have seen, it can be understood in the context of an inward-looking desire for seclusion evidenced by, for example the development of the Minsters within tenth

---

[86] Allott, letter 51, p. 67.

[87] BHE IV.1

[88] R. Krautheimer, *St Peter's and Medieval Rome*, especially p. 23 onwards.

[89] For a discussion, see OEC, pp. 100-5.

[90] M. Gelling, *Early Charters of the Thames Valley*, nos 22, 23; H.P.R. Finberg, *Early Charters of the West Midlands*, no. 76; C. R. Hart, *Early Charters of Northern England*, no. 34; H.P.R. Finberg, *Early Charters of Wessex*, no. 424.

century Winchester.[91] For such properties, the intrusion of official and other secular visitors with their rude entourage must have been most unwelcome and it is likely that their hospitality was reserved for fellow clerics, like Lupus and those depicted in the Colloquies.

We shall see below how some religious houses saw a commercial advantage and were prepared to share in the opportunity, no doubt in a genteel and reasonably discreet way. We do not know how much they preferred to cater for the wealthy, but an indication is given by the Winchester grant cited above, where paupers qualified only if there was money left over from official visitors. If we once more step a little outside our period it is clear from the description of the road to Santiago that along the main routes provision of facilities of any kind became a highly developed commercial operation. Where there were people there was money, and whilst charity and common humanity mingled with other motives, enrichment of the monastery was not easily ignored. The attitude to poor travellers is well set out by the letter of Dungal [D36.1]. Whilst a little tongue in cheek, it includes a serious element of truth. They must have been resented by many.

Secular Accommodation

Even the amount and quality of secular accommodation could vary. We do not know what sort of facilities institutions like the *Schola Saxonum* could provide early in their histories and the descriptions are too vague to help. The fact that there was a quarter, the burgus, suggests that there were several buildings were available but we do not know what facilities they provided [D35.1 and 35.2]. Were there hospices managed for visitors or were they merely groups of aliens living close together for mutual assistance?

Eddius tells us that Pope John provided Wilfrid and his party with free lodging when they reached Rome around 703. The Pope gave him 'a very warm welcome' and free accommodation [D12.12]. This seems to have been an honour reserved for the important few for Wilfrid himself seems to have been offered no such hospitality on earlier visits. If it was a special courtesy to him it must have reflected either an increasing stature or a Papal desire to handle him tactfully. Wilfrid does not seem to have been in one of the *Xenodochia* which had been developed for the pilgrim trade but the account was more specific for one of Boniface's later visits. When he returned to Rome from Germany, he was lodged in one of the pilgrim hostels [D20.2]. Others lodged with the Pope or were given the opportunity to do so, such as Aldhelm and Lanfranc when the latter wrote to Pope Alexander II in 1072/3 asking to be relieved of the cares of office. Lanfranc went to on regret that he had been unable to take up the invitation but still

hoped to do so. The timing is interesting; Christmas was an important period but the Pope seems to have assumed that an Alpine crossing in the depths of winter would not present a difficulty. Since, however, Lanfranc had no intention of going again, the Pope may not have been too considerate.[92]

If he existed at all, among those who travelled seeking a medical cure was the Spaniard afflicted with a spasm allegedly caused by drinking from the Ebro.[93] He reached Fulda in search of a cure and he was 'received into the pilgrim's hospice'. He found more than hospitality, for he was cured as well. More familiar secular accommodation could be available for when St Lebuin was in Frisia, before he started his ministry, he 'was received into the house of a widow called Abarhilda and enjoyed her hospitality for some days'.[94] Not everyone fared as well, and certainly one person who might have had cause to complain was Charlemagne's envoy to Byzantium who according to Notker 'was given accommodation with a certain Bishop. The Bishop spent all his time in fasting and prayers, and he mortified the flesh of the envoy by never giving him anything to eat'.[95]

On occasion, large parties had to be billeted, sometimes compulsorily. Towards the end of our period, in the reign of Edward the Confessor, Godwin tricked Alfred by this simple device, splitting up his men so that they could be overcome easily. [D71.2].[96] This particular occasion was a deliberate trap but the wording does not suggest anything unusual in such an arrangement when a large party was on the move and it accords with the expectations of those in the Colloquies. Others were not so lucky. Even a king could have difficulties as when Lothar arrived in Rome in 869 and, according to the Annals of St Bertin, had a poor reception, being given substandard and dirty accommodation [D41.5]. This was definitely an insult. Royal visitors could expect better as when Charlemagne arrived unexpectedly at a Bishop's house. There was panic and everyone ran round in circles cleaning up for him [D34.1].

Receiving hospitality might be a mixed blessing for secular as well as religious travellers. They also would be expected to give gifts. Cnut was reported to have made lavish gifts both to the monasteries and the poor of

[92] M. Gibson, *Letters of Lanfranc*, no. 1; Z. N. Brooke, *The English Church and the Papacy*, pp. 127-8.

[93] Talbot, p. 225 (Life of St Leoba). The quality of the water in the Ebro seems to have changed over the years. In the Santiago guide we read that it was good: 'At Logrono, runs an enormous river, called the Ebro, which is pure and abounds in fish'. (Gerson et al., II, p. 19.) In that work it was the neighbouring rivers that travellers were warned against, between Estella and Logrono. Perhaps the chronicler was confused as to the exact river, or maybe Spanish tummy could strike anywhere.

[94] Talbot, p. 230.

[95] Notker, ch. 6.

[96] From the *Encomium Emmae*, trans A. Campbell, chs. 4, 5; given in extract in EHD, no. 28.

[91] For an outline, see M. Biddle, '*Felix Urbs Winthonia*: Winchester in the Age of Monastic Reform', in D. Parsons, *Tenth Century Studies*, pp. 132-140.

St Omer when he passed through on his way to Rome[97] and this was clearly behaviour expected of other wealthy or royal travellers. We may note the approving terms in which the *Chronicle* reported Æthelwulf's progress 'in great state' [D43.2] and even Macbeth broke with reputed Scots thrift for he 'distributed (or rather scattered) money at Rome'.[98] This was all part of the role of early medieval kingship and others had to follow suit. We do not know whether Archbishop Sigeric responded to the warm invitation to visit St Bertin despite passing so close. The letter extending it recalled how generous Archbishop Aethelgar had been on his visit a year or so before and clearly expected more of the same. Did Sigeric oblige [D59.1]?

Tents

To provide shelter many Anglo-Saxon travellers did what their modern counterparts can do: they took tents with him. The need is demonstrated by the many references to tents. When Willibald had crossed the Channel and landed on the banks of the Seine, he and his band of friends put up their tents [D24.2]. St Boniface pitched camp when he first landed at the mouth of the Canche and was in camp at the time of his martyrdom for he came out from his tent in order to urge his followers not to resist [D20]. Willibrord used his tent as cover when he told one of his companions to dig a trench to obtain water [D25.3]. St Boniface even had a tent in death for when there was a threat from the Saxons the priests at Fulda took his relics with them and fled, keeping the body safe in a tent. [D21].

Two tents are mentioned incidentally in wills. In 1003/4 Archbishop Ælfric left his books and his tent to his former monastery of St Albans. A little later, 1042/3 Ælfric Modercope left to Bishop Ælfric '... my tent and my bed clothing, the best that I had out on my journey with me'.[99] Even near a town, it might not always have been possible to obtain a roof over your head and some people might have stayed with their tents in an undeveloped site in or near the city. We have an example of this in Gregory of Tours when a Bishop waited in his tent for three days to see Chilperic [D1.4]. Another person who preferred to use a tent, even though he could have afforded something more solid was Gerald of Aurillac who in the second half of the tenth century, pitched his tent, along with everyone else, in the customary field. Similarly, 'on his way back from Rome, as he was going past Pavia he made his camp not far from the city.' Scenting the opportunity for trade, some of the Venetian traders came to Gerald's tent trying to sell him cloaks and spices [D62.6]. A tent need not be a cheap or simple affair but could be valuable enough to be diplomatic gifts, like those given to Charlemagne by the King of Galicia and by the 'King of Persia'. [D39.3 and 39.6].

Some might have to manage without even a tent for whilst travelling in search of a site for his monastery, later founded as Fulda, St Sturm had to traverse wild country and take sensible precautions at night, building a thicket of brushwood to protect his ass. He himself seems simply to have slept on the ground with no more than vegetation for cover [D26.3].

The size of parties

Even when a hospice was available, how many people could be accommodated? It might be very few for when Donatus of Fiesole founded the hospice for Irish pilgrims at Fiesole 'in honour of Saint Brigit in the city of [Placentinae] for the monastery of Bobbio' in 850 there was provision for only two or three people [D40]. This presumes either only a trickle of people at any one time or provision only for the sick and the important. We have a little evidence of the size of parties and some were clearly substantial. Boniface's party was large enough to need more than one boat when it crossed the Channel although that may be because he embarked in a small swift ship [D20.2]. We know from Bede that there were more than eighty Englishmen with Ceolfrid but this almost certainly included lay helpers as well as monks [D30]. It is unlikely that there would have been permanent accommodation for that number along the road and they must either have carried tents or divided themselves into the lucky few who had a roof over their heads and the rest who made do with the trees, hedges and anything they had with them. We may suppose that life on the road was much the same as it was in the time that Peter of Blois penned his highly coloured description of the entourage of Henry II [D85]. Whilst his account smacks of hyperbole and dramatic effect, it nevertheless represents a basic reality and squabbles over accommodation must have been a feature of larger and especially secular parties. Some parties were smaller. Although he was not off to Rome but to the Rhine, Willibrord gathered eleven others with him; an apostolic twelve in all, but was that fortuitous, planned or not literally true? 'So he embarked on a ship, taking with him eleven others who shared his enthusiasm for the faith'.[100] Willibald left England with a band of friends but the number of his companions varied. When he left Rome for the Holy Land some two years later, he left with only two companions and they were not his kinsmen. By the time he reached Emesa they numbered seven. Earl Tostig's party in 1061 was big enough for him to split it into two, with his wife going ahead accompanied by her own escort and most of his men. He lingered in Rome to complete his business and followed later. Although the total number is far from clear, the large size of the party is indicated by the notables included in it and by the narrative of the attack [D74.1].

[97] Campbell, *Encomium Emmae*, ii. pp. 210-11.

[98] For Macbeth, see the *Chronicle of Melrose*; H & S, II. 152.

[99] Both references are in Whitelock, *Wills*, nos xviii and xxviii respectively.

[100] Talbot, p. 6.

Food and Begging

The clerics whose journey is incorporated in scattered paragraphs of the two Colloquies clearly enjoyed some facilities but a number of passages show that they also had to be prepared to scavenge and beg [D52.5 at ch. 27 and 53.17]. One paragraph of the shorter version describes them setting out on an early morning scavenge for food for the day. They had to be careful to thank their hosts for what they had received, for their own sakes and for those who came in the future. This need for begging is shown by the narrative of Willibald's journey to the Holy Land for there we are told that when they were in Phygela they had to beg for bread. [D24.3]. The reference there to the public fountain brings to mind King Edwin's provision of water and drinking bowls for travellers [D17.5].[101] Food shortage if not scavenging is indicated on Willibald's departure from Emesa (the modern Hums, in Syria), this time with a safe conduct, when his party was split into small groups both for control and to ease the search for food [D24.5]. Gerald's servants seem to have taken what they wanted from beside the road, although their master was more scrupulous in compensating the local people [D62.3].

Organisation, Leadership and Guides

There is little in any record of an actual Anglo-Saxon journey to indicate how parties were organised along the way but the Colloquies [D52 and D53] tell us a lot. This material has to be handled with caution for as indicated above the present text is a jumble of passages taken from several underlying originals. It is hard to distinguish the various elements with any certainty for although many must relate to the journey to Rome some undoubtedly relate to more local travel within the confines of a diocese. This uncertainty may not matter very much for it is probable that the same features and organisation were common to both. It is clear that the party described in them was large enough to require and have some internal structure. It had a head (*princeps*) who acted as a spokesman and negotiator when they arrived in Rome and earlier in the story (though later in the text), he is seen giving orders about the conduct of the party. The order implies the existence of a second-in-command, playing the role of an adjutant. There is another officer, a 'divisor' whose job it is to divide the rations. We must not infer too much formality or rigidity about these arrangements and especially the titles. The present Colloquy is a school text and it had certainly undergone many changes before it reached its final form. What we must understand is that a party the size of Ceolfrid's or Tostig's required some sort of formal organisation to keep it on the road. We should not envisage an early medieval hippy colony on the move. What we do not know is whether such 'officers' were drawn from the group itself or whether there was the equivalent of

the modern day courier, a professional who had done the journey before and knew the ropes. Senior ecclesiastical travellers, Archbishops and suchlike, probably preferred to pass from one religious centre to another wherever possible and the provision of Bishop Deodatus as a guide for Wilfrid after he left Dagobert's court may have been as much as a social help as a guide. Deodatus stayed with him until they reached Perctarit's court and from there he was sent on by the king with guides to take him to Rome [D12.7]. The Bishop's presence must have opened many doors, for he would have played a double role for Wilfrid as both guide and adviser (one is tempted to say minder). It may be that assistants in his entourage acted both as guides and 'fixers', and surely general factotum must have been the role assigned to the Anglo-Saxon Deacon Ealdwulf when he accompanied King Eardwulf back to England [D39.7 and 39.8]. He was not a senior figure acting as an envoy and he was not returning permanently to England for he was captured by pirates on his way back to Rome. In a similar way, Benedict Biscop, a seasoned traveller, was engaged by the Pope to act as interpreter for Theodore [D17.9]. Such evidence as there is suggests that by at least the end of the ninth century, a corpus of professional party leaders had emerged, visible in the *Chronicle* entry for 889, when 'In this year no journey was made to Rome, except by two couriers whom King Alfred sent with letters.'

How did one set about the day's walk or ride? Even with a list of towns to be passed, without maps or road signs the traveller could easily be lost. James Boswell shared the experience in 1773, while crossing the Isle of Skye, which to him was featureless and barren. He observed that 'A guide, who had been sent with us from Kingsburgh, explored the way (much in the same manner as, I suppose, is pursued in the wilds of America) by observing certain marks known only to the inhabitants.'[102] The Colloquy indicates that local guides must have been available and that is borne out by only real experience. In the later Colloquy, in paragraph 12 of *Retractata*, the traveller asks the way and has the services of a local guide thrust upon him, plainly of doubtful quality [D52.2 at ch. 23]. There is rather more in the longer version. *Fabulis* 15 copies *Retractata* exactly but in *Fabulis* 23 we have a picture of the party setting off, asking about the way and about any dangers on the road. A parallel to this exchange is recorded by Gregory of Tours in a story of a Deacon going to Rome and asking the way from St Hospicius [D1.2].

Whilst we have no record of an Englishman engaging local guides on an actual continental journey we know that they existed within England, for another traveller, who crossed mainland Britain, was Asser, who tells of how he reached King Alfred in Sussex with the help of guides from that area [D48.4]. The man from Chartres who guided Richer on his journey and coped so well with the

---

[101] BHE II.16. Both the public fountain and the provision of wayside springs are still common in Mediterranean towns and mountain areas, such as the Pyrenees.

[102] James Boswell, *The Journal of a Tour to the Hebrides*. The remark comes towards the end of his long entry for Monday 13 September 1773.

hazards of the dangerous bridge must have been another example of this kind of professional guide [D61]. He had been sent by a learned cleric Heribrand, from Chartres to Richer at Rheims, and Richer's account is of the journey back to Chartres, when the *chartrain* was clearly in charge and Richer an obedient passenger. This must have been a typical relationship and a similar role was probably played by Witto who as well as taking messages for Alcuin across Europe and back to England, went to Rome in 798 almost certainly accompanying Arno of Salzburg as a guide.[103]

Also on the Continent though somewhat later, we meet guides in the record of the crossing of the Great St Bernard in December 1128 by Rudolph of St Trond and Alexander, Archdeacon of Liege. They hired local guides, *marones*, who were available to help negotiate the pass: they are mentioned by name again in the account of St Odo's crossing [D62.4]. They had to be paid handsomely for their services: 'Then the *marones* of the mountains came of their own accord to the pilgrims and offered for a large reward that they should try and open up the road'.[104] As their first attempt to cross the passes in early January failed, they had to hire more guides and after spending a night on the mountain, crossed successfully. This offering of services by the *marones* accords with the similar passage in the longer Colloquy quoted above. One may speculate, incidentally, whether they had tents with them for the overnight stay or whether there was some other form of rough shelter provided? Though this example is from the mountains, it is reasonable to suppose that there were local guides in other areas of difficulty. Sitwell identified the normally hostile Saracens with the *marones*: whoever they were, they seem to have offered assistance at the right price [D62.11].

A guide might be needed not only for a short stretch of the way, but for the journey as a whole, or for a large part of it. On his first journey, in perhaps 654, Wilfrid was sent on his way from Lyons with 'guides and supplies'. As we have seen he was later given the assistance of Bishop Deodatus for the journey south from Dagobert's court to Perctarit's and thence, with a new set of guides, from his court to Rome.[105] This is a rarely documented example of what must have been a common practice, of passing well regarded or important visitors from one set of guides to another, both to help them on their way and also keep them under control. With his record of meddling, the second reason alone may have been good enough grounds for providing Wilfrid with a guide. When Archbishop Theodore was entrusted to Benedict Biscop in 688, the latter was selected and asked to be an escort because he knew the way. Part of it would probably also have been known to Abbot Hadrian who had previously travelled within France on diplomatic missions.[106] These escorts were chosen because of their knowledge and experience of the route as a whole rather

than for detailed local knowledge of the kind offered in either the Colloquy conversations, or in the actual crossing of the Great St Bernard. It may be that the record of Sigeric's journey embodies the skeletal notes made by some such professional courier which were prepared as an aide memoire for the return journey or for the benefit of a colleague.[107] It is unlikely that the Archbishop whose journey brought them into being had more than a passing interest.

Guides could be arranged in advance. Between 748 and 754 King Æthelbert of Kent wrote to St Boniface and sent the bearer under the protection of some agents of the Saint who were returning to him.[108] Similarly, about 961 Count Arnulf of Flanders wrote to St Dunstan on behalf of ambassadors whom he was sending to the English Court. At the end of the letter, he specifically asked for them to be guided on their way.[109] A prudent traveller would ask permission in advance, as in 839, when the English king, often assumed to be Æthelwulf but more probably Egbert, nearing the end of his life, asked leave to cross the Frankish kingdom, on his way to Rome [D41.1]. Royalty were usually well looked after by the foreign ruler, as perhaps were senior clerics, being given a fitting escort.[110] It may well be that the purpose was not simply courtesy but a reasonable desire to keep an eye on any important political figure travelling across one's territory. Such folk might be unwelcome or carry inconvenient messages.

Although it anticipates the examples in the next section this is a convenient point to introduce one more example of such control, of high ranking travellers, this time to prevent rather than assist passage. In 864 Charles the Bald sent a high ranking embassy to Rome but its members were refused permission to cross into Italy and were turned back [D41.4]. No passage was possible until Louis had been persuaded to relent. The text is not precise but the plain reading is that the Pope was informed of the blockade before Rohad reached him, presumably by the people who had turned back.

Maps

How did a traveller manage who had no guide to help him? This section cannot be concerned with the origins of medieval cartography for that is too vast and complex a subject. Nevertheless a few comments can be made. Some knowledge of maps had been preserved from the ancient world and the concept of mapping had not been entirely lost. Writings show that people could still think in terms of maps, as in Alfred's *Orosius* where the outline description of Europe almost oblige the modern reader to see it as an image [D47.2]: in much the same way, so do the descriptive passages by Adam of Bremen [D76.1].

---

[103] Moore, p. 77.
[104] Tyler, pp. 28-9.
[105] Eddius, ch. 28.
[106] BHE, IV.1.

[107] Stubbs, *Memorials*, pp. 391-5.
[108] Emerton, *Letters*, p. 178.
[109] Stubbs, *Memorials*, p. 359.
[110] Nelson, *St Bertin*, sa 855.

The latter's description of the boundary of the diocese not only reflects the bounds attached to English charters, but suggests that the author, and by implication his reader, was able to appreciate a mind's eye image of a large stretch of country [D76.1]. Bede recorded that Benedict Biscop brought back with him from Italy the 'works of the cosmographers' although they might help the traveller very little in a practical way.[111] Later, Charlemagne owned maps engraved on metal [D34.2], which must have been seen at his court by the Irish geographer Dicuil. Finally, we have the tenth century Anglo-Saxon world map Cotton Tiberius B.V. f 56v which contains a recognisable if distorted image of the British Isles, set in a fair relation to continental Europe.[112] In spite of these examples, it seems that there was no mental need which maps had to fill. As Harvey observed

> We must accept that drawing and using maps, even of the simplest kind, did not come naturally to people in medieval Europe …. Medieval people simply did not think of drawing maps for the innumerable purposes for which we are apt to take them for granted. Thus for instance the complexities of the ownership or arable strips in open-field farming would be set out in elaborate written descriptions; directions for a journey would take the form of a list of the places to be passed through.[113]

One writer may be mentioned who makes us feel that he at least saw topography in terms of a pictorial image, if not of a map. In three chapters of his Life of Alfred, Asser wrote of places being to the right hand side of a particular location or of the island of Britain. In chapter 35 he described how two Viking 'counts, with a great part of the (army), rode out to plunder, while the others constructed a defensive earthwork between the two rivers Thames and Kennet, on the right hand [southern] side of the same royal estate'. In the passage in chapter 79 which we have already considered he tells us that he arrived at Dean in West Sussex to meet King Alfred. Dean lay in 'the region of the Right-Hand [southern] Saxons which is called Sussex in the Saxon language'. Finally, in chapter 80, he used the same idiom in describing his own native Wales, observing that '…at that time and for a long time before, all the regions of the right-hand [southern] part of Britain belonged to King Alfred and they belong to him still' [D47]. Those districts are then listed and identified as the kingdoms of South Wales. In all these descriptions Asser was using the convention followed later in the Middle Ages of placing the east at the top of a map, so that south fell to the right-hand side. His terminology is not an abstract geographical concept

but a very practical observation which but for lack of evidence we might think was based upon some familiarity with actual maps. Common though the convention was for world maps in later centuries, his words must surely give us a rare example for its date in relation to local or national geography.

In addition to maps and Asser's pictorial approach, there were a number of specific geographical descriptions. There is an eighth century description by the Lombard Paul the Deacon of the regions of northern Italy.[114] King Alfred was at least aware of Ptolemy's writings, if not his world map, as is shown by his interpolations to his translation of Boethius' Consolations of Philosophy.[115] From them he displayed a very reasonable comprehension of the ordering of the world [D47.1] but although Alfred was himself a well travelled man, his journeys had been in his early years and we must not presume that he remembered too much in detail. In the eleventh century we have several descriptions of parts of northern Europe given by Adam of Bremen.[116] Whilst all these works give a good general picture we must doubt whether they were widely known to the average traveller and even if they were, they would be of little use to an individual trying to find his way to a particular place. For our purpose it is sufficient to say that no Anglo-Saxon map exists to show the route to Rome either within England or on the Continent. Indeed, it is clear that the concept of a map as a directional tool did not exist. Why else should Anglo-Saxon Charters be followed so often by a detailed description of the boundaries? A society familiar with maps would have attached an equivalent of the plans which accompany any modern land registry. Once local knowledge was exhausted, the traveller's best aid in finding his route was probably a simple list of places to be passed, like the record of sub-mansiones which Archbishop Sigeric either stopped in or passed through [D59.2]. This must have been compiled for a purpose and it is to be expected that centres like Canterbury retained a record of the main places on the route. There is no mention in any of the records of physical signposts, such as crosses, and place names give us very limited help for whilst the incorporation of a cross in a town or village name could indicate that it had served as a traveller's guide it need not do so, but might do no more than record the existence of a preaching place. One name does suggest that the cross had served as a guidepost; Christian Malford in Wiltshire, identified by Cameron as the 'ford with a cross'.[117] A few tantalising relics remain that point to what might have happened. On the edge of the village of Nevern on the pilgrim track to St David's in Pembrokeshire a crude cross has been cut in the rock face beside the path significantly

---

[111] BLA, ch. 15.

[112] Conveniently reproduced with an interpretation in D. Hill, *An Atlas of Anglo-Saxon England*, maps 1, 3 and 4.

[113] Harvey, *Maps,* at Chapter 5 generally and p. 86 quoted. By way of parallel the author remembers as an undergraduate in about 1957 being stopped in the market place in Cambridge by four Asians in a car, who wanted to know the way to Huntingdon. They had driven from the ferry at Harwich *en route* to Leicester, and all they had was a list of towns on the way. At the centre of each town they asked the way to the next one.

[114] Paul the Deacon, Waite (ed.), MGH SS Rerum Langobard, also in translation by W. Dudley Foulke.

[115] These were identified by W.J. Sedgefield in his 1900 edition.

[116] *History of the Archbishops of Hamburg-Bremen*, trans. F.J. Tschan, Bk. I, pp. 6-10; Bk. II, pp. 62-68; Bk. IV, pp. 186-220.

[117] K. Cameron, *English Place Names*, p 131. I am grateful to Dr David Hill for this reference.

just above the crossing of the stream that flows beside the churchyard. As it is not properly a shrine and is not apparently connected with any cult feature one possible reason why it was cut was to reassure or guide the pilgrim on his way. This must be a later medieval example but were such features common along the way to the more popular destinations at an earlier period? Time and human activity will have erased them.

The truth is that the traveller would be guided and cared for in a wide variety of ways from the important cleric or noble travelling in a substantial group who would be passed from one safe hand to another, whilst knowing little of the underlying mechanics, down to the poor and isolated individual who had to seek his way by the age old practice of asking about the road from one village to another.

Passports, Safe Conducts and Letters of Introduction[118]

It was not enough to be told or to know the way. The traveller needed permission to pass through the territory of another ruler. There were two levels. In general terms, travel had to be authorised and in particular, the individual traveller might need consent specific to himself. What were the problems?

Political Difficulties

The political climate had to be right, and that depended upon treaty relationships, which could ease or block the travellers' path. In 790 Alcuin wrote to Colcu about the disruption in communications between England and the Empire, complaining that there was a blockade which prevented ships from crossing the Channel [D38.2]. The embargo presumably affected all English shipping but even if it did not, there were plainly obstacles in the way for travellers or messengers. It is interesting that the name Colcu is Irish and although the priest had been in York it is possible that he was no longer there when this letter was written.

Although we must not assume that political squabbles necessarily stopped all movement they undoubtedly created difficulties and a greater need for a traveller to be able to account for himself. The Popes faced considerable difficulties in maintaining contact with their Frankish protectors and on occasion they had to resort either to smuggling letters through Lombard territory by bogus or genuine pilgrims or to use the sea route to circumvent it altogether. The former was adopted in 753 when Stephen II had a letter to Pepin smuggled past the Lombards by a pilgrim [D28.1]. This passage is interesting not only for demonstrating Papal tactics but in indicating how pilgrim

traffic could proceed despite a political embargo. This might not always be the case as we have seen with the Channel blockade of the late 780s but it generally held. Right at the end of our period Tancred was still using the same deceit in Italy though then his motive and that of his companions was to seek their fortunes rather than to trade [D83].

The problem of interference had to be faced again in 773 by Pope Hadrian, causing him to send his envoy to Charlemagne by sea, to the south of France [D39.1]. Clearly the ban applied to that particular group, for others could go through and covertly take messages The ban could even apply to particular people rather than all travellers, as we saw above when Charles' envoys were stopped at the frontier in 864 [D41.4]. Both this and the letter to Pepin make clear that the way might be blocked to particular individuals or groups while other travellers could have normal passage. It was not a new technique for a total blockage over half of Marseilles seems to have been imposed by King Guntram in a dispute with Childebert [D1.3] and as we shall see later, even the Alpine Saracens learned to tax rather than stop travellers [D51.1, sa 951].

Personal Identity

Even if there were no political problems, the traveller had to be able to prove who he was and that he was in a foreign territory legitimately. In obtaining permission for his own journey the individual might have to prove his status and possibly submit to interrogation. He was not free to wander where he liked. It was important for the genuine pilgrim to establish what he truly was and not be taken for a spy, a merchant or a simple beggar. Once he had done that, he had some hope of assistance. This is evidenced in both fact and fiction. In the shorter *Colloquy* (*Retractata*) the travellers had to explain themselves in quite a thorough interrogation [D53, paras 20-21]. These theoretical exercises matched reality. A close equivalent to the request in the Colloquy is given by William of Malmesbury when he related that Aldhelm had to receive permission from Kings Ine and Æthelred to leave England and go to Rome [D16.1]. Like Boniface, above, he also received assistance. A licence not only gave permission to proceed but could also be a request for assistance. One such letter was from Saint Boniface to Count Reginbert, written 732-754, explaining that his servant was carrying letters to and from Rome [D22.16]. The wording indicates that there was nothing special about the person or the request. It was a routine matter, which would presumably be matched by the issue of a formal letter or token. A traveller might not only carry letters but might take verbal messages or be empowered to negotiate business on behalf of a principal. He would need to establish his credentials and the *sigilla* referred to above would serve this purpose also. Higham plausibly suggested that the seal of Archdeacon Boniface was used in this way by a representative at the Synod of Whitby

---

[118] For a recent treatment of this subject, using material from a rather wider period, see Neil Middleton, 'Early Medieval Port Customs, tolls and controls on foreign trade' *Early Medieval Europe* 13, pt 4, pp. 313-58.

ILLUSTRATION 1: THE 'BONIFACE' SEAL FROM WHITBY. THE LEAD SEAL OF ARCHDEACON BONIFACE, REPRODUCED BY COURTESY OF WHITBY MUSEUM. THE SEAL ITSELF IS 2CM IN DIAMETER, BUT WITH A SURROUND, THE OVERALL SIZE IS 3CM DIAMETER.

(below and illustration 1).[119] Such a 'seal' was not intended to be attached to a document but established one's right to be in the particular place.

Failure to make proper arrangements could lead to serious problems as Willibald and his companions discovered in the Holy Land. They had difficulties at Emesa where their lack of authority lead to a charge of spying, followed by imprisonment. Later they had occasion to go through Emesa again and we have already seen that this time they were more careful to obtain letters [D24.5]. The need for a safe-conduct was not confined to the Holy Land, for when in 733 Pope Stephen II had to negotiate with the Lombards about the future of Ravenna he 'at once sent his envoy to that blasphemous king to get a safe-conduct for himself and those who were to travel with him'.[120] Shortly after, the Pope himself wanted to visit France

and consent was needed for that too, though there is no reference to an actual document being issued [D28.3]. A little later the Edict of 750 by Aistulf, in Pavia, records an attempt to bring border arrangements up to a proper standard. If they worked, control would have been very tight [D64]. The neglect that it suggested stands in marked contrast to the more orderly scene revealed in the later regulations, again from Pavia, dated 1010-20, referred to above. Note there the prohibition on the taxing of pilgrims, as opposed to merchants, who had to pay. Despite these examples, the references are insufficient to show whether an individual safe-conduct was still needed in lands where there was treaty protection or whether that general cover was sufficient provided that other criteria were satisfied.

There were three kinds of travel document, to use a neutral term. The first was the personal letter, written in the traveller's home country, asking for help along the way or acting as a more specific letter of introduction at the destination. Although we have no direct evidence, it is likely that this kind of general request would be of most value to travellers passing through several jurisdictions or journeying to visit a particular person or place, such as the Pope. The second type, a parallel to this, was the safe-conduct specific to an individual but issued by the ruler of a particular jurisdiction. Such was the pass given to Pope Stephen by the Lombard King Aistulf, considered below. This would be of use only within that territory and would have to be replaced by another once the frontier was crossed. The third, and the hardest type to identify, was like the second issued by the ruler of the jurisdiction but which was not specific to any particular individual. It would have no value beyond the frontier and the authorities probably intended that it would be returned when the traveller left, for re-issue to the next visitor. In practice, many were probably lost or forgotten. The shorter *Colloquy* suggests that this was some sort of simple token, the idea being similar to that of a signet ring traditionally given as a symbol of authenticity to a messenger. They have been seen as passports, but they were most likely not intended for frontier crossings but only for local internal use. They are probably better seen as a form of entitlement card, though not one personalised for the holder. A modern parallel is the security pass issued to the visitor to a large office block, which simply demonstrates that the holder is on the premises legitimately.

Of the first type, we may instance two documents printed by Stubbs. These were recommendations of a quite general kind, in the form of open letters addressed to anyone along the traveller's route from whom help might be needed. In the first an unidentified author wrote an open letter to all faithful Catholics, establishing the credentials of the bearer as a genuine pilgrim. Having been a soldier he had turned to pilgrimage and all those living along his way were asked to help him.[121] Whilst this letter is undated, the second

---

[119] N.J. Higham, *The Kingdom of Northumbria*, AD 350-1100, p. 135.
[120] LP8, ch. 18, pp. 59-60.

[121] Stubbs, *Memorials*, p. 381.

dates from between 992 and 1001 when Bishop Wulfsige of Sherbourne addressed a letter to all Bishops, Abbots, Dukes and all members of the Holy Church explaining that the bearer was on life long pilgrimage as penance for killing a relation.[122] There is nothing in either letter to suggest that the particular individuals were going to Rome but whether their journeys were national or international they indicate the need for a wandering pilgrim to be able to explain himself in order to claim assistance along the way. Whether, like Boniface, one was going to the Pope or simply going to a centre of pilgrimage, there was clearly a procedure to be observed.

The second type, a parallel to this, was the safe-conduct specific to an individual but issued by the ruler of a particular jurisdiction. Such was the pass given to Pope Stephen II in 753 by the Lombard King Aistulf, allowing him first to visit the king and later to cross the Alps [D28.4]. This would be of use only within that territory and would have to be replaced by another once the frontier was crossed. A variant of this was a letter of introduction which could help, not only at frontiers but on other occasions or the journey's end. Boniface took such a letter to Rome with him, given to him by Bishop Daniel and the Pope was not prepared to spend time with him until he had seen it [D22.1]. When he was sent to Germany he was given first an introduction to Charles Martel, and then Charles issued another for his own dominions, specifically 'sealed with our ring'.[123] Similarly, when Ceolfrid set out in 716 his successor Hwaetberht hurried after him as soon as he was elected and gave him, in Bede's words, 'a letter of recommendation to Pope Gregory, some lines of which we think it well to include in this book as a record' [D30.1]. Such part of the letter as Bede then incorporates in his narrative says very little that is specific but sings the virtues of Ceolfrid and explains that after labouring for more than forty years 'He has set out again as a pilgrim for the sake of Christ at the end of his days and with death looming high.'[124] These letters were not idle formalities, as is shown by an entry in the *Chronicle* for 995. Two priests tried improperly to persuade the Pope to give them the pallium due to Archbishop Ælfric, but one of the reasons for their failure was that 'the pope refused to do that, for they brought no letter, neither from the king nor from the people, and ordered them to go'.

Although it is not so relevant to the long distance journeys with which this book is primarily concerned, another need for a safe-conduct came on a change of regime. Supporters of the old king might not want to stay where they were, but go home. Thus, at the end of the Confessor's reign, the dying Edward said to Harold:

Likewise I also commend those men who have left their native land for love of me, and up till now have served me faithfully. Take from them an oath of fealty, if they should so wish, and protect and retain them, or send them with your own safe conduct safely across the Channel to their own homes with all that they have acquired in my service.[125]

The third kind of pass is quite elusive. It would not be personal to any particular individual. It would have no value beyond the frontier and it was probably intended that it would be returned when the traveller left, for re-issue to the next visitor. In practice, many were probably lost or forgotten. This is what the clerics in Paragraph 23 of *De Raris Fabulis Retractata* were asking for, 'a sign carved and written with your name' [D53]. They sought a token with the ruler's name or emblem inscribed on it. I believe that the numerous lead tokens discovered at Billingsgate in London were examples of the same thing, collected and ultimately buried there because that was a landing point where they would be issued and returned. I follow Higham in identifying the 'Boniface' seal from Whitby to be another example and draw attention to much later medallions found in Denmark, notably one from Ribe which it is suggested was a passport issued to those going in and out of the city. 'Passport' is not quite the right description for that is personal to the holder. As suggested above, a better comparison is the anonymous security pass issued to any contemporary visitor to a government or corporate office block. It simply signals the wearer's right to be where he is.[126] The size of these seals is compatible with such a use. The pre-Conquest examples discussed by Archibald range from 1.5 to 2.6cms diameter and the Whitby 'Boniface' seal, 2cms.[127] It is not surprising that many were struck by known moneyers, for the two productions go together.

Most of the references to passports imply that they were given without payment but we must suspect that travellers who were not well connected might sometimes have had to pay for those as for everything else. Bernard the Wise had a similar experience in 867. He and his companions obtained letters of safe conduct from the 'sultan' at Beneventum, but when reached Alexandria, they found first that they had to pay six *aurei* before they were allowed to disembark. Having paid that unjust demand, they then found that the 'Prince of Alexandria' would not honour the documents but obliged them to pay thirteen *deniers* for new ones.[128] It may be that the distance from Italy to Egypt was a factor but a more likely explanation is greed.

[122] Stubbs, *Memorials*, p. 408.

[123] Emerton, letters nos. XII and XIV.

[124] BLA, ch 19, p. 205.

[125] VER, pp.79-80.

[126] For the Billingsgate and other tokens, see Marion Archibald in Alan Vince (ed.), *Aspects of Saxo-Norman London*, II, *Finds and Environmental evidence*, pp 326-46; comment on the Boniface seal appears in N.J. Higham, *The Kingdom of Northumbria AD 350-1100*, p. 135; the Ribe medallion on display in the National Museum in Copenhagen, is referenced 13774 and is 18mm diameter, but two other examples are referenced D2070 and 1319 (letter 23 August 2000 to the author from Michael Anderson at the National Museum of Denmark).

[127] Archibald, in Vince, *London*, p. 336-42; R. Pickles of Whitby Museum, pers. comm.

[128] Thomas Wright (ed. and trans.), *Early Travels in Palestine*, pp. 23-4.

The sources do not enable us to establish whether the traveller needed these documents even when there were treaty arrangements in place. Human experience suggests that they were, even if only to show that the holder fell within the terms of the treaty, and this is supported by the tenth century regulations from Pavia. Since these provided for the provision of a safe conduct even though there was a treaty in force, it is most likely that the personal obligation to prove one's bona fides remained even in the context of a treaty [D64]. A particular passage in the eleventh century regulations at Pavia is worth noting here, for despite a general treaty regulating trade, individual Anglo-Saxons 'are to receive a safe conduct (*sigillum*) from the master of the treasury that they may not suffer any annoyance as they come and go' [D53, clause 3]. It is interesting that there is a change of term from *epistola* in 750 to *sigillum* in the eleventh century and to compare the latter with the original text of paragraph 23 of the shorter and later version of the Colloquy:

We ask … for a sign (*sigillum*) with your name carved and written (on it) that we may be refreshed and helped by all in your name.

Et sigillum cum tuo nomine sculptum et scriptum rogamus, ut ab omnibus in tuo nomine adivvemur et reficiamur.

It may be that with increased communication a less personal seal became more common than a letter, but the slight indications are that the two always existed in parallel. The brief extract above suggests a badge or a token rather than a letter and echoes the custom recorded by Gregory of Tours of envoys carrying consecrated wands as a badge of office [D1.5]. Unfortunately on the occasion mentioned they revealed the true nature of their journey and their diplomatic protection failed, with the usual results of rack, torture and prison.

Even if holding a valid pass the traveller had to be open in his movements. Within England the laws of Ine (AD 695) emphasised the need for a traveller to let locals know that he was passing through by making as much noise as possible [D14.2]. There might be other obstacles on the way, those imposed by political disputes. Some travellers, not strictly pilgrims, might be political refugees, and we have a reference to these in a letter from Charlemagne to Æthelheard, Archbishop of Canterbury, dating from 793-796.

So, depending upon that friendship which we established once in faithful words, when we were together, we have sent to your friendship these wretched exiles, praying that you may condescend to intercede for them with my dearest brother King Offa, so that they will be allowed to return to their native land in peace and without any kind of unfair treatment, and be able to serve anyone whoever. For their Lord, Hringstan, has died. It seems to us that he would have been faithful to his Lord, if he had been allowed to stay in his own country. But to avoid the danger of death, as he was often said, he fled to us; and was ever willing to purge himself with an oath from any [charge of] disloyalty. We kept him with us for some little time, not out of enmity but in the hope of reconciliation,.[129]

This sort of individual and his retainers had to be kept under observation, until they could be eventually be returned when any threat that they might have posed had ended. During the various wars between the Franks and the Lombards, the passes were often closed at the *clusae*, the guarded security points. This may seem obvious as the Alps lend themselves so much to that tactic but checkpoints were set up at less dramatic points. The *Royal Frankish Annals* record other frontier controls. In 826 there were negotiations between the Emperor and the Bulgars to resolve the issue. There was similar friction at the western frontier of his empire for the next year the Emperor had to attend to a revolt on the Spanish border that threatened the stability of that region [D39.10 and 39.11]. We may assume that arrangements to monitor travellers existed on all land frontiers and among the duties of the border guards would be checking the credentials of travellers to sort out the pilgrim from the merchant, winkle out the spy and collect tolls. Even in England with its seaboard frontier there was a coastal equivalent for in 789 it was the reeve making a routine check of approaching shipping who was killed by the Vikings [D45.1]. Although the circumstances were different because of his ambiguous conduct, Thorkill had to obtain permission before he entered port [71.2].

The smooth operation of treaty arrangements was stressed by Cnut in his famous letter of 1027 and such agreements must have been crucial at border crossings [D69]. It may well be that one of the reasons why English travellers appear to have increasingly concentrated upon the direct route to Rome used by Sigeric amongst others was because the advantages given by the chain of agreements and the consequential facilities which developed with the passage of time, outweighed the uncertainties of the longer but easier route by the Rhone and Mont Cenis. It may be significant that in his letter of 1027 Cnut used the singular '*in via Romam*' not a plural form, which would have suggested a variety of routes, but this may be reading too much into the words [D69]. It would, however, match the singular usage of the *Via Francigena*, further south, where traffic narrowed to a single route.

Even if a traveller had adequate documents, the services of a guide or minder like Bishop Deodatus could smooth the way or even be critical. Not all barriers were correctly operated and officials could take full advantage of all the opportunities presented for bribery and petty obstruction, so that, for example, it needed the tact, the money and perhaps the seniority of Count (later, Saint) Gerald of Aurillac to get past one greedy official at Piacenza who had to be bribed before he would let the party proceed [D62.4]. His bullying echoes the earlier complaints

---

[129] H&S, III, 487.

recorded in the Santiago Guide where there is a graphic account of the toll collectors searching even 'in the breeches' of the travellers when they objected to paying illegal tolls [D82.1]. There could also be general unrest, with threats from bandits as well as unscrupulous officials and boatmen. On this, we may pause to note the gloomy pictures of travel in Italy painted by Bernard 'the Wise' in 867 and William of Malmesbury for the 1040s in the time of Gregory VI [D74.3, 73.4]. In judging them we must remember that William wrote after the end of our period and also judge how much rhetoric there is in both their words. Our evidence for the period on this aspect is certainly thin and the routes may have become more dangerous in the eleventh century, as Tostig was to find. A prolonged break in communication seems unlikely, and people seem to have taken the risk.

Smuggling

The traveller of whatever sort had to pass the checkpoints and answer in the fashion recorded in the *Colloquy*. Sometimes they did so deceitfully. As so often Gregory of Tours gives us a vivid picture of the sort of deceit that had to be watched for, with letters possibly hidden in shoes [D1.8] or writing tablets [D1.6]. Travellers frequently wanted to smuggle material, usually letters but sometimes goods, across a frontier. One wonders whether the pilgrim taking the papal letters in 753 used the device recorded by Gregory of Tours of laying a letter below the wax of his writing tablet. Duplicity was no bar to Sanctity, for that device was essentially the same as that adopted by Willibald when he engaged in his little bit of smuggling [D24.6]. He was more lucky and succeeded in his trick.

Money and Finance

This is possibly the most difficult aspect of all and deserves special study. Travellers left little evidence of their daily transactions on their journey, although there are incidental references to their paying for goods and services. Worse, whatever they did must have changed over the years, not only according to the wealth and status of each traveller, but because our period extends from a time when England had little or no conception of coinage to one when it was normal and abundant. We have very little idea how the earliest travellers paid their way, if indeed they did so in any fashion other than exchange of gifts. One must suppose that when St. Augustine travelled north he would seek accommodation from local clergy, whom he would reward with presents rather than cash payment. He probably found that whatever coin he had with him became increasingly useless once he was beyond the Channel, if not before. Biscop, Wilfrid and other southbound travellers must have been equally perplexed, starting off with little notion of coinage but increasingly meeting it on the way. One must assume that gifts and bullion were always acceptable, even in areas where coin was familiar. However inconvenient gift giving may

have been as a form of payment, its principles must have applied. It is unfortunate that although McCormick has demonstrated the changing routes from the evidence of coin deposits, they tell us nothing about how day by day transactions were made.[130]

The utility of coin changed with the years, and we shall see below Lupus of Ferrières' concerns over having the right sort of money [D46.3]. If by the eleventh century the road to Rome was as commercially developed as the road to Santiago, hard cash was needed and the traveller could not rely upon charity alone. Whatever his rank, he might have to pay his way, either by commercial payment, or by suitable gifts. He had either to take enough money with him or beg for more, or for food and other supplies along the way as we have already seen Willibald had to do. Even at the very end of the journey and in the shadow of the cathedral, the Santiago pilgrim passed the shop that sold him souvenirs and necessities for the return journey. In telling how his French countrymen ('*gens Gallica*') enter 'the basilica of the Apostle' the author recalls how they would pass a mixture of what we would now call useful and souvenir shops [D82.4]. In Rome the journey's end was much the same. Having arrived at St Peter's food and lodging had to be arranged. Both versions of the Colloquy record this and there are hints elsewhere. Both of them set out the sort of welcome that awaits the travellers, with the practical arrangements coming before the opportunity to pray [D52 paras. 16; 53, end]. The thought that the footsore travellers would have clothes good enough to barter with would seem unlikely were it not for their earlier begging of the very same articles [D53, para 12 (begging), para 13 (paying)]. *Vestimentum* is used in both paragraphs and it would seem that the clothing was being begged from Paul to pay St Peter!

Money might be needed on the way back, as much for souvenirs as for the cost of travel. In the will of Theodred, Bishop of London who died in 951, we learn that amongst his possessions were two chasubles, which he bought in Pavia, almost certainly on the way back from Rome. Æthelnoth certainly purchased relics of St Augustine there in 1022 on the way home, paying a hundred talents of silver and one of gold for them [D49.2].[131] As a talent was eighty pounds weight, that was a considerable amount of money but yet it must have represented only a minor part of his total expenses. One wonders whether a man of his eminence was able to borrow money in Italy against future revenues due from England in an early banking transaction. There is no sound evidence for this but a hint may be found in a grant of 762 by Dunwald to St Peter and St Paul, Canterbury [DA33.1]. What underlies this wording? Was the intention to make a set-

---

[130] McCormick, *Origins*, pp. 357-361.

[131] For Theodred, see Whitelock, *Wills* I, and for Æthelnoth, GR, ch 184. For the value of a talent see J.H. Hessels (ed.), *Leiden Glossary*, at pp. 31, 202. William tells us that the arm was displayed in a silver casket with presumably a contemporary inscription.

off of an asset in England against a transfer of funds to Rome?

There were a number of ways by which money could be obtained. The very poorest people might have to beg every inch of the way but one must question what their chances were of completing their journey. At the other end of the scale royal or episcopal representatives must have been adequately funded and we have met the references to the lavish spending of Æthelwulf, MacBeth and Cnut. There were many variations in between. When Boniface set out on his first journey to Frisia, he put his plans before Abbot Winbert and was given whatever money was felt to be enough [D20.1]. One can only assume that the sum was enough for we have no further reference to funding but he may well have received more money in Rome from Papal largesse. The money might not be enough, and might run out. St Odo of Cluny was managing on a limited budget, and would have run out had he not had the good fortune to meet a fellow monk who had spare money and borrowed from him. [D62.2]. One person who certainly did not have enough was Eadburh, the widow of King Beorhtric. After a feckless life in both England and abroad, she died in penury in Pavia. Her story is related by Asser, who adds the detail that although she was reduced to begging, she still retained the services of one slave boy to the end.[132] She should not be regarded as typical, for she had been living abroad, not just travelling. The linked problems of money and horses combine in two illuminating stories. In one, we have a letter from an unknown applicant to an equally unknown recipient, in which the former asked for money. It is not altogether clear what happened but we can piece the story together. The traveller went overseas but ran out of money. He then bought a horse for thirty shillings, paying for it by bonding himself to the vendor. He then rode home on the horse. So far, so good. Unfortunately the horse died and the rider was no longer able to sell it and repay the money which he owed. At some stage he turned to a cleric called Remius who lent him some of the money he needed. Perhaps the bond was transferred to the cleric. Unable to repay, the writer had to turn to the recipient of the letter, known only as N, asking him in the most despairingly obsequious terms to pay off the debt or the writer would be at risk [D60]. This episode echoes the concepts of a bond enforceable across frontiers as shown in the *Ordinance of the Dunsaete* [D14.11], and across the Channel, and reinforces the possibility of primitive transfer arrangements already hinted at by Dunwald's will.[133] The other horse story is simpler. In 1075, a little after the end of the Anglo-Saxon period, Lanfranc wrote to Roger Earl of Hereford urging him to do his duty by his King and Lord and not rebel. At the end of this important

matter he slipped in a little paragraph: 'You are asked to see that Beringer, who brings you this letter, has a just settlement with those men whom he accuses of having stolen his horse.'[134]

The transmission of money is illustrated in a letter of Alcuin. Writing from England to 'his son Joseph' in Ireland, he first asked for political news and then got down to finance. He had earlier sent Joseph five pounds of silver 'for bartering or selling its equivalent or exchanging: could he now either have it back or have its equivalent in goods'. Odwin was to bring it, having, one may guess, taken over the letter making the request. More than that, Alcuin must have been using Joseph as a banker for he asked also for the return of another five pounds of his silver, which by implication he had sent over before. There must have been either further cash or credit, for he asked for the supply of clothes and other goods 'for the use of my boys'. Finally, one Eanfrith was to report to Joseph, so that Joseph would know him, and he also was to remit money (via Odwin?) that he had been collecting at the monastery, and, with Frotgoneg, money he had collected from Wurmec's township [D38.1]. There seem to have been three financial operations run in parallel: using Joseph as a banker; authorising Joseph to trade with funds deposited; engaging Eanfrith to collect and remit money both by himself and with Frotgoneg. The money could go astray. Ordericus Vitalis tells of the death abroad of William of Montreuil, the founder of Evroul. On his deathbed he appointed two men of St Evroul to be his executors, but one of them, Anquetil of Noyer, embezzled the money.[135]

Sometimes the money was gathered but never used, for the journey might be abandoned part way or even altogether. In the 790s Alcuin wrote to Eugenia telling her to spend her money on the poor rather than undertake the long and risky journey to Rome [D38.5]. Later, in 1056, It was said that Edward the Confessor, King of England, had vowed to attend the Council in Rome and had gathered money for the purpose. In the event, the situation in his kingdom did not allow him to be away for so long and he sent ambassadors to the Pope, with the plea that he be released from his vow. The Pope agreed, on condition that he gave to the poor the sum that the journey would have cost him and that he founded a monastery in honour of St Peter. As a result, the considerable sum was put to quite a different use altogether, the building of the great abbey of Westminster [D75]. This is not a credible story and is not supported by the *Vita Edwardi Regis* which stated that the money came from tithes [136] due to the king, but even if incorrect, it does give an idea of what might happen and how much it was thought that an official journey

---

[132] Asser, ch. 15.

[133] For our period, it is impossible to be certain of arrangements for the recovery of debtors over a distance, but not long after it the Anglo-Norman Custumials of Exeter provided for the summoning of 'foreigners'. (J.W. Schopp (ed.), clause 30, on p. 29).

[134] M. Gibson, *Letters of Lanfranc*, no. 31.

[135] M. Chibnall, *The Ecclesiastical History of Ordericus Vitalis*, Bk III, p. 61.

[136] VER p. 44. 'Ex decimis' which Barlow translated as 'out of the tithes of all his revenues'.

might cost. Another aborted journey was that proposed by Adulf, 'Chancellor to King Edgar' in remorse for the accidental death of his son. St Æthelwold persuaded him not to go, but instead to give the money to help in the rebuilding of Peterborough Abbey.[137]

Raising money for the journey might involve the sale or mortgage of assets. As early as about 800 we have a form of short-term mortgage, when Æthelric wanted to go to Rome. He first checked with the Archbishop and King that he was free to do what he wanted with his lands. Then, discreetly making no reference to borrowing money, he 'entrusted [his lands] for my friends to keep when for the relief of my soul I sought St Peter and St Paul. And when I came back to my country, I received back my land and repaid the price as we had previously agreed that we might be mutually at peace' [D33.2]. The agreed price could include capitalised interest, but more likely the lender received his recompense from having the use of the land for the period of the loan. Before 912, Werthryth, wife of Cered, disposed of all her property to a kinsman, Cuthwulf, and presumably used the cash raised for the journey to Rome.[138] Later, about 1050, a Danish nobleman Askyll gave all his property to Peterborough and retired to Rome. It is quite likely that 'gave' is a euphemism for 'sold', and that the purpose was to finance the journey.[139] Another early arrangement comes in the will of Æthelnoth and his wife Gaenburg. They made elaborate arrangements for their property, including its disposal should they venture on a pilgrimage [D77]. The effect would be that the sale of their property would finance the journey.

Finally, at the very end of the Anglo-Saxon period Ulf and Madselin, husband and wife, provided for the cost of the journey from capital by mortgaging an estate for eight marks of gold, to be repaid if they returned. If they did not, the Bishop kept the land but had to dedicate any surplus value to the good of their souls [D78.3]. Æthelric and Ulf cannot have been alone in adopting a form of mortgaging to raise money for that particular purpose. Other people might contribute to the cost, and we have noted the Exeter Guild Statutes, which provided financing for the southbound merchant although it is not clear whether the contribution was towards an individual adventure or a joint enterprise. If there was no help from others, an individual might have to sell up and raise the money that way.

I have referred above to ferry crossings, for which money was needed, and the cost of buying horses, but another specific cost was that of the boat trip across the channel, and although we have no record of its payment, from Marseilles to Italy when that route was used. When Boniface was on his first voyage to Frisia, he went to

London where he found a foreign ship and duly paid his fare before they set sail [D20.1]. Willibald did the same, though the account is more lively and suggests that the narrator had himself sailed from or was familiar with harbours [D24.2]. Although there is no specific mention of money, Benedict Biscop must have had to pay the master of the merchant ship that took him from Lerins to Rome.[140] Payment might not always be so simple: Aldhelm obviously annoyed the sailors by haggling over the price of the Bible and that led to an argument over the price of his passage [D16].

All the journeys mentioned in the last paragraph originated in England and payment would be made in local coinage. Once abroad, that could no longer be the case. It is probable that along the better frequented routes a variety of coinages was known and accepted, but it is more likely that the traveller was in the hands of money changers. It is not clear how arrangements for changing money developed. There is a specific but late reference to such transactions in the description of the facilities around the Cathedral at Santiago, for in the passage already quoted money changers were said to be in business along the Via Francigena. There is virtually no earlier evidence. In the summer of 849 when Lupus of Ferrières was planning a journey to Rome on Royal business he wrote to an unidentified cleric Reginfredus, asking him not only for hospitality as he passed through the other's territory but for a supply of Italian money [D46.3].[141] Lupus explained that he had none of his own but had been told that in Italy only Italian money would be accepted. The passage is inconclusive. Lupus may have panicked; he may have wanted a way of reminding others of his important mission; he may have been clever and prudently tried to obtain money from a fellow cleric rather than pay the charges levied by whatever money changers there were. We cannot be certain and can only note that, for whatever reason, he wanted to have a supply of the right money and that a deposit of foreign currency was held in at least one ecclesiastical city on the way to Rome. That must have been the case for most royal and major ecclesiastical centres where the local ruler controlled the currency.

A few travellers may have been able to raise some money by limited trading, but this would only be feasible if what they had to sell was of high value and took up little space. Travellers from the north might find this difficult. Precious manuscripts could be taken either as gifts, but also, if suitable, of a type that could be exchanged or sold. Unfortunately this is poorly documented. Travellers returning might sell spices or similar high value goods, and Alcuin's letters mention many of these sent as gifts taken by the messenger. One wonders what Willibald did with the balsam that he smuggled out of Palestine. Did he

[137] *The Peterborough Chronicle of Hugh Candidus*, W.T. Mellows (ed.) (Oxford 1949), pp. 29-30, 188.
[138] Birch, no. 537.
[139] Kemble; *Cod Dip* IV. No. 86, p. 140.

[140] BLA, ch. 3.
[141] The letter is in L. Levillain, *Correspondance de Loup de Ferrières, edite et traduite ...*, vol. ii, number 75; Duemmler, no. 66.

give it away, or did he sell it?[142] It might not necessarily have been used to finance his travels as McCormick assumed, even if only because he could only profit from it when he was safely on the return journey and most of his expenditure met.

It may be that with more frequent use, people were able to form an estimate of the cost of a journey to Rome but that must always have been difficult. Even the best planned arrangements could go wrong and the cost of a journey further afield particularly one lasting for some years, could be totally unquantifiable.

Ships and the Sea

There are few graphic accounts to life on board ship or the techniques of sailing. Most of the references are bare, even formal, such as those from the lives of St Boniface and Willibald already cited. They do not suggest first hand experience or great familiarity with seamen. Most references are even less informative, simply telling us that someone 'took ship' whilst some were almost poetic, like the beginning of the report by the Papal legates of 786, cited above. Wilfrid seems to have taken the shortest Channel crossing when he could, as when he returned from Gaul in 666 and was forced ashore in Sussex.[143] An observed touch, from a narrator who must have been on board ship, comes from that story for when the Saint's boat was being rowed back and 'while the priests were praising God with psalms and hymns, giving time to the oarsmen', the storm arose that left the travellers stranded on the sea shore [D12.4]. They presumably adopted a strongly rhythmic chant similar to the stresses of later sea shanties. Those personal elements occur rarely in the factual record, but when we read them they bring us close to the emotions of the travellers themselves. In 678 he more probably sailed direct from Northumbria to Friesland, following a westerly wind.[144] I discuss elsewhere the possibility that Wilfrid returned by the sea route round Spain in 658 after nearly being executed by Ebroin [D12.3].

Personal experience may have underlain Alcuin's poem *Carmina* IV which recalled his own travels on the Rhine [D37]. Although those were river and not deep sea descriptions, they are relevant to the whole problem of travel, for rivers could be an important route. Aidan must have had some experience on the water, for even though a flask of oil, holy or otherwise, was unlikely to quell a great area of rough sea, his advice has a ring of experience [D17.8]. The story does tell us that following the coast was regarded as a normal way of taking a valuable person – a princess – from one part of the country to another and presumably more pleasant, as well as quicker, than the land

route that Utta took going south. If this was so, there is no need to assume that travellers to the Continent necessarily took the straightest crossing: they too may have followed the coast to a port more convenient for the next section of the journey on land. We do not know, for example, which route Augustine took from his (probably) last major call in Tours and he may have hugged the Channel coast rather than going north east overland.

One later writer who does seem to have had either first hand experience of sea travel or at least have lived amongst those who had, was the author of the *Encomium Emmae Reginae*, writing in 1040-42 [D71]. Although his literary style was heavily influenced by Virgil's Aeneid there is a mass of detail in his writings, like the references to the clouds rolling up behind the ships and the use of topsails; from being caught in a storm at sea and anchoring for the night; mooring and un-mooring the boats, from feeling the silence of a boat on a smooth sea. These must have come from the author's own experience rather than reading Virgil or from talking with sailors. The reference to seeing boats anchored and supported by poles, upright against an ebbing tide cannot be a literary echo of the tideless Mediterranean and must reflect personal observation [71.7]. This is probably the first written reference that we have to this technique.

Language and Communication

We may assume that Latin served as a pan-European language for a limited number of people. Even amongst the clergy, knowledge of it might be limited to the liturgy without competence in conversation. With the exception of Jews, for most travellers, their native language was the only one that most people possessed and it might not have taken them very far. Ohler noted that even in England four languages were spoken in the eighth century, so that difficulties might arise even before the Channel was crossed.[145] Although they must have been aware that they would have to communicate with locals along the way, at least for basic requirements, there is little open recognition of this. Bede remarked sadly, in passing, that some of the monks who had accompanied Ceolfrid stayed at Langres after his death, to be with his tomb, although they would be 'in the midst of a people whose language they could not understand' [D30.3]. There is another reference to the difficulty of language in the dispute which separated St Columbanus and St Gall, for the latter had learnt to speak the local languages and wished to stay where he was whilst the restless Columbanus wanted to move on.[146] One wonders how effective a missionary could be if he had no ability and seemingly no desire to learn the local languages but preached through an interpreter [D7]. The problem appears with the unfortunate Bishop Agilbert. He exasperated his king, who 'grew tired of his foreign speech', facing a problem which must have

---

[142] McCormick, *Origins*, p. 133, presumed that he sold it but that is not stated.

[143] Eddius, ch. XIII.

[144] Eddius, ch. XXVI

[145] N. Ohler, *The Medieval Traveller*, pp. 74, 77.

[146] See G.S.M. Walker; *S Columbani Opera*, p. xix.

been common in the early days of the Conversion.[147] A fictional but still useful reference comes from a little after the Conquest. It comes in the story of the former servant of Harold Godwinson, named Saebeorht, who went to Rome shortly after the Conquest, 'Hoping as Harold had done to moisten with his tears the resting places of the Holy Men, to listen to strange languages which he did not understand...'[148] Curiously, he seemed to relish rather than fear the experience [D79].

Commerce always eases difficulties and we may presume that along the more popular routes traders learned a smattering of the basic words needed to communicate with people of the more common nationalities who passed. Pointing and a rudimentary sign language could be assisted in part by bilingual or parallel texts and the classic examples are those setting out basic terms in Latin and Old German, exemplified by Vatican M/S 566.[149] The latter provides equivalents for parts of the body, people and other common words or terms so that travellers could prepare themselves by learning simple exchanges, just as the poor linguist does now. Two comments may be made on the Vatican document. The first is that it confirms the value and accuracy of the fictional exchanges set out in the two English Colloquies. Second, the format is interesting, for it tacitly assumes that people familiar with Latin, such as clerics, could not rely upon finding accommodation among other Latin speakers. The assumption is therefore that the accommodation was secular, indicating a network of inns by the ninth century. We have already seen Saint Lebuin lodging in the house of a widow, and he cannot have been unique in being given that sort of opportunity. There are similar texts and word lists from St Gall, where numbers of pilgrims must have presented particular problems.[150] Even the author of the Santiago guide gave some help, though he did so in disparaging terms. Of the Navarrese he wrote that their language was 'savage' and he then gave examples of familiar Latin words with the Navarrese equivalents [D82.2]. Despite his critical attitude, the information would be useful to the traveller. These word lists would supply the basic vocabulary needed for simple transactions and we may assume that anyone who had made the journey and returned would become a useful source of information for the next person to go. Whether or not the traveller had the benefit of word lists in advance, he had to manage somehow and it is not by chance that there are so many indications that long distance guides and mentors were used to save the escorted traveller from difficulties. Nor is it is surprising that people banded together not only for security but as a way of overcoming their logistical

and language problems. If a group could find or have appointed as its leader someone who had made the journey before, knew the ropes and could speak some of the language, its difficulties were much reduced.

The Two Latin Colloquies

It is worth a slight diversion to consider the longer Colloquy in this context. Like the shorter version, it contains much conversational matter of use on a journey but it does not provide a true parallel text of the kind considered so far. However, it does have a number of Welsh (or Cornish) glosses, which have been much studied for other purposes. Attention has centred upon who wrote them and where but it is worth asking why they were entered. It seems to be accepted that the manuscript was written in England not in Wales and it has been assumed that the glosses were written by an ex-patriate Welshman living or studying at an English ecclesiastical centre. If these glosses are seen as one of a type of parallel texts, this is not necessarily the case.

The most interesting of the glosses fall in paragraph 7 which consists of a list of over forty-five names for tools: axe, bill hook, sickle, wagon body, adze, spade, rasp and so on [D52.1]. Almost all of them have their Welsh (or Cornish) equivalent entered above. We must remember that the text is probably not in its first formation but is a reworking of an older version. Parallels, without the glosses, appear elsewhere as for example in the St John's College Manuscript immediately preceding the passage, which Stevenson took as the beginning of the shorter Colloquy. The choice of words glossed suggests a landholding rather than an administrative or liturgical interest and it may have supplied a vocabulary for English members or servants of an English house who had regular business in Wales. The fact that the glosses are both linear and interlinear (which indicates continued use and rewriting) suggests that the need for a vocabulary lasted for some time.

I will conclude this section by returning to the account of Saebeorht's journey which I referred to above. Even though it must date from just after the Conquest and is also very probably fictional, it embodies many of the elements that we have been considering. It also suffers from the dominant vagueness of the *Vita Haroldi* from which it comes, as in the lack of a route, simply described as 'after many wanderings', or names of the actual places visited. In the story, and after Harold's death, a servant of his named Saebeorht living in Chester decided to copy his master and visit not only Rome but the Holy Places in Palestine as well.

... because he knew that Harold had done so, he undertook the hardship of a pilgrimage embracing voluntary exile from his native soil in order to merit becoming a Holy Man and a servant of God. Whereupon with naked feet he departed from the confines of the City of Chester,

---

[147] BHE, III.7.

[148] M. Swanton, *Three Lives of the Last Englishmen*. The Latin is in W. de G. Birch: *Vita Haroldi*.

[149] E. Steinmeyer & E Sievers, *Altdeutsche Gesprache; die Altochdeutsche Glossen*, vol. 5.

[150] E. Steinmeyer & E Sievers, *Die Althocdeutsche Glossen*, vol. 3, p. 1 (Codex S Galli 913).

leaving there the treasure which he had hoarded for so many years, taking only a portion for the crown of his Heavenly Kingdom and abandoning the rest dug up on the surface of the ground ... And hoping as Harold had done to moisten with his tears the resting places of the Holy Men, to listen to strange languages which he did not understand ... (eventually he) ... returns to his native land as Harold had done.

He spent the rest of his life as a respected hermit in Oxfordshire.[151]

---

[151] J.S. Matthews; 'From Chester to Rome: An Early Medieval Journey', in *Transactions of the Lancashire & Cheshire Antiquarian Society,* vol. 94*,* 1998; *idem*, 'The construction and content of the *Vita Haroldi*', in Gale R. Owen-Crocker (ed.), *King Harold II and the Bayeux Tapestry* (Boydell, 2005), pp. 65-92.

CHAPTER 6

THE ROUTES TO ITALY

The evidence suggests that there were originally four principal routes for travelling between Italy and the British Isles, especially England. Most used was the direct route. Initially this took an almost direct line from south eastern England across the Channel to Etaples (Quentovic) and thence across eastern France, the Jura and over the central Alps by the Great St Bernard into northern Italy by Aosta and Pavia, but after the sack of Quentovic by the Vikings it moved slightly to the east, to pass through St. Omer. Next there is the route which ran through northern France, Paris and down to the Rhone valley either to a crossing of the Sea of Liguria direct to Rome or a crossing of the Alps by one of the lower western passes. I call this the central route. Both were used in the early period as we shall see. There was next a more easterly route using the Rhine and the central Alps which seems to have been favoured by Irish travellers, especially early in the period. Irish travellers need separate study though as a generalisation it may be said that the surviving evidence provides little precise record of through traffic as opposed to monastic settlement. Some Anglo-Saxons used the eastern route but the evidence suggests that when this was so it was used there was a particular reason which over-rode the usual consideration of speed offered by the direct route. It seems to have been more used if there was a political need, as for Eardwulf's visit to Aachen in 808 or a particular person to be visited such as Alcuin, or like Witto in about 794, or if political danger dictated it, as may well have been the case for Bishop Wilfrid.[152] Last, there was a western route, which ran from further along the Channel coast, more likely to the mouth of the Seine, to Tours and thence to the Rhone valley, with once more the choice of a crossing into Italy either by the sea or the western Alps. English travellers seem to have used it little, if at all, after the end of the eighth century, and this accords with a general decline in its use identified by McCormick.[153]

It is often hard to determine whether a route was the direct or the central because a number of the references are solely to Pavia where many of our travellers died or rested after the exertions of the Alpine crossing. This was the meeting point for both the Great St Bernard and Mont Cenis crossings and unless there is some other named point, one has to guess the way from other clues. Tyler argued that many travellers were deterred by the greater

obstacles of the shorter route and may have preferred the longer way over the Mt Cenis but the evidence is not good enough to enable us to say with certainty that this was true for Englishmen.[154] The Mont Cenis route was undoubtedly used by continentals. The balance of such evidence as we have all points to a preference for the direct route as the preferred way to and from England and in truth, the main argument in favour of the predominance of the direct route after about 700 is the total lack of reference to the central. I have assumed that when we know a journey was made quickly, it probably followed the direct route.

There were, no doubt, many minor variations on these routes, taken for a variety of reasons. Friends or particular sites might be visited, or there might be local obstruction by unrest or truculent officials. There might be contrary winds in the Channel or outbreaks of illness to be avoided on land. Facilities at particular places might vary, or even disappear as when the direct route changed after the destruction of Quentovic at the very end of the ninth century and switched to St Omer.[155]

Although it will scarcely feature again, for lack of evidence, we may pause briefly to consider also the possibility of travelling by a true deep sea route round the Iberian peninsula. This was used earlier. The trail of archaeological finds along the western seaboard of the British isles demonstrates contact with the Mediterranean world but that by itself is not conclusive for they could have been brought across western Gaul by the Loire or Garonne and been transhipped at the Biscay coast.[156] We know from the Life of St Columbanus that this was done. Some are particularly tantalising; one such is the St Menas flask found at Meols on the Wirral which probably dates from the fourth century onwards when the shrine became popular, to the middle eighth when it was sacked. The find site is such that the flask can only have come by sea.[157] There is slight evidence for trading round the Iberian coast in Gregory of Tours for he recorded the looting in

---

[152] The reference to Witto is in a letter of September 798, see E. Duemmler, *Alcuini Epistolae*, MG Epp Karol Aevi II. p. 253.

[153] McCormick, *Origins*, pp. 77-82.

[154] Tyler pp. 18, 21-23 on the various routes.

[155] For the significance in this for Alfred's travels, see P. Grierson; 'Grimbald of St Bertin', in *English Historical Review* 55, 1940.

[156] See for example C. Thomas: *Celtic Britain* pp. 57-60 and Fulford: 'Byzantium and Britain: Post Roman Mediterranean imports' in *Medieval Archaeology*, 33, pp. 1-6. At p. 4: 'Thus we can see the British material on the periphery of an expansion of trade originating in the East Mediterranean and peaking between *c.* 475 and 550.'

[157] 'Miscellaneous notes' in *Journal of the Chester & North Wales Archaeological Society*, NS xliii, 1956, pp. 48-9.

Septimania of ships from Galicia [D1.7]. We have only one firm piece of literary evidence for this route in the Anglo-Saxon period, that of Arculf's return from the Holy Land shortly before 700, reported by Adamnan. The reference is brief but if we assume that Arculf would not have passed through the straits of Gibraltar unless he intended to round the Iberian peninsula, we may be sure that that he intended to land on the Biscay coast of Gaul. Bad weather took him probably right round the west coast of Ireland to land somewhere not too far from Iona. As there is some evidence for a seaborne trading connection between western Britain and the Mediterranean, we may perhaps surmise that Arculf took a passage on a merchant ship bound for western France. His journey must have been made not long before the Arab crossing of the Straits of Gibraltar and their conquest of Andalucia [D10].

The deep sea route can be considered once more as a possibility in the first of Wilfrid's return journeys and I return to this below but the archaeological evidence bears out the reasonable supposition that the sea route to northern Europe was already in decline by the turn of the eighth century and finally went out of use either at the time of or as a result of the Islamic conquest of North Africa and Spain. Certainly, I cannot find any indication of its use from Anglo-Saxon sources and the next record is the Viking raids in the 840s when Seville was attacked as part of a voyage into the Mediterranean.[158] Further attacks deeper into the Mediterranean followed from 858-9 and into the next decade. More peaceful Scandinavian travellers made the round trip, by the Dnieper in the east and Gibraltar in the west, from at least the eleventh century.[159] The deep sea route used by Arculf and possibly Wilfrid seems to have passed out of use, for a number of reasons which have been much discussed, after about 700 and as noted above it can virtually be ignored here.

A salutary reminder of the variable quality of the evidence is the mention of the English merchant Botto in Marseilles as late as 781[D32]. The reference makes clear that he was a merchant and that the town was still a functioning port at that time. What chance brought him there and does his presence indicate a trading link with his home country? Were there other English people whose names have not survived? Ganshof's demonstration that seaborne activity continued through the period, and that the upper Rhone was still in use as a route south, albeit in decline, until at least 953 supports the argument that Anglo-Saxons could have gone that way if they had wanted to, crossing over the Mt Cenis if preferred. There must have been other reasons for their presumed preference for the direct route.

The questions to be answered are whether, when and why there were changes in the routes, especially from the western and central to the direct route.

The changing routes

The western land route seems to have been much less used and was probably abandoned altogether as a through way not long after 700. Abbot John had hoped to return to Rome via Tours but, except for Oswald, he was the last we know of to go that way. As noted above, Oswald had a special reason for diverting to Fleury on the Loire, having spent part of his youth there.[160] Possibly Willibald passed that way in 721 but we simply do not know. All that is certain is that he crossed France from the Seine. He may have turned southwest to the Loire or he may have followed the Seine to Paris and then taken the central route to the Rhone valley. After then, silence, at least for known individuals. This does not accord with the foundation of the hostel in Auxerre in 725, specifically for pilgrims going to Rome but there is no reason to suppose that this was founded with English travellers in mind. Whilst Wilfrid was taken there while he was ill in 704 there is no record of any later English traveller to Rome using it thereafter. Alcuin's plea for Archbishop Æthelheard to visit him at Tours was unsuccessful.[161] The lack of information does not, of course, mean that Tours was not visited in its own right, and it certainly was although the evidence is scanty. Visits probably never ceased or were only temporarily interrupted by disturbance, for much later, in 1013, Queen Emma visited Tours with Abbot Ælfsige whilst in exile.[162] What seems certain is that whatever the importance of Tours as a centre of pilgrimage in its own right it was not seen as a place to visit on the way to Rome.

Once the impetus of the Anglo-Saxon mission had passed, English travellers do not seem to have used the most easterly route along the Rhine unless there was specific reason for doing so. That seems to have been the case only rarely. In 1061 Tostig followed the Rhine while undertaking a diplomatic mission but he seems not to have travelled the lower reaches of the river. Although his movements are far from clear, Cnut seems to have preferred to follow the Rhine, but given a starting point in Denmark that is to be expected. Similarly, we have no record of journeys through Paris and down to the Rhone in the later years. Although the record of places visited tends to leave a void between the Channel coast and Italy, such indications as there are – notably Sigeric's route and the unusual diversion taken by Oswald – suggest that the direct route was predominant by and probably well before 800.

[158] There is little secondary material of value on the Viking raid on Seville and few contemporary north European references. Three of the Muslim chroniclers have been translated in Dozy, *Recherches,* vol. II and a fourth is used extensively but not translated in E. Levi-Provencal, *Histoire de L'Espagne Musulmane,* vol.II.

[159] See A.A. Vasiliev; *The Russian Attack on Constantinople in 860;* H.R. Ellis Davidson, *The Viking Road to Byzantium,* (London, 1976), chapter 5.

[160] Macray, *Ramsey Chronicle,* pp. 24-5.

[161] For the invitation, see *Vita Oswaldi,* in J. Raine, *Historians of the Church of York* I. p. 435 and II, p. 27. For Alcuin's request to Æthelheard, see Allott, *Alcuin,* Letter 20, p. 28.

[162] W.T. Mellows, *Peterborough Cronicle,* pp. 48-9.

Before we turn to the second question, why there was a change, we need to answer another. Was there a replacement of one by another or was there a narrowing of choice? Here it is worth recalling the remark of Eddius that Bishop Winfrid had unfortunately taken the 'most direct route to Rome'.[163] That was in relation to 678 and we must remember that barely eighty years had passed since the first specific contact that we know about – Augustine's mission. It was only twenty-five years since the first known journey of an Englishman, and neither period seems long enough for the establishment of a route so well known that it could be referred to in such casual terms. We do not know for certain of anyone who had actually made the journey by the 'most direct route' before that date. Yet in Eddius' words it suddenly springs into common parlance as if without precedent. The remark must also be compared with other statements. In contrast, Eddius referred to his hero's first visit to Rome some twenty years before as 'a road hitherto untravelled by our people'.[164] Does the difference between the two reflect the creation of a new, direct route or was Eddius thinking only of journeys by clerics or was he simply being inconsistent? Another statement made not much later indicates a feeling about the number of people who were making the journey. In 747 St Boniface advocated a ban on English women going to Rome, because so many fell by the wayside, accidentally, or in the mistaken hope of an easier life. His words are often quoted but in assessing them we must remember the moralist's tendency to exaggerate and also the simplistically distrustful view of women held by many of the clergy. Nevertheless, for what it's worth, he wrote, 'There are very few towns in Lombardy or Frankland or Gaul, where there is not a courtesan or a harlot of English stock. It is a scandal and a disgrace to your whole church' [D22.12]. The same feeling may have underlain Alcuin's advice to Eugenia, though she may not have been flattered by the possible implication [D38.5]. Whether Boniface's allegation was strictly true is not the point, and one suspects a degree of righteous exaggeration, but what he was doing was tracing in the barest outline the direct and surely the most popular route from England to Rome. His words were echoed three centuries later by Cnut, in his letter to the English people, where he spoke of 'the road to Rome.'

We must remember the weakness of our narrative sources in that they not only tend to commemorate the lives of a few great men, but that many of those men were clerics. Can we assume that they took the same routes as those taken by other travellers? Augustine followed an ancient and well known through route which had not passed out of use by the sixth century and joined ecclesiastical and civic centres important in the late Roman world. He needed to gather information about Britain from those centres. The Loire valley is also a natural and easy route for someone going to the north, following the current and these factors may have dictated the course of the early missions. Were there

nevertheless other routes which had also not passed out of existence and which were used by other, commercial, folk? That takes us back to the old question of how St Gregory's English slave boys reached Gaul. Intriguing though it is, our records do not provide evidence for a solution.

The sources do not give us evidence of specific traders going to Rome though there is some indication that they went and that they followed the same direct road. We cannot tell from them whether they used the Rhone-Sea route as well. The existence of the merchant Botto and Ganshof's demonstration that the Provencal ports functioned well into the tenth century pose a challenge to McCormick's argument which we cannot resolve here. It may simply be that both the written record and the coin evidence, which McCormick uses, are insufficient to give us a conclusive answer.[165] The provisions of the Exeter Guild Statutes [D57] and international treaties, such as that in 796 between Charlemagne and Offa [D34.3] apply equally to any continental route and do not necessarily mean that journeys were made as far as Italy. In Cnut's letter of 1027 he announced agreed exemptions from tolls for English traders specifically negotiated with the Emperor, the Pope, King Rudolph and the other princes 'through whose territory the road to Rome is situated'. How much emphasis can we place upon those two words 'the road'? Translation is treacherous and the Latin words do not carry the connotation that it is easy to give them in English. The most that we can infer is that because the Latin used the singular *via*, one main route was used rather than several. The direct route was, in truth, the trunk road used by many other northern Europeans, especially Carolingians, as is witnessed by the record of a journey by Charles the Bald, noted a little further below. Are we justified in reading this passage as telling us that there was, for Englishmen, by that date, just one route? It is probable that over the centuries, the variety of routes adopted at the start narrowed into a concentration upon one direct line, no doubt with local variations in detail. After the middle of the eighth century the western and central roads seem to have fallen into disuse as arteries. The reasons for this narrowing of choice remain obscure and deserve particular study, especially against the background of economic growth and change throughout Europe. I suggest only the outlines of possible answers. The most immediately attractive explanation is the increasing exposure of the southern end of the western and central routes to Saracen attack. This has to be considered in two phases. The first is the period of Saracen raiding, mainly from Spain, which introduced much conflict in the eighth century. This had dramatic but probably largely localised effects. Particular sites were raided, occupied and re-occupied, some several times, but it is hard to gauge the effect upon travellers. We do know that a similar pattern of raiding in northern Europe by the Vikings did not bring traffic to a halt and there is no reason to suppose that the hazards of Saracen raiding alone would be sufficient to turn English travellers away from

---

[163] Eddius, ch. 25.

[164] Eddius, ch. 3.

[165] McCormick, *Origins*, pp. 357-361.

the Rhone as a through route. It failed to have that effect upon others. That said, it may well be that incidents like the pro-Saracen stance taken by Duke Mauront, hostile to the Franks, and the sacking of Avignon in 737 by Charles Martel as a result, may have made a greater impression than we can now judge. It was during this period that King Offa of Mercia issued the enigmatic fake *dinar* found in northern Italy.[166] It is hard to believe that this was intended to a gift for the Pope. It was most likely produced as a statement by Offa that he was a player on the European stage, although one would expect such a statement to produce more than one coin. It could have been made, very probably as part of a small issue, to enable travellers to pass more easily through areas controlled by or greatly influenced by Moslem rulers. Muslims were active in southern France as well as in coastal waters and any traveller heading for Rome along the central route via the Rhone and the short sea journey to the Italian mainland, might well have had to treat with them at some point. Although the findspot was probably in or near Rome, since that is where it is first recorded, the likelihood is that whoever lost it had made at least part of his journey through the Rhone valley and the Ligurian Sea. At that date there was no Muslim presence in the Alps, which might have made it of no immediate use there.

The second phase, of settlement in and around Frejus, accompanied by Alpine raiding, from the late ninth century onwards could have been more of a deterrent were it not for the fact that the evidence suggests that English traffic had ceased to use the Rhone valley before these permanent bases were established.[167] One may question the effect of even that activity for two reasons. The first is that as observed below it was spasmodic and within that, Saracens seem to have learned the value of taxing traffic rather than simply plundering it. The second is that raiding, especially seasonal raiding, is not an efficient way of creating a blockade. That is not its purpose. Inevitably, only traffic unlucky enough to be caught in the sweep suffers. The rest passes without hindrance and if I am right in supposing that travellers continued to pass through in the winter, the Saracen impact might well be less crippling than the sources suggest.

As in all human judgements, the perceived level of danger was as important as the actual danger involved, and the latter varied more rapidly in response to political circumstances, than the former. What determines peoples' movements is their perception of the risk, and from the second half of the eighth century, the exposure of the Rhone valley to Moslem attack cannot have helped. The perceived risk may have driven English travellers further east even though those more familiar with actual conditions may still have seen the route as feasible. There

were substantial periods of peace in between the wars. In addition, at the height of their power later on the Saracens threatened all the Alpine passes not only in the west but in the centre and spasmodically the east so that if one was to run the gauntlet anyway, why not do so by the easiest route? Moreover, wherever they were, the Muslims seem to have learned to feed off the through traffic by exacting tolls, rather than to kill it [D51.1] and we may recall the decree of the Bishop of Aosta in 960 charging tolls on goods coming to the town from merchants who must have passed through lands which for some years had been at least spasmodically under Muslim control. We do not know how much greater the risk was in the Rhone valley than further east; still less do we do know how much more serious potential travellers saw it to be.

Apart from the notorious and sometimes dangerous changes in the flow of water, a potential disadvantage of the Rhone, which may have increased as time passed, was its role as a frontier. How safe was a traveller passing along it from the agents or forces of both of the adjacent rulers? Would one authority honour a safe conduct or a passport issued by the other? Would the traveller in effect be obliged to duplicate his security arrangements and would he risk having to pay two sets of tolls? If these were real threats, the Rhone's advantage as a waterway would be lost and if he had to go by land the traveller might just as well take the shorter route. In a similar way, the demands of the many small states along the Rhine, each of whose rulers demanded tolls, may have deterred travellers from using that route unless they had to for some over-riding reason.[168]

We consider the dangers of the road later on, when considering the routes taken by particular people, but it is worth noting here how few express warnings there were about them. In one of the few, Boniface uttered a quite practical piece of advice when he advised Abbess Bugga to wait before setting out for Rome [D22.4]. This was a warning about a specific threat rather than the more general warning of dangers that might have been expected if he was just trying to discourage her. There is too little evidence to support an argument that danger from widespread Muslim settlement was a major factor in determining the route. For Englishmen the western and central routes had become less popular as through ways to Rome before that became serious and if their activity had an effect it must have been in the earlier raiding phase. Support for the argument that the question of route may still be one of choice rather than real danger in the eighth century and even later lies in the fact that the west facing passes and even the sea were still used by other nationalities for both military and commercial as well as religious traffic. To give but a few examples: in 756, Abbot Warnehar took a message from the Pope to Pepin asking for help. He took the sea route to avoid the Lombards who were the aggressors [D28.4]. He was followed a few months later by the Greek envoys

---

[166] Illustrated by Gareth Williams, 'Mercian Coinage and authority' in *Mercia, An Anglo-Saxon Kingdom in Europe*, Michelle P. Brown and Carol A. Farr (eds), opposite p. 211 and pp. 218-9.

[167] See the *Enclycopaedia of Islam* under 'Fraxinetum'.

[168] Christopher Brook, *Europe in the Central Middle Ages 962-1154*, p. 75

John and George who crossed to Marseilles to establish whether Pepin was coming and then had to return to meet him at Pavia. Another emissary, Peter, took the same route in 773.[169] A century later, in 877, the Annals of St Bertin tell how the Empress Richildis fled back from Italy via the Mont Cenis and Maurienne, taking her treasure with her. Those Annals also relate the flight of Pope John who left Rome in May 878 for Arles by sea, for Lyons and Troyes where he met Louis. He returned via Maurienne and the Mont Cenis. These events preceded the settlement phase of Saracen activity in Southern France and the Alps and they suggest that if English travellers had wished to go by the Rhone valley there would have been no external impediment of that kind. Once the Saracen colonies were established and at the height of their power from about 890 to 960 then there was no doubt good reason for avoiding at least the southern part of the western and central routes. Although passage was resumed by the later tenth century [D62.1], it still remained out of favour with English travellers. In this context, Alcuin's request for a visit provides indirect evidence that English pilgrims still reached Tours for he seems to have regarded a diversion that way as quite feasible for Æthelheard.

Given that people had a choice, we now have to consider why they came to prefer the direct route to the central or western. The last two were both longer, the western especially so, for it involved either a land crossing of northern France or a longer Channel crossing. In addition, neither was ideal for a journey from England whose ecclesiastical centre was at Canterbury, although that was an influence only for travellers going on church business. We should not overlook the commercial pressure that may well have been exerted by Canterbury's control of the port of Sandwich.[170] If we consider the additional length of the western and central routes we may have sufficient reason for their losing their attraction as through ways. Nevertheless, although the direct route was shorter than the others for an Englishman, as Tyler pointed out, it had a considerable disadvantage that could easily outweigh that. The traveller had not only to cross the Great St Bernard, higher than Mt Cenis, but also the Jura which was itself a considerable barrier.

The Rhone route with the Mont Cenis was longer but had only one and an easier mountain barrier. If one was not in a hurry why not take life a bit easier? We will return to that, for the travellers' purpose may be one of several critical factors. Safety was certainly important, especially when it was provided by the familiarity of use and treaties negotiated between rulers. The arrangements negotiated by Offa and reported by Cnut cannot have been unique but there seems to have been no equivalent to assist in the turbulent Rhone valley. In all modes of transport, guides,

and the centres that provide them come to know a particular route and they will use and adapt that rather than explore alternatives. Although it is not a reference for a journey from England to Italy, it is worth pointing to the similarity between Sigeric's route and that taken by the Charles the Bald in 877, via Quierzy, Compiegne, Soissons, Rheims, Chalons, Ponthion, Langres, Jura crossing, Orbe, Vercelli (where he met the Pope), Pavia and Tortona.[171] This is as near to the direct route as one can get and must help to indicate the advantages it offered through its long standing and frequent use.

Travellers meant business, especially if they were officials moving fast on affairs of church or state rather than indigent pilgrims. It may be that there were economic forces at work by which older routes were deliberately fostered and adapted to take the new traffic, and McCormick pointed to the growth of inns along the developing routes.[172] Unfortunately none of the treaties made to ensure the safety of travellers is cast in twentieth century economic terms but their provisions, like those of the agreement between Offa and Charlemagne, may have had far reaching consequences. Another influence on the routes may have been the rise of Venice as a commercial centre, gaining under Byzantine patronage at the expense of Provence.[173] Its outlet through Pavia coupled with a swing of power and commerce towards the Rhineland in Carolingian times could have pulled the trade routes eastwards away from the west facing passes. The requirements and groupings of travel parties have already been explored in this paper and we may now simply note that correspondence like that between Charlemagne and Offa makes clear that religious and lay travellers mixed freely on the same roads. Any change in direction for one group would necessarily affect the other. Granted that hospices were founded for the needy rather than for the commercial, a detailed study of the foundation and prosperity of those institutions might throw much light on the changing patterns of pilgrim traffic.

The explanation for the predominance of the difficult direct route probably springs from two pressures. The first was the nature and needs of the travellers. The greatest need of the majority of those recorded was to complete their journey and their business as quickly as possible and return to England. Few if any were engaged in lifetime spiritual wandering. Even those whose motive was simple piety wanted to reach the steps of St Peter's as soon as they could and this dictated the direct route. The second pressure was the need for security on the way, especially for those on official business. A safe journey is always preferable to a dangerous one even if physically harder. From an early date English kings were anxious to enter into treaty arrangements that ensured the safety of

---

[169] Both missions are reported in *Royal Frankish Annals*, sa 756 and 773.

[170] See N. Brooks, *Early History of the Church of Canterbury*, p. 23; P. Sawyer, *Anglo-Saxon Charters*, no. 808.

[171] Nelson, *St Bertin*, sa 877.

[172] McCormick, *Origins*, p. 398.

[173] A.R. Lewis, *Naval Power and Trade in the Mediterranean 500-1100*, (1951) especially pp. 112-3, 123-4, 179-80.

officials, pilgrims and merchants alike. Such agreements fitted naturally with marriage alliances which resulted in a network of treaties and other arrangements providing for the welfare of travellers. The role of the church must not be overlooked, for although there appears to have been little co-ordination in its efforts, as an institution it was also anxious to assist travellers on their way. We must add to that the inability of the disintegrating Carolingian monarchy to control the southern areas of France, quite apart from the Saracen problems discussed above. Those two factors of speed and security were probably decisive in securing the predominance of the direct route.

We do not know much about the travels of the ordinary people whose story is not told but the trail of hospitals and the known tendency of unprotected people to come together for safety, as well as a few chance references, taken together indicate that for good reason they followed in their more notable companions' footsteps.

CHAPTER 7

A REVIEW OF THE EVIDENCE ABOUT THE ROUTES AND INDIVIDUAL TRAVELLERS

This section provides a brief note on each traveller in chronological order. The first section is based upon Moore's list.

The record of individual travellers, *c.* 600 – *c.* 800

1. We have evidence from our early sources for a number of journeys between England and Italy. Some travellers used the western route. Of these, the first of whom we have any record is St Augustine. We can trace his path through Bede.[174] St Gregory gave him an introduction to the Bishop of Arles, indicating a sea crossing, and he then followed a logical though winding path through the Rhone and Loire valleys before reaching the Channel coast.

2. This initial sea crossing was paralleled by the unfortunate Bishop Romanus of Rochester, who was drowned at sea off Italy.[175] We cannot tell from the reference whether he was on the way to Rome when this happened or on the way back and we can only presume that it was part of a crossing of the Ligurian Sea.

3. Although we cannot be sufficiently certain of their movements to include them in this catalogue, there is a reasonable inference that the Rhone route was followed by the messengers dispatched to and from England in the years following Augustine's mission. According to Bede, in June 601, Pope Gregory wrote to Vergilius, Bishop of Arles, asking him to assist Augustine should he pass that way. Since the letter was written at about the same time as the mission headed by Mellitus was sent to England, they probably all took the same route.[176]

4. It seems most likely that the Lombard St Birinus took the sea and central route on his way north after being consecrated in Genoa, for we learn from William of Malmesbury of a miracle at sea when he walked on the waves to go back for vestments he had forgotten [D9]. William based his narrative upon a twelfth century Life but I think it must represent an early tradition for by that date the Ligurian Sea crossing had been out of use for so long that it would be an unlikely later invention. As the miraculous walk must have taken place shortly after setting out on his voyage rather than in the Channel we may assume that he followed in Augustine's footsteps [D9]. William tells us

that he settled in Wessex in 637 so the journey must fall between his consecration in 634 and then.

5. We next have Benedict Biscop who in all made five journeys to Rome from England.[177] We know of them from Bede in both the Ecclesiastical History and the History of the Abbots. His first journey was in 653 when he and Wilfrid, to whom we shall return, travelled across France to Lyons. There they separated with Benedict going ahead direct to Rome while Wilfrid stayed with the Archbishop Annemundus, incorrectly named Dalfin.[178] We do not know which route either of them took from then on but it is unlikely that they would have doubled back to take the straight-line crossings of the Great or Little St Bernard. They might have struck further south to take the Mont Cenis at 6893ft but it is equally likely when they were already so near, that they took the sea route. In going as far as Lyons both Benedict and Wilfrid must have known of the deep sea route used by Augustine and we can tentatively assume that both completed the journey by sea. We know nothing of Benedict's return journey which Bede passes over quickly. We return to Wilfrid below.

Within a short time Benedict was off again, in 666. We do not know his route south but after being in Rome for a while he moved to Lerins, off the coast of Provence. He may have known of it by repute only but it is equally likely that he had passed or even briefly visited it on his first journey. After two years there he returned to Rome and it was whilst there that he was asked by Pope Vitalian to escort the new Archbishop Theodore and Abbot Hadrian to England. We consider them next.[179]

6. Bede tells us that they left Rome on 25 May 664 for England.[180] They sailed to Marseilles and thence by land to Arles. There they split, Theodore going direct to Paris, presumably to learn about Britain from Agilbert, then Bishop of Paris. Hadrian, after being detained by Ebroin on suspicion of political intrigue, visited the Bishops of Sens and Meaux. We can only speculate why Hadrian was detained but Ebroin may have had a wary eye on the Emperor Constans II in Sicily.[181] Since Hadrian

[174] Augustine's route can be traced in BHE. I. 24.
[175] BHE II. 20.
[176] BHE I. 28.

[177] BLA ch 2 - 12 and BHE IV. 1.
[178] Eddius, ch 3.
[179] BLA ch. 2-3.
[180] BHE IV. 1.
[181] For a summary of Constans II's activity at this time, see Peter Llewellyn, *Rome in the Dark Ages*, pp. 157-9.

had travelled in France twice before he may have been suspected to be a possible centre of intrigue. No more is said of Benedict but Theodore and Hadrian do not seems to have rejoined until both had reached Canterbury, Theodore first. Theodore at least went from Paris to Quentovic (Etaples) for the Channel crossing.

7. Bede tells us in the *History of the Abbots* that Benedict, on his third journey in 671, collected books along the way and gave them into the care of friends, who delivered them to him on his return at Vienne.[182] This probably indicates a Rhone-sea route though he could have crossed by one of the western Alpine passes. Of his fourth continental trip we know nothing save that he 'traversed the provinces of France', and there is no indication that he went to Rome.[183] We cannot establish the route of his next trip to Rome in *c.* 676/8 when he was accompanied by Ceolfrid but on his return he brought back with him John, Abbot of St Martin's whose death we will consider later.[184] From the account of John's uncompleted return to Rome we can conclude that Benedict's return route this time was by the western Rhone – Loire, perhaps after another sea crossing, for he called at Tours. Of his fifth and last Roman trip we know nothing except that it was completed before 685.

8. In between his outward journey with Benedict Biscop and Ceolfrid's last attempt, to which we will turn below, we have the later journeys of Wilfrid. Eddius tells us little of the routes taken and as we have seen, for his first outward journey with Benedict we have to infer much from the people he visited. In 653 he left England from Kent and was escorted by Biscop to Lyons where Wilfrid stayed with Archbishop Annemundus whilst Biscop went on ahead. Eddius only tells us that he was then provided with guides and supplies but from Lyons he, like Benedict, had the choice of either going by sea or crossing the western Alps.

The description of Wilfrid's return journey is intriguing. The first part was again to Lyons but once there Wilfrid found himself caught up in internal politics with his patron on the losing side. He incurred the wrath of Ebroin, was nearly executed and it may well be that like Hadrian he had difficulty in completing his journey by land. He may in fact have caused the difficulties that they faced not so long afterwards. Eddius is rarely precise but his wording suggests that it is possible that like Arculf some thirty years later, Wilfrid took the deep sea route home, round the Iberian peninsula [D12.3]. Eddius does not mention any northward journey by land and as persona non grata it would be unlikely. For Arculf the sea route may have been choice but for Wilfrid there may have been no option.

These journeys suggest that the sea and western or central routes were the norm at that date, at least for travellers

going south-north and that is not surprising given the unifying influence of the Imperial past and the advantage offered by the river currents.

9. Wilfrid's next journey, in 678, can be reconstructed in outline. Unlike Winfrid, to whom we shall return, Wilfrid crossed to Friesland and thence to the Court of Dagobert, King of the Franks, who offered him the See of Strasburg.[185] When Wilfrid refused, he sent him on his unspecified way with presents and a guide and we know no more until he reached Perctarit, King of The Lombards. This journey must have involved a land crossing of the Alps, perhaps over one of the central or easterly passes in the summer since he left Friesland 'at the first sign of spring'. There may have been several reasons for this route but the friendship with Dagobert and the hostility of Ebroin were plainly decisive.[186] Eddius tells us that the return journey was also by the Alps (in 680) [D12.9].

10. This route back throws light on that taken by Wilfrid's unfortunate near namesake Winfrid who was mistaken for him by Theodoric (King of the Franks) and 'the wicked Duke Ebroin'.[187] Eddius' comments here are interesting for they suggest that a well known and established route was already in place for the journey to Rome. He says that arranged for him to be waylaid. Unfortunately, 'Bishop Winfrid ... happened to be on the selfsame route ...' and suffered the treatment intended for Wilfrid. When he reached Rome, Wilfrid found that Cenowald's envoys had got there first, which implies that Wilfrid's easterly route must have been lengthier and slower and that by that date there was a well established direct route which we will see in detail in 990 when we turn to Archbishop Sigeric. Wilfrid may have added to his journey time by delaying at Dagobert's court and there is a hint of that in the text.

11. In 688 Cadwalla gave up his kingdom and set off for Rome. On the way he granted thirty solidi for the construction of a church at the modern Samer in the Pas de Calais, an indication that he at least went near there, and further south was entertained by Cunibert, King of the Lombards, in Pavia.[188] The route could have been either the direct one or the central but was probably the former. The English connection was strengthened by the fact that Cunibert's wife was an Anglo-Saxon, Hermelinda.

12. In the *Miracula St Bertini* we read of a monk, identified by Moore as St Bertin who joined a group of Englishmen on their way to Rome.[189] If it was indeed the Saint this must have been before his death in 698, possibly some years before. At Langres they joined some merchants from Verdun and travelled with them for a while until the

[182] BLA ch. 4.

[183] BLA ch. 5.

[184] BLA ch. 6.

[185] Eddius, ch. 28.

[186] Levison, pp. 50-51.

[187] Eddius, ch. 25.

[188] The journey is recorded in ASC and Bede HE V. 7.

[189] *Lib. Miraculorum*, Holder-Egger (ed.), *Mon. Bertiniana Minora* MG SS XV. I p 511.

latter turned off for Spain. The identification with Langres gives us another example of the use of the direct route at an early date, perhaps as early as the journeys of Winfrid and Cenowald.

13. Wilfrid's last journey in *c.* 703 seems to have been made by the eastern route for it was almost certainly on this trip that he again visited Willibrord in Frisia. An eastern route by the Rhine would be understandable in view of the previous political context but the choice may have been for personal reasons and not political as the return route was almost certainly central. There is then a rhetorical description of the return journey: 'he made his way homewards by paths rough and smooth, over hill and dale, till after a long journey he reached the Kingdom of Gaul' [D12.13]. There indicates an Alpine crossing and one is tempted to assume one by the western Alps as Wilfrid, taken ill on the way, was carried in a litter to Meaux. This location is compatible with the central route although it need be only a small diversion from the direct. It is this which suggests that friendship rather than political necessity was the main reason for the outward route.

The wording of chapter 50 implies that the faithful Eddius may not have gone on this trip for there is a contrast which may well be deliberate between the opening *We* and the subsequent *They* as well as the use of the third person '*he* made his way homewards' [D12.12]. That might explain an air of vagueness that hangs over the geographical details and the stock piece account of the rigours of the path. The account might not be as reliable a source for the route as for the others.

14. One traveller who took a western route was Abbot John, Abbot of the monastery of St Martin's, who was brought from Rome in 680 by Benedict to teach the Roman way of chanting to the monks at Wearmouth. A second task was to report to the Pope on the orthodoxy of the English faith. In due time he set off on his return and although we have no date for this it must have been after the Synod of Hatfield in 679. Sadly, John died on the way and his body was taken to Tours [D17.10]. This represents a considerable diversion from the shortest way but it followed the ancient route taken by St Augustine and may further have been justified by a desire to visit the home town of the Saint after whom his own Abbey was named and which was itself a great centre of pilgrimage. Benedict must have accompanied him on the way north at the expense of a longer journey than was necessary, but again it may have been an easier way along the rivers for someone laden with treasures from Rome. One senses also that for him the aim was always the journeying rather than the arrival.

15. In a cryptic passage, Bede tells us that Theodore's successor Berthwald was consecrated on 31 August 692 by Gudinus, Bishop of Lyons.[190] Moore made the

identification and interpreted the entry in the *Liber Pontificalis* to mean that Berthwald travelled to Rome for his Pallium although having done so, he did not catalogue him amongst his travellers.[191] If he did go, it seems that the route was Rhone and sea or west Alpine.

16. In his account of Aldhelm's journey to Rome in about 701, William of Malmesbury implies that the Saint sailed from Wareham or somewhere nearby. He records that Aldhelm founded a church there and then sets him on his way, noting only that he crossed the Alps both ways, south and north[192] [D16]. There is some doubt why Aldhelm went. In contrast to William's reason, Fabricius, his first biographer (d1117) says that he was invited to Rome by Pope Sergius because of his reputation for scholarship. Fabricius was a Tuscan, later at Malmesbury and Abingdon, but probably drawing on a different tradition for his source.

17. Before 705 Æthelwald set off with two companions, one of whom was his brother. One died on the journey but the other two returned to their home country after an interval of two winters. Æthelwald wrote a poem celebrating their achievement, which Anderson acclaimed as a rare record of such a journey by someone made at first hand.[193] Alas, its 184 lines leave the reader despairing for any topographical fact, however slight. Their route is unknown save that they seem to have crossed the sea, been untroubled by robbers and crossed hills, though that last feature may have had a spiritual rather than a real significance.

18. One of Benedict's successors as Abbot of Wearmouth also attempted the journey to Rome.[194] Ceolfrid as a youth had accompanied Benedict there on an earlier trip and he determined to end his days in the city. Bede was unusually informative in his desire to do justice to his subject for he gave the date of departure, the size of the party and the route: a unique wealth of detail. Ceolfrid left the Wear on 4 June 716 and died at the age of 74 on the 25 September in Langres, a place which indicates an intention to cross by the central Alps, probably the Great St Bernard. He had in fact travelled slowly and had left the journey too late, for a winter crossing might well have been fatal for him even if he had attempted it at a better time. Bede [D29.4] tells us that more than eighty Englishmen had accompanied him, giving us an indication of the size of one pilgrim party. It may be that the size of the party was swollen because of the valuable manuscript that Ceolfrid was taking to Rome (the *Codex Amiatinus*) but there is no sure evidence for that. This large group disintegrated on his death, some

---

[190] BHE V. 8 tells us that he was consecrated by Godwin, Metropolitan of Gaul (a Goduine metropolitano episcopo Galliarum).

[191] Moore, p. 38, n. 3, for the significance of the wording in *Liber Pontificalis* [Vita Sergii]: 'Hic (Sergius) ordinavit Bertoaldum Britanniae archiepiscopum ...'

[192] GP, V ch 217, p 363; for his motive, see *Vita Aldhelmi* in Boll SS VI May.

[193] G.K. Anderson, *Literature of the Anglo-Saxons*, p. 224. The text is in R. Ehrwald, *Aldhelmi Opera*, pp. 528-533.

[194] Ceolfrid's expedition is set out in BLA chs. 16-23 and in the *Anonymous Life* [trans. EHD no. 155].

members returning home, some staying where they were and the rest continuing the journey. Bede implies that they succeeded in doing so and certainly the *Codex* itself by a roundabout route eventually reached where it is now.

19.   Boniface visited Rome three times in all, but only once from England. In 718 he left London for the Canches, south of Boulogne, and Quentovic.[195] That suggests a direct route but we are told no more except that he crossed the 'snowy peaks of the Alps' probably by the Great St Bernard. He reached Rome by May for he left on the 15th of that month. We can discount an eastern route south for we are specifically told that on his return journey, after meeting Liutprand in Pavia, he crossed into Bavaria, which was until then unknown to him.

20.   We can now turn to a traveller who must rank as one of the greatest wanderers of the period, Willibald. It is most unfortunate that his biographer gave us such a wealth of detail about the Holy Land and the route there and back from Italy but so little about the first part of the epic journey, from England to Rome. What little she does say is confusing and open to varied interpretation. We are told that he left from Southampton and landed in France on the banks of the Seine near Rouen.[196] After that, we know only that he visited various sacred places as he crossed France until he reached the unidentified town of Gorthonicum, possibly Chortina in Liguria. No mention is made either of sea or Alps, but the phrasing of 'and so going by degrees from place to place' suggests the slow pace of travel on land rather than a partial sea journey.[197] In his article on the Life and Legends of St Richard (Willibald's father) M. Coens speculated that the word *Gorthonicum* could be a simple derivative from the land of the Goths, that is Provence, and drew a parallel with a passage in the *Vita Wynnebaldi*, 'per vastam Gallicaniae ruram'.[198] We do not know. The first certain location is Lucca where his father died. This is where our difficulties begin for from there in a standardised description Willibald crossed over the vast land of Italy until he reached the snowy peaks of the *Alpium* where he escaped ambush. In his translation, Talbot adopts *Apennines* without apparent difficulty or comment. Moore preferred to read *Alpium* as *Alps* and commented that the biographer had put Lucca north of the Alps.[199] Holder-Eggar shared that view.[200] The narrator was very possibly mistaken or it may be that in the narration she or Willibald became confused between the outward and the return sequence. On the other hand, she may simply have used *Alpium* as a generic word for any mountain range. This explanation would fit with contemporary usage for when writing his *History of the Lombards* just before the end

of the century, Paul the Deacon in describing the regions of Italy, used the word to cover three different areas.[201] In addition to the range we now call the Alps he referred to the *Alpes Cottiae*, meaning the transverse barrier running across Italy, and also to the southward spine running down Italy, *provincia in Apenninis Alpibus conputatur.* Of these the first would contain the snowy peaks and glaciers and be met before Lucca but with some confusion as to the difficulties of the terrain, the travellers would certainly have more Alps to cross before they reached Rome. I do not think his biographer can simply be accused of erroneously copying from the *Life of Boniface*, conventional though the phrasing may be. The diminished party reached Rome in November 721.

Willibald's return journey many years later is again given in detail. He left Rome at Easter to revisit Lucca, then went on to Pavia and Brescia, possibly over the San Bernardino and on to Eichstatt. Useful though that information is for travel generally it does not help us with routes to and from England as that was not his destination.

21.   From a letter written by Cuthbert Abbott of Wearmouth to Lullus in 764, we learn that in 758 Hunwine (Hunuin) 'my priest' (*meum presbyterum*) visited the latter on his way to Rome, taking him presents. This was presumably an eastern journey.[202]

22.   Alcuin went to Rome from England twice. He went as a young man with his great teacher Ælbert and there is a reminiscence of this in a letter he wrote in 799.[203] In it he remembered that on that journey he had stopped at Pavia and there heard Master Peter of Pisa dispute with a Jew Lull. That suggests a direct crossing though in view of other evidence it could be that it was more easterly. Alcuin may have been familiar with an Alpine route through Lucca, for Ætheltrud, the daughter of Æthelwald King of Northumbria bought the Church of San Dalmazio in that town in 782.[204] Whilst there is no direct evidence that Alcuin visited Lucca it would not be surprising if he had, given the Northumbrian connection. For his second visit in 780-1 we have a record of his meeting with Charlemagne in Parma at Easter.[205] This indicates an Alpine crossing but Parma is too far south to indicate any particular pass.

From these bare fragments we must turn again to a poem, *Carmina* IV [D37], which Alcuin wrote at a date generally thought to be about 781-2 whilst at York but about to leave for Aachen in Charlemagne's service.[206] This is a curious and enigmatic work and it has been variously interpreted.

[195] Talbot, p. 38.

[196] Talbot, p. 157.

[197] Talbot, p. 158. The Latin is 'gradatim ex parte peragrantes supervenerunt'.

[198] *Analecta Bollandiana*, xlix, 1931.

[199] Moore p. 60 n 6.

[200] *Vita Willibaldi*, MG SS xv I, p 91 n 10; Talbot, p. 158.

[201] Paul the Deacon, bk II, chs xv, xvi, xviii (pages 71 onwards in Foulke's translation.)

[202] EHD, no. 186, p. 832.

[203] For the dating of this letter see Moore, p. 73 n. 3, 4. The letter is in MG Epp Karol Aevi II, no 172 and a translation is in Allott, Letter 75, p. 91.

[204] For a brief discussion, see OEC pp.102 -3 and note 37.

[205] W. Arndt, *Vita Alcuini*, p. 190.

[206] E. Duemmler, MGH Poetae Latini Medii Aevi I.

Duckett by implication makes it a memoire of either his first or second journeys to Rome but Kleinclausz relates it to another journey, which can otherwise only be inferred and whose purpose is unknown.[207] This was made not later than 778 to Charlemagne's court. Its existence rests upon a hint by Alcuin's biographer that he and Charlemagne had met before Easter 781 but as Moore indicates, there could have been another journey at another time.[208] The poem is worth examination for if it does record an actual journey, albeit in a romantic mode, it has a much neglected importance. I do not think that either of the descriptions given above quite fits it. It is certainly written to praise Charlemagne and his court but there is more to it than that. It is, I believe, partly a practical document for it is addressed to an unidentified fellow scholar/poet presumably seeking to follow Alcuin's own footsteps to the court and tells him in poetic form roughly how his journey will go and what to expect. It is therefore partly akin to a letter home describing the journey. Its detail on travel by river is probably of far more interest to us than practical use to its contemporary recipient. The poem could have been written at York before Alcuin left for Aachen, or it could have been written afterwards; there is internal support for both views. If the poem was written whilst Alcuin was at York, why write it, unless the recipient was in another English centre? If written whilst Alcuin was at Aachen, to a recipient still in England why the word of introduction in line 28? Alcuin could have made the introduction himself. It may be that the dating is wrong and it was written after Alcuin himself had left for Tours.

If written later, it is possible that it was an elaborate introduction to a visit by a particular individual to Aachen and the elaborate style suggests a parallel with the letter to Charlemagne introducing Æthelheard in 801. If so the guidance failed for the Archbishop landed at St Judoc's where he met Alcuin's messenger and Alcuin certainly did not meet him in person. Æthelheard may have turned eastwards after the landing at S. Judocs to visit the Emperor but we cannot be certain. Whatever its background, the poem can tentatively be regarded as the record of an actual journey which Alcuin himself had undertaken, visiting and taking shelter in many of the Anglo-Saxon missionary centres in the Rhineland rather than just a sentimental and idealised recollection of friends abroad and if that is what it is, it has not received the attention it deserves as a travel document. What we do not know is whether it is the record of a journey only as far as Speyer or whether it is the northern part of the journey which Alcuin himself had made to Rome. It may well be that Alcuin had taken this slightly dog-legged route before.

23.   In 794 Alcuin wrote to Bishop Higbald to tell him that he had detained Witto (known in correspondence as Candidus) on his way to Rome and asked for his return

to him when the journey was over. The date of the letter suggests that Alcuin was still at Aachen at the time, not Tours, and this indicates a Rhine route rather than the direct. Presumably the choice was influenced by the desire to make contact, possibly deliver letters, at the expense of speed.

24.   In 786 a Papal embassy reached England after being delayed by storms and at the beginning of their report they dwell upon their experiences.[209] They do so in such formalised terms that we cannot establish whether their sea route was simply cross channel or longer, across the North Sea but whichever it was they seem to have shown a distaste for the water. If their only obstacle was a short lived contrary wind in the Pas de Calais or the North Sea their rhetoric was a little excessive but at that date any longer sea journey direct from the Mediterranean is inconceivable [D31].

25.   In the letter of 796 which Charlemagne wrote to Offa he also mentioned a group of political exiles led by a priest called Odberht, who '… have sought sanctuary with us, so that their case may be heard and judged in the presence of the pope and your distinguished Archbishop (Æthelheard) …'[210] His complaint involved, among other matters, the improper mixing of pilgrims and merchants,

The record of individual travellers c. 800-1066

Paradoxically, after the relative wealth of detail given in the earliest sources, we are given less information for the rest of the period and apart from the problematical poem by Alcuin discussed above there is a great gap in the detailed record after the death of Ceolfrid. The *Chronicle*, for example, records that people set off and returned on either church or state business or for private devotion but that is all. There is no description and the only detail is incidental. We have to wait until the end of the tenth century before we again have much useful data in the return route given for Sigeric.

26.   Alcuin gives us a clue to the route taken by the considerable party of Æthelheard, Cyneberht, Ceolmund and Torhtmund in 801 which has been considered above.[211] He wrote to Æthelheard about the journey and we learn that his messenger met them at St Judoc's near Quentovic, at the start of the direct route.[212] Alcuin invited the party to visit him at Tours, but since they wrote afterwards we can infer that the invitation was not taken up. Although we cannot be certain, it seems more likely that Æthelheard turned eastwards after his landing and went either to Aachen or some other convenient meeting point. After Alcuin's letter of introduction, anything less would have given offence [D38.10].

---

[207] Duckett, *Alcuin, Friend of Charlemagne*, p. 33; Kleinclausz, *Alcuin*, p. 36.
[208] Moore, p. 73.
[209] EHD, no. 191.
[210] Allott, letter 40 p. 52; Moore p. 78.
[211] Allott, letter 51, p. 66 and letter 20, p. 28.
[212] EHD, no. 207.

It may also be that Æthelheard had to attend to the unfinished business over Odberht and his companions, referred to above, though that could have been at Rome with Papal intervention. The Emperor had meanwhile given an assurance that there was no mischief afoot: 'Regarding the priest Odberht, who desires on his return from Rome to live abroad for the love of God, as he often says and did not come to accuse you …'[213]

27.   According to the *Royal Frankish Annals*, Eardwulf, king of Northumbria, met Charlemagne at Nijmegen on the Rhine and went from him to Rome, presumably by the remainder of the Rhine route and over the central Alps.[214] He returned the same way, within the year, as we have seen. For his return he was given as escort, for part of the way at least, two abbots from northern France as well as the Anglo-Saxon Deacon Ealdwulf who was already in Papal service and whose adventures on his return give us such a tantalising glimpse of the hazards of long distance travel in this period.[215] We do not know whether his original intention was to go to Rome or whether he sought help from Charlemagne but later changed his plan and thus no firm conclusion can be drawn from him about the preferred route.

28.   Asser tells us that about 810 Eadburh, Queen of the West Saxons died in penury in Pavia after having been expelled from the nunnery given to her by Charlemagne.[216] She may have wandered around in north Italy, but *prima facie* the location suggests a crossing by the St Bernard.

29.   We can be fairly sure of both the outward and the return routes taken by King Æthelwulf on his visit in 855-6 with the young Alfred. He was away from England for two years but he seems to have spent most of his time either in Rome waiting for the election of a new Pope, or in Charles' court [D43.2]. The annal refers to a betrothal in July and the obvious month is July of 856, on the return. This is not an entirely satisfactory solution for it leaves Æthelwulf and presumably the rest of his considerable party staying with Charles from July until October for no apparent purpose. Why should he do that? If he was betrothed at Charles' court in July 856 he could hardly have stayed in Rome for a year, but spent a shorter time there and far longer with Charles. Although it is not the best reading of the text, is it possible that the July in question was that of 855 on the outward journey? This makes better sense of the journey and accords with the *Chronicle* for it would imply a late spring departure from England, a stay with Charles leading to the betrothal in July and a late summer crossing of the Alps. Æthelwulf could then re-cross the Alps as late as September 856 in time to marry Judith in October and return to England before a winter crossing of the North Sea. Unfortunately, this solution presumes an error or at best an

ambiguity in the *Annals of St Bertin*. The problem matters less for our purpose as the route itself is clear even though the timing is not. His purpose is generally attributed to a rather foolish piety, which caused him to leave England at a critical time, with the result that he effectively lost most of his kingdom. The more this is considered the less likely it becomes, and, taking the version in the *Liber Pontificalis* into account, it is more probable that his departure was caused by political troubles rather than simple piety.

30.   In 888 another Queen died in or near Pavia, Æthelswith, Alfred's sister. As noted earlier, hers was a problematic journey. Her husband, Burgred had fled to Rome in 874 where he died shortly afterwards. Many commentators have suggested that she accompanied him then, and that her death in Pavia was on a return journey home.[217] The *Chronicle* is ambiguous [D45.8]. Text E stated that she had been travelling with Ealdorman Beocca, who was taking the annual alms to Rome, whilst text A records both journeys but as separate incidents. F added that she was on her way to Rome. Of the three versions, a combination of E and F seems most plausible. To accept A one must deny F and explain why after fourteen years she decided to return home. Her marriage had been a political one, and given the internal turbulence of Mercia after her husband's exile, it is quite possible that she stayed in England as much to keep an eye on family interests as because it was her homeland. Impending mortality may have caused her to go to Rome later, in a way that was far from uncommon. Whichever way she was going, it is most likely that she took the direct route over the Great St Bernard. This would be especially so if she accompanied a party which was carrying money, for that would presumably take the shortest and safest way.

31.   Under both 921 and 923 Flodoard recorded that numerous Englishmen were killed in the Alps by Saracens. We do not know which particular passes were involved for their power fell over all the western crossings and on occasion threatened those further to the east.[218] These passages are often quoted, but out of context their use can be misleading. Flodoard covered the fifty-nine years 919-978 and in that span he recorded only five occasions when Saracens closed the passes and attacked travellers attempting to go through. That happened in 921 (Anglo-Saxons), 923 (Anglo-Saxons), 929 (Unspecified), 933 (Local raiding), 940 (English & French). For 933 he recorded no attacks on *travellers* and although there were further attacks in 936 and 939 he gave neither the nationality nor the location. By 951 the intruders had obviously learned better ways for in that year he recorded that they had occupied the roads but took tribute from travellers before allowing them to proceed. An incident in 931 when Robert Archbishop of Tours was killed is attributed by Flodoard's editor to the Saracens but that

---

[213] EHD, no. 197.

[214] Sa. 808.

[215] Levison, *England and the Continent*, p. 114.

[216] Asser, ch. 15.

[217] See, for example, Ian W. Walker, *Mercia and the making of England*, pp. 58-59.

[218] Tyler, p. 53-55.

may be no more than giving a dog a bad name for there is no other reason to suppose it. Flodoard carefully says he was killed by robbers (*a latronibus)* and since he is usually exact in attributing blame one would have expected him to blame the Saracens if he had known that they were responsible. The fact is that over a period of fifty-nine years Flodoard recorded only three episodes when Anglo-Saxons specifically were attacked in the Alps but one of those references is most important for the attack in 940 on a combined party of Anglo-Saxons and French took place at St Maurice which the Saracens had occupied and that of course was on the direct route before it crossed the Great St Bernard.

32.   At some time before he died in 951 Bishop Theodred of London probably took the classic St Bernard route, for in his will he bequeathed the white and the yellow chasubles 'which I bought in Pavia'.[219] We do not know whether he bought them on the outward or the return journey but the latter is more likely and the entry in the Appendix is made accordingly.

33.   About 958 Oscytel, Archbishop of York, had to collect his Pallium and took Oswald with him. We do not know his route on that occasion but Oswald went again in about 972 as Archbishop himself, with a priest Germanus.[220] On the return journey Oswald made a detour through Fleury, where he had spent some time before and Germanus stayed there. The text makes it clear that Oswald and Germanus took a more circuitous route back (*divertit)* and by implication that Oscytel took the usual short one.

34.   One major figure who met disaster in the Alps was Archbishop Ælfsige who died in 959 on the way to Rome [D56]. He suffered from frostbite and died despite drastic attempts to save him. Unfortunately the detail given is insufficient to enable us to determine the precise route.

35.   The next year, Ælfsige's successor had an easier and successful journey. In 960 Dunstan too had to go to Rome to collect his Pallium [D58]. The *Anglo-Saxon Chronicle* does not report his trip and all that we know of it is that John of Worcester, writing much later, said that he set off in the third indiction and returned 'by peaceful stages'. That is not conclusive but it does suggest that the journey followed the carefully planned direct overland route which we see from the record of the next Archbishop to go, Sigeric.

36.   Next, after 960 we have a note of the return journey of Æthelwine [D70] who had gone first to Jerusalem, by a route unknown to us, but who returned through Italy with the secondary purpose of collecting a pallium for St Dunstan. His path is given as through Apulia, Rome and Lombardy. He must then have crossed one of the Alpine passes, but we do not know which.

37.   Æthelgar must have followed the direct route before 990 for we have a request in a letter to his successor, Sigeric that he visit St Bertin on his way.[221] In inviting him, the writer recalled the visit of Æthelgar and his generosity.

38.   The classic description of the direct route comes in 990 with the account of the stages of the return journey of Archbishop Sigeric across north Italy and over the Great St Bernard [D59.2]. We do not know the time of year he travelled but as the account suggests that he spent only a few days in Rome, he was probably making a summer trip and wanted to return before the passes became difficult in the winter. The list of *submansiones* reveals a route as straight as possible across north Italy, the Great St Bernard and eastern France. His route has been extensively studied, most thoroughly by Ortenberg, and the places he passed through have been plotted with some precision.[222] Whether they were places where he actually stopped overnight is another matter for they may represent no more than a list of options some of which could be quickly passed by a traveller in a hurry. There is nothing in the text to suggest that Sigeric stayed the night in each place mentioned or even that he stopped there. In the same way, the modern traveller might talk of going from Manchester to London via Crewe and Watford but that need not mean that he will stop in those two towns on the way. The mention merely sets out the route, and that was all important both as a guide for any successor and, if he wanted one, a reminder for the Archbishop. The list of *sub-mansiones* need do no more than indicate places where the traveller could stop if he wanted to. If that conclusion is correct, it follows that no deduction can be drawn from the list about the length of time that Sigeric himself or anyone else took over the journey. The various records show that people stayed where they could as the day's journey dictated or where accommodation was to be had. Archbishop Ælfeah appears not to have been in a usual stopping place when he was robbed in an un-named village [D66].

39.   William of Malmesbury tells us that Ælfeah went to Rome to get his pallium in 1005, and crossed the Alps. We know no more but may guess the direct route [D66].

40.   It is always dangerous to turn from recorded fact to literature though the particular reference lies half way between fact and fiction. At the end of *Njals Saga* we have the journeys of Flosi and Kari to Rome. Neither started from England but passed by or through on the way and so provide evidence either of actual journeys or what were considered to be the likely route that a traveller would have taken. Kari sailed to Normandy, crossed the continent on foot over the Alps and after receiving absolution for his sins returned by the same way. He then sailed to Iceland via Dover and a westward sea course that skirted Wales and the western coast until Caithness. Flosi took the same

---

[219] Whitelock, *Wills*, I.

[220] Macray, *Ramsey Chronicle*, pp. 24 - 5.

[221] Stubbs, *Memorials* p. 388.

[222] V. Ortenburg, 'Archbishop Sigeric's Pilgrimage to Rome in 990', *Anglo-Saxon England* 19 (1990), pp. 197-246.

outward route but having received absolution from the Pope himself he returned by the 'east route' presumably the Rhine to Norway and thence back to Iceland. The saga is not fiction but equally it is not unembroidered historical fact and it must therefore be used with caution. In his paper, Springer took it as an authentic record of a route and there is no reason why it should not be so: the only query is whether it truly represents a late tenth century route and that depends upon the date chosen for the various elements in the Saga.[223]

41.   At some time before 1020, Archbishop Lyfing must have gone to Rome and brought back both letters and verbal messages for King Canute, for the king said so in his proclamation of 1020 [D68.3].

42.   Although it gives us only a clue, we know that in 1022 Archbishop Æthelnoth also purchased goods in Pavia on his return journey, in his case some parts of the body of St Augustine.[224]

43.   One famous royal visitor was Cnut but it is unfortunate that the records throw so much confusion on his route or routes. The difficulties are summarised by Lawson.[225] The prime source is the letter which he wrote in 1027 while in Rome and dispatched in advance of his return, through Archbishop Lyfing. In that, he quite clearly stated that he had gone to Rome from Denmark and intended to return to England by the same route [D68, D69]. This wording suggests a longer sea journey than a mere cut across the Channel, and an indirect route is supported by William of Malmesbury, who when writing of Lyfing stated that he went with the king from Denmark [D70].

Against all this we have the eulogistic description of his rich gifts to St Omer as he passed through, said to have been witnessed by the author of the *Encomium Emmae*, then a monk there [D72]. We also have the statement in Goscelin's *Translatio Sancte Mildrethe Virginis* that Cnut passed through Canterbury both on his way to and his return from Rome.[226] To go to Rome from Denmark via Canterbury and St Omer may seem a curious route and Lawson's solution is to posit another visit in 1030 which accords better both with the *Chronicle* entry under 1031 and his campaign in Norway in 1028-9, also reported in the *Chronicle*. It is nevertheless curious that if there were two visits that the *Chronicle* only reported one, for the absence of the King for a considerable period of time would be a significant and recordable event, more so than the absences of Bishops. On balance the simplest solution is probably a route to and from Denmark in 1027 (dated by the letter) with another visit to the continent at much the same time, direct from England, which may not have taken

him as far as Rome or away for as long, and therefore have aroused less comment.

44.   Another cleric who almost certainly used an Alpine route was Ulf, Bishop of Dorchester, who had to attend the Council of Vercelli in 1050 to defend himself against a charge of simony [D45.12].

45.   We do not know the route taken by Archbishop Robert of Canterbury in his very quick visit to Rome in 1051 but when he fled the country the following year he probably took the direct route for he was again in a hurry [D45.13, 15]. He left from the Naze. He may well have taken a more central route for his return in 1053, since he died at Jumièges. It is probable that he was not intending to return to England, at least not immediately, but was seeking a safe haven in his old monastery.[227]

46.   It is hard to reconstruct the route taken by Earl Harold, son of Godwin, in either 1056 or 1058, most probably the former. Grierson has set out the most probable accounts leaving the choice open between the direct route and a politically inspired path through Germany and Hungary with a crossing of the Alps by an eastern pass, probably the Brenner.[228] Either is possible. His presence in St Omer on the return journey as soon as November seems unlikely but equally there is no need to dismiss so readily the possibility of a winter crossing. On balance, the longer route seems more logical.

47.   Next we have the adventures of Earl Tostig and his family who set out in 1061 and as far as we know reached Rome without incident. According to the *Vita Edwardi Regis* their route took them through Saxony and the Upper reaches of the Rhine. We may assume that they crossed the Alps by an eastern pass but we do not know whether they sailed to the mouth of the Rhine or whether they took a land route south east after the shortest sea crossing. The party was a large one with eminent members including Archbishop Aldread and, to judge by the return, had a measure of protection. In spite of that they were attacked on the return journey not far from Rome and stripped of nearly all he had so that they had to return to the city. The composition of the party is indicated by the story of the knight Gospatric who, clad in noble garments and riding in the van, offered himself as Tostig thus enabling the others to escape [D74.1, 2].

48.   Last we have the unfortunate Burgheard, who so nearly completed the journey. From a donation to St Remi made by his father Earl Ælfgar, we know that the son died there on the return journey. The location suggests the direct route.[229]

---

[223] Springer, *Medieval Pilgrim Routes*, at p. 102 ff & 120.

[224] OEC, p. 103.

[225] Lawson, *Cnut*, pp. 102-4.

[226] D.W. Rollason, *The Mildreth Legend, a study in early medieval hagiography in England* (Leicester 1982).

[227] See GP, p. 35. For a succinct narrative see F. Barlow, *Edward the Confessor*, pp. 104-26.

[228] P. Grierson, *A Visit of Earl Harold to Flanders in 1056*. EHR, XL, 1936.

[229] Sawyer, *Charters*, no. 1237.

CHAPTER 8

SUMMARY

Every society needs a golden age and in these days of passport controls, visas and political barriers it is all too easy to imagine a golden age of travel when the pious pilgrim put his knapsack over his shoulder and strode off towards the first of a series of welcoming hospices. The evidence suggests that this picture is far from true. In an agricultural society, manpower is a most important resource and the local landlord might well not take kindly to well behaved industrious peasants taking themselves off to Rome for perhaps a year or more, or even for ever. This would be true of the higher orders as well, and one wonders what motives underlay the advice which persuaded Chancellor Ealdwulf to stay at home and not go to Rome in penance for accidentally killing his son, but be persuaded to stay and restore a church instead.[230] Losing troublemakers was a different matter and in the documentary appendix I have reproduced the Laws of King Edgar which cover one particular kind of disobedience [D14.6].

Once on his way, life on the road was not easy though as the years went by conditions probably improved. I have suggested a concentration upon one route and that was not the result of whim or chance. For any traveller, personal security is critical and one striking feature is the network of treaty relationships which ensured the minimum of interference. By the eleventh century, Cnut had, by treaty arrangements, formalised the direct route as 'the way' to Rome and the concentration of travellers of all nationalities is echoed by the term *Via Frankigena* for the route from the Alps south into Italy. Security and usage develop in relation. The more that people used the direct route, the better the arrangements became, and the better the arrangements the more people would want to use the route.

Even on this route the traveller had to prove his bona fides, both on the way and perhaps at the end if he had business to transact. A runaway could only cause trouble especially whilst still near home and no ruler could allow unfettered movement across his territory. Merchants and pilgrims had to be identified and treated appropriately; tolls had to be collected and spies intercepted. A safe conduct might be needed or a letter of introduction, or the company of a known figure who could speak for the traveller and whose presence would open doors. The traveller needed money, for free accommodation might not be available and lodgings might have to be bought. Food and clothing had to be bought or begged and entry to the Holy Places might require money for gifts. Physical dangers claimed many lives as did political ones arising from warfare as well as local disorder, although evidence for the latter is less common than might be expected.

That said, it is easy to exaggerate the impact of bandits or raiders in the Channel or the Alps. People seem to have travelled in relative security. There are a few cases of serious interference but should one interpret entries like Flodoard's as evidence of the abnormal? The normal is rarely recorded. William of Malmesbury's gloomy description of conditions in Italy are generalised and second hand at best. Bernard the Wise was making a point, not dissimilar to comments made by modern travellers unfortunate enough to have been mugged in a foreign capital. What is surprising is that there is no mention of robbery in saint's lives. Those who offended them in other ways were taught the error of their ways: witness the fate of the 'keeper of the field' who challenged Willibrord. A few horses were stolen, and other disasters occurred, mostly remedied by the power of the Saint, but their money and possessions were generally safe on their journeys. Yet if they had been robbed, there would have been a prime opportunity for the Saint to show his power and to drive home the moral lesson that crime doesn't pay. The roads seem to have been safer than popular imagination would suppose.

Even if relatively safe, the route was hard, success uncertain and the conditions were often squalid. It is a testimony to the zeal and determination of those who took it that they did so, and so often returned.

---

[230] W.T. Mellows, *Peterborough Chronicle*, pp. 29-30.

ILLUSTRATION 2: THE RHONE FROM THE AMPHITHEATRE AT ARLES
THE RHONE WAS A MUCH USED ROUTE BUT ITS MASSIVE FLOW POSED PROBLEMS FOR TRAVELLERS ESPECIALLY WHEN IN SPATE,
BEFORE IT WAS TAMED BY LOCKS

ILLUSTRATION 3: THE VIEW FROM THE RIDGE AT LANGRES, WHICH MOST TRAVELLERS WOULD HAVE PASSED
AND WHERE CEOLFRID DIED

ILLUSTRATION 4: MOUNTAIN SCENERY IN THE JURA

ILLUSTRATION 5: BOURG ST PIERRE, JUST BEFORE THE
GREAT ST BERNARD PASS
BOURG ST PIERRE WAS THE LAST STAGING POST BEFORE
THE SUMMIT

ILLUSTRATION 6: THE ARCH OF AUGUSTUS AT AOSTA, DATING FROM THE FIRST CENTURY BC. ANGLO-SAXONS MUST HAVE BEEN AWARE THAT THEY WERE ENTERING A NEW WORLD

ILLUSTRATION 7: LOOKING SOUTH FROM THE APENNINES
ONCE ACROSS THE PO VALLEY WITH ITS SWAMPS AND DISEASE, THE TRAVELLER HAD TO CROSS THE APENNINES

ILLUSTRATION 8: ROME, CITY WALLS
WOULD THE ENGLISH TRAVELLER HAVE COMPARED THE WALLS OF ROME WITH THE REMAINS OF ROMAN WORK IN ENGLAND?

ILLUSTRATION 9: THE SAXON BURGH AS IT IS NOW (SEE PAGE 16)

APPENDIX 1

THE TRAVELLERS WHOSE ROUTE IS KNOWN OR CAN BE GUESSED, IN CHRONOLOGICAL ORDER

a. = ante *p.* = post *c.* = circa

W/C = Western Route, Rhone-Loire, or Central route.
D = Direct
E = Eastern
O = Other

NAME	DATE	W/C	D	E	Other/Comment
Augustine	596	X			Rhone, Loire, N. France
Romanus	*c.* 630	X			
Birinus	637	X			
Biscop/Wilfrid	653	X			Rhone
Wilfrid, return	658				Deep Sea?
Biscop	666	X			
Biscop, return Theodore Hadrian	668	X			
Biscop/Ceolfrid	676		?		
Biscop, north John	678	X?			Rhone?
Wilfrid	678			X	
Papal Envoys	678		X?		
Winfrid	678		X		
John, south	680	X			Died at Tours
Wilfrid	680			X?	
Cadwalla	688		X?		
Bertwald	692	X			
Englishmen	*a.* 698	X?			
Arculf, north	*c.* 695				Deep Sea
Aldhelm	*a.* 701		X		
Wilfrid	*a.* 703			X	
Wilfrid, north	704	X			Alpine, central
Offa, Cenred, Egwyn	709		X*		

* Offa, Cenred and Egwin passed through Lucca but we do not know their route there. The city is far enough south to be the terminus of a sea crossing or the winding route along the coast from the south of France. It is nevertheless worth recording that they passed through the town and may well have made the more usual Alpine crossing. There is no hint of a sea crossing from the mouth of the Rhone to Italy.

Ceolfrid	716		X		
Boniface	718		X		
Willibald	721	X			Landed in Normandy
Hunuin	758			X	Rhine
Ælbert, Alcuin	*a.* 762		X?		
Witto	*c.* 794			X?	
Embassy	768		X?		
Alcuin	780	X?			
Alcuin	781			X?	Central Alps?
Odberht	796			X?	
Æthelheard	801		X?		
Æthelheard, return	802		X?		
Eardwulf, south	808			X	Via Charlemagne's court
Eardwulf, north	808?			X	
Ealdwulf, north	808?			X	
Ealdwulf, south	809?	X?			'Taken to Britain'
Eadburh	*a.* 810		X?		Died at Pavia
Æthelwulf	855			X?	
Æthelwulf	856			X?	
Æthelswith, Beocca	888		X		
Englishmen, south	921		X		Alpine crossing
Englishmen, south	923		X		Alpine crossing
Anglo-Saxons	940		X		Alpine crosing
Theodred, north	*a.* 951		X		
Ælfsige, south	959		X		Alpine crossing
Dunstan, north	960		X?		
Oscytel, north	*c.* 972		X		
Oswald, Germanus, north	*c.* 972	X			Loire route
Æthelwine	*p.* 960		X?		
Æthelgar	988		X?		
Sigeric, south	990		X		
Sigeric, north	990		X		
Ælfeah	1005		X?		
Æthelnoth	1022		X		
Cnut	1027			X	
Ulf	1050		X		
Robert, south	1051		X		
Robert, north	1052		X?		Finished at Jumièges
Harold	*c.* 1056			X	
Tostig	1061			X	
Burgheard, north	1062		X		

Appendix 2

List of Travellers between England and Italy, who are known to have gone, their motives and the sources

KEY TO THE CODES USED IN THE TABLE

Code	Principal motive
1	Collect Pallium
2	Church Business
3	Royal Business
4	Pilgrimage
5	Refugee
6	Taking alms or messages
7	Legal
8	Study or cultural
9	Medical
10	Trade

Moore's List to AD 800 as amended and expanded to include travellers other than Englishmen and unknown messengers, and to exclude those who did not go from England.

DATE	TITLE	TYPE	NOTES – COMMENTS – SOURCE
c. 580	Merchants	10	Thorpe, Ælfric's Catholic Homilies ii, 120-1
597	Augustine	2	BHE; ASC
598	Laurentius	2	BHE I: 27
598	Petrus	2	BHE I: 29 It is not clear what happened to Abbot Peter – was he the Peter drowned off Gaul in 602? See BHE I: 33.
601	Mellitus, Laurentius Justus Paulinus	2	BHE I: 29 Justus & Paulinus spent their careers in England, dying in 627 & 644 respectively.
601	Messengers	2	BHE I: 30
610	Mellitus	2	BHE II: 4
610?	Mellitus	2	BHE II: 4 On his return north he brought back letters from the Pope. Mellitus stayed in England, dying here in 624.
a. 624	Messenger	2/3	BHE II: 8 An unknown messenger brought a letter from Rome to Archbishop Justus, authorising him to consecrate Romanus as his successor in Rochester. This was preceded by one from Justus to Rome and referred also to letters from King Æthelwald.
624	Messenger	2	BHE II: 8

p. 624	Messenger	2/3	BHE II: 10 A little after 624 another letter arrived, again by an unknown messenger, from Pope Boniface to King Edwin, urging his conversion.
624-7	Romanus	2	BHE II: 20
634	Messengers?	2	BHE II: 18
634	Messengers	2/3	BHE II: 17-18 There were other letters at this time. In 627 Pope Honorius sent the Pallium to his namesake in England (BHE II. 18) but there must have been an earlier letter for in II. 17 we are told that the Pope heard of the Northumbrian conversion and sent Paulinus the Pallium and Edwin a letter, both of which followed the Pope's earlier letter urging the conversion. There was close contact between Rome and its latest mission at this time.
c. 637	Birinus	2	BHE II: 17; GP, ch. 75. Did Birinus bring the letter from Pope Honorius received in England by King Edwin in 634?
653	Wilfrid Biscop	2/8	BLA 1, 2; Eddius 3.
665	Biscop	2/8	BLA 2
667	Wighard	1?	BHE III: 29; ASC; BLA 4
667	Messengers	2	BHE III: 29. 'given to the bearers of this letter for delivery to your excellency..'
668	Biscop Theodore Hadrian	4/8 2 2	BHE IV: 1. Theodore & Hadrian also remained in England.
671	Biscop	2/8	BLA 4
675	Messengers	2	Eddius 51; ASC.
687-701	Monks	2	BLA 15. They obtained privileges for Wearmouth.
678-9	Wilfrid Eddius	2 2	Eddius 26-33
678	Winfrid	2	Eddius 25
678-9	Biscop Ceolfrid	2/8	BHE IV: 18.
678	Coenwald Hilda's Envoy	2 2	Eddius 29. Cenwald left after Wilfrid but made a faster journey.
680	Biscop Ceolfrid Abbot John	2/8	This was the return journey for the two Englishmen.
p. 680	Abbot John	2	BHE IV: 18. This was his return journey, when he died.
684	Wilfrid's envoy	2	See Moore, p. 29, n. 7 on the evidence for this messenger and his date. We can assume that the messenger completed the round trip safely.
685	Biscop	2/8	I have followed Moore in adopting 685 but only with reservations. BLA 9 says that Biscop appointed Eosterwine Abbot shortly before he set off on his fifth journey to Rome. That was in 682. The foundation stone for the Abbey Church of Jarrow is dated 24 April 684 or 685. Could Biscop have missed the ceremony? On the other hand, Biscop returned after March 686 when Eosterwine died. The earlier date would make a very long journey and 685 is more likely, were it not for Bede's statement that he left shortly after the appointment. A departure after April 685 also makes quite a quick journey for someone collecting relics which might not be immediately to hand. I am inclined to put the dedication and his departure in 684. The return cannot by much later than 686 for Bede states that Biscop suffered from creeping paralysis for three years before his death in January 690.

688	Cadwalla	4	BHE V: 7; ASC.
a. 692	Oftfor	4/8	BHE IV: 23 could be taken to imply that Oftfor went to study as well as a pilgrim: 'Meanwhile I wish to speak of Oftfor, who having devoted himself to reading and studying the Scriptures in both Hilda's monasteries, wished to win greater perfection, and travelled to Kent in order to visit Archbishop Theodore, of blessed memory. When he had continued his studies under him for some while, he decided to visit Rome, which in those days was considered an act of great merit.'
692	Berhtwald	1	See Moore p. 38, n. 3 for a study of the consecration.
c. 693	Messengers?	2/3	Pope Sergius sent letters to the English Bishops and also to Kings Æthelred, Alfred and Adulf.
a. 698	Anglo-Saxons	4	The reference is in *Libellus Miraculorum*, Mon Bertiniana Minora, Holder-Eggar (ed.) MG SS XV I p. 511.
687-701	Hwaebert	8	BLA, 18.
a. 701	Aldhelm	2/4	William of Malmesbury (GP, chs. 218, 219) stated that Aldhelm stayed with the Pope. He may have stayed some time since he persuaded the Roman mob that Sergius was not the father of a new born baby (because the baby said he was not.)
a. 705	Æthelwald	4?	Ehrwald, *Aldhelmi Opera*, pp. 528-33.
a. 701	Wilfrid's envoy	2	The messenger must have returned, bringing Sergius' reply, cited in Eddius, ch. 51. See Moore, p. 40 n. 4. He may also have brought the letter to Ceolfrid, Abbot of Monkwearmouth, asking for a monk of his house to be sent to Rome. (H & S, III, p. 248-9)
703?	Wilfrid Acca	2	Eddius, ch. 50. The text suggests that Eddius did not go on this particular journey.
703?	Bertwald's envoys	2	Eddius chs. 50-53. Remarkably, there was only one cleric among them: 'and one mere deacon, so to speak, and others, all without any rank of ecclesiastical dignity…' [Ch. 53]. The probability is that the archbishop's representatives also returned safely, but there is no specific evidence to that.
705	Wilfrid	2	Eddius, 57. This was Wilfrid's return journey. He died in England, despite his thoughts of ending his days in Rome.
a. 705	Two pilgrims	8	Cited by Levison; *England and the Continent*, p. 134, citing Æthilwald, *Carmina Rhythmica*, Ehwald (ed.), ii 107. They returned before 705, with 'volumina numerosa'.
a. 706	Egwyn	2	*Vita Egwini*, I. 26. The authority for this first visit to Rome is late tenth or early eleventh century and gives as its origin a dispute in his diocese.
709	Egwyn, Coenred, Offa	4	ASC.
680-713	Northumbrian nuns	4	Moore, p. 49. The abbess of Whitby wrote to the abbess of Pfalzel, near Trier, asking for hospitality for a party of nuns on its way to Rome.
716	Ceolfrid	4	BLA 16-21. Since Ceolfrid died before he crossed the Alps, he himself should not be included, except by intention. However, the expedition as a whole has a place, for Bede specifically tells us that some of the party continued the journey to Rome.
716-8	Wethburga	4	The reference is in Tangl t I no. 78. She stayed for a long time, if not the rest of her life, for she was still there up to 738 when Bugga finally went. For a discussion, scc Moore pp. 54 -5.
718	Boniface	2/4	*Vita Bonifatii*, ch. V.

c. 719	Pega	4	AA SS Jan. I, (1643), 532-3.
721	Willibald Wynbald Family	4 4 4	*Hodoeporicon,* p. 157 in Talbot's translation.
721	Daniel	2?	ASC. 'In this year Daniel went to Rome.'
a. 722	Friends of Bugga	4?	Letters of Boniface, Tangl, p. 21: Moore, p. 54.
a. 725	Nothelm	8	BHE, preface. This must have been an earlier visit than that recorded in the ASC, when he received his pallium.
726	Ine Æthelburgh	4	ASC. 'Ine went to Rome with his wife Æthelburgh where he lived in plebeian state like a labouring man.'
c. 728	Wynnebald		*Vita Wynnebaldi,* p. 108: Moore, p. 61. This seems to have been a family or sentimental visit home.
730	Wynnebald and his brother	4 4	*Vita Wynnebaldi,* p. 108: Moore, p. 61. This was his return to Rome.
a. 733	Egbert Egred	4? 4?	Plummer, BHE I. p. 419.
735	Egbert		ASC. I have deferred to Moore in accepting that Egbert did go to Rome, though it is not obvious why he should have done so at that early date. The text clearly creates problems for translators. Whitelock, Garmonsway and Swanton adopt 'received his pallium from Rome'; Moore 'received his Pall at Rome'. *The original is* 'Her onfeng Ecgbriht pallium æt Rome.'
736	Messenger	1	ASC. Nothelm does not seem to have gone to Rome for his pallium and the text is quite different from Egbert's in the previous year, though Swanton adopts the same formula for both in his translation: 'Her Nophelm ercebiscop onfeng pallium fram Romana biscope.' Whitelock: 'In this year Archbishop Nothelm received the Pallium from the Bishop of the Romans.' The pallium must have been brought by a messenger.
737	Forthere Frithugyth	4 4	ASC. 'In this year Bishop Forthere and Queen Frithugyth journeyed to Rome.'
738	Marchelm Marcwin	4/8	These two brothers had come to Rome with Boniface to study and the probability is that they had not come directly from England. The reference is in Liudgeri (later Abbot of Utrecht); *Vita Gregorii* I p. 75: 'And there were two boys who with the consent of their master (Boniface) who was teaching them, namely Marchelm and Marcwin, English brothers, whom he led there with him.' See Moore, p. 67.
738	Lullus Kinsmen	4/8	Letters of Boniface, Tangl no. 98. Lullus went to Rome in a mood of repentence after a severe illness, came under Boniface's influence there, and returned with him to Germany.
738	Bugga	4	Letters of Boniface, Tangl no. 105. Bugga toured Rome and saw all the Holy Places with Boniface and then returned to England. 'A few years ago, the most venerable abbess Bugga, after she had visited all the most Holy Places of prayer in Rome available to her and thence returned back here to her own country and to the nunnery of Holy ladies which she had previously kept under ecclesiastical rules...'
p. 740	Cuthbert	1	The existence of Cuthbert's visit depends upon two late sources, Gervase of Canterbury writing in the 1190s and Ralph de Diceto who died in 1202. We cannot be sure whether he went or not. For – he may have already been Bishop of Hereford and there is a late tradition that he changed burial customs after a visit to Rome. Against – he may not have been Bishop of Hereford and if he had gone it is odd that there is no contemporary record or earlier tradition. See N. Brooks, *Church of Canterbury,* p. 80 onwards.

c. 750	Cuthwin	1/8?	Moore, p. 72, n. 3, citing MS Paris Latina 12949, where it is stated that he returned with an illustrated life of St. Paul.
c. 750	Philip of Zell	4	*Vita Phillipi* p. 796. He was 'of the race of the English, who for love of God and leaving his family and country behind, travelled to Rome'. See Moore, p. 71 n. 4. He settled at Zell after leaving Rome.
751	Lullus	4?	See Moore, pp. 66-7, for a discussion of Lullus' confusing movements.
751	Bregwin	4?	Tangl no. 117.
757 or 758	Forthred	2	Birch, 184: trans EHD no. 184. Pope Paul I admonished King Eadberht for seizing three monasteries that belonged to Forthred, as Forthred had told him.
758	Hunuin	4?/6	Letter of Cuthbert, abbot of Jarrow, to Lul, trans. EHD no. 185. Hunuin took presents to Lul when on his way to Rome and then on to Beneventum, where he died.
766	Messengers	1	ASC reports that Archbishop Jaenberht received the Pallium. There must have been messengers announcing his appointment and then bringing back the Pallium.
a. 767	Ælbert Alcuin	4	Allott no. 75: MG Poet. Carol. I, p. 206: MG Epp. Karol. Aevi II, no. 172.
780	Alcuin	1/3	*Vita Alcuini*, MG SS XV, p. 190. See Moore, pp. 73-4.
782	Negotiators	2	The negotiators reflect the purchase of the church of S Dalmazio in Lucca for the daughter of the king of Northumbria. Since the purchase was completed we can assume their return. See Ortenburg, *OEC*, pp. 102-3 for a full account.
a. 785	Pyttel	4	Moore cites Pyttel's journey in *Vita Liudgeri*, Pertz (ed.) MG SS II p. 408.
c. 785	Envoys	2/3	H & S III, p. 440-2. Since we have the Papal response to Offa's letter, there is a fair presumption that his messengers returned safely. See Brooks, *Canterbury*, p. 117.
786	Papal Envoys	2/3	H & S III, pp. 447-62, trans EHD no. 191. The Papal legates were George, Bishop of Ostia and Theophylact, Bishop of Todi, accompanied by Abbot Wigbod.
c. 787	Anglo-Saxons	4	*Chron. Cassinense.* The party included a deaf mute who received a double cure when praying at the tomb of St Benedict at Monte Cassino.
a. 793	Autbert Sigulf	4/8 8	*Vita Alcuini* MG SS XV, p. 189. Sigulf went indirectly, for he went from England to Gaul to his uncle Autbert, who sent him on to Rome after an unspecified interval. It is not clear whether he returned to England. He took an easterly course through Metz, where he studied chanting. He succeeded Alcuin at Ferrières in 804.
c. 794	Witto	4	Dümmler p. 253
795	Odberht	4	Moore cites MG Epp Karol aevi II no. 100. Whilst in political exile, Odberht went to Rome for the love of God.
p. 796	Messengers	2	H & S, III p. 586. Messengers went from King Coenwulf to the Papacy and back again over the quarrel with Archbishop Wulfred.
797	Wada	2	H & S III, p. 523.
798	Sigeric	4	ASC
798	Bryne Cildas Ceolbert	2 2 2	H & S III, p. 523.

B Travellers from AD 800 onwards

c. 800	Æthelric	4	Birch no. 313, Trans EHD no. 81. [D33.2]
801	Æthelheard Cyneberht and party	2/4 2/4	Allott no. 20; ASC; Jaffé 2505-6. It is possible that Bishop Cyneberht of Wessex took with him the letter from King Cenwulf about the Abbey of Abingdon. For the background and authenticity see Stenton, *The Early History of the Abbey of Abingdon*, p 23-5.
802	Messenger	2/3	Lamb, *Archbishops of Canterbury* p. 144. 'After Æthelheard's departure from Rome it would appear that the Pope received another letter and gift from Cenwulf which the Pope acknowledged in effusive terms.'
808-9	Eardwulf	3	RFA
809	Ealdwulf	3	RFA
c. 810	Eadburh	11	Eadburh ended up in poverty as a vagrant. Asser ch. 15
814	Wulfred Wigberht	2 2	ASC. The *Chronicle* does not say why they went but Wulfred had quarrelled with the king over church property and although the rift had been healed one must assume that Papal support or intervention was needed. Roger of Wendover asserted that they went 'on the affairs of the English Church'.
817	Messengers	3	H & S III p. 587. King Cenwulf wrote to Rome about his dispute with Archbishop Wulfred over the lands of some Kentish monasteries.
817-18	Pilgrims	4	LP as evidence of the English community [D35.2]
p. 830	Helmstan	2	Birch 424. Lamb, *Archbishops of Canterbury*, p. 167. Helmstan succeeded to the See [of Winchester] 'by command of the king' prior to setting out on an embassy to Rome where the Pope signified his approval of the king's nomination. The authority for Helmstan's journey to Rome really depends upon the unusual wording of his profession of faith.
c. 834	Messengers	1	ASC; JW. It is unlikely that Archbishop Ceolnoth went to Rome for his pallium but since the *Chronicle* explicitly states that he received it, we can assume that messengers went and returned.
836	Messengers	3	The *Book of Hyde* records that Egbert died 'and Adulph, the monk sub-deacon of Anglia, was appointed king'. An embassy was then sent to Leo to ask that the king's son be made king. The Pope approved. This account is followed by John of Wallingford.
c. 850	Rich Thegn	9	Ælfric, Life of Swithun, *Ælfric's Lives of the Saints*, W. Skeat (ed.), vol. 1 p. 455. (Lines 193-201): 'There was a certain thane in England very rich in possessions/ who suddenly became blind; then journeying he to Rome/ desiring to pray for his cure from the Holy Apostle/ he dwelt at Rome but was not cured/ for four full years; then he heard of Saint Swithun/ what miracles he had wrought since he (the thane) had journeyed thence/ then made he much haste, and returned to his own country/ and came to the Holy Man, and was there healed/ and returned home with perfect sight.' The reader must judge the actuality for himself.
851	Messengers	2	Jaffé 2609. Messengers must have taken letters. Jaffé quotes from Coll. Brit Leon ep. 14.
853	Alfred Messengers	3?	Asser ch. 8; ASC. Some of his escort must have returned without delay. They probably brought the letter from Pope Leo to Æthelwulf, telling him that Alfred had arrived safely and been received well. [GR II 42, n. 4].

854	Messengers	2	Simeon, *History of the Kings*. 'Archbishop Wlfere received the Pall'. It is possible that Alfred's party both asked for and returned with it, but the timing would be so precise that it seems more likely that one leg at least was performed independently. The northern messenger would in any case be coming from York and might not go overland through Wessex at all.
855	Æthelwulf Alfred	3/4 3/4	Asser ch. 11.
858-67	Englishmen	3/4	LP9, p. 232, 'In [Nicholas'] time.... some of the race of the English came to Rome, and in the oratory of Christ's confessor Pope St Gregory, ...placed 1 silver panel weighing ...lb'.
874	Messengers	3	WBB p. 1; EHD, no. 221. We have no record of the messengers who brought the letter from pope John VIII to Burgred, King of Mercia, warning him of the consequences of the immoral behaviour of those in his kingdom, but the letter starts by saying that the Pope has heard ill reports. It may well be that it was brought by English messengers on their return journey.
873-5	Messengers	2	EHD, 221, [D44].
874	Burgred	5	ASC; Asser ch. 46
877-8	Messenger	2	WBB p. 3. Whitelock noted that this letter of John VIII to Æthelred, Archbishop of Canterbury, 'has obviously been written in response to one from the Archbishop which has not survived.' It may well be that the exchange represents a round trip by an English courier who took one letter out and brought back the response.
882	Messengers	2/3	ASC(E) recorded that Pope Marinus sent the *Lignum Domini* to King Alfred in words which suggest that his messengers arrived in England before Sigehelm and Athelstan set off. It may well be that on their return trip the Papal messengers accompanied the Englishmen on their way and acted as their guides.
882	Sigehelm Athelstan	6 6	ASC. Sigehelm and Athelstan 'took to Rome and also to St Thomas and St Bartholomew the alms which King Alfred had vowed to send thither when they beseiged the host in London.' If they did in truth go to India they may well have been disappointed for the remains of St Thomas were probably moved to Edessa in 394. The fate of St Bartholomew's remains is even more obscure. (Farmer, *Oxford Dictionary of Saints*, pp. 374 and 29-30). Wherever it was that they went, Sigehelm at least returned safely for he survived to be killed in battle in 904 (ASC [A]. There is no record for Athelstan.
887	Æthelhelm	6	ASC and Asser ch. 86: 'ealderman Æthelhelm took the alms of the West Saxons and of King Alfred to Rome.'
888	Beocca Æthelswith	6 4/6	ASC. Beocca was accompanied by Queen Æthelswith when 'he took the alms of the West Saxons and of King Alfred to Rome.'
889	Couriers	3	ASC.
890	Beornhelm	6	ASC. The Abbot 'took the alms of the West Saxons and of King Alfred to Rome.'
891-6	Messengers	2	WBB p. 37. This letter must also have been written in response to a lost letter from Plegmund, also carried by an unknown courier – perhaps the same person on a round trip. The reply reads '...but because, as our esteemed brother Plegmund has told us'. The courier may well have brought Plegmund's Pallium (Gervase is almost certainly wrong in asserting that he went to Rome for it.)
908	Plegmund	2	Æthelweard's *Chronicle*. According to Æthelweard, Plegmund, 'After a period of three years Archbishop Plegmund dedicated a very high tower in the city of Winchester. ... In the course of the same year the Bishop just mentioned conveyed alms to Rome for the nation and also for King Edward.'

a. 912	Werthryth	4	Birch 537.
921	English	4	Flodoard, [D51.1].
923	English	4	Flodoard, [D51.2].
a. 926	Athelm Oda	4? 4?	*Vita Oswaldi*
927	Wulfhelm	1	ASC (E). 'In this year King Athelstan drove out King Guthfrith and Archbishop Wulfhelm went to Rome.' An entry in the Confraternity Books of St Gall (P. Piper (ed.)) suggest that he may have gone by a more easterly route but this cannot be relied upon.
c935	Alfred	3	Alfred was sent to Rome to answer a charge of treason with Edwin the Ætheling, against Athelstan. The party was presumably a big one, with guards to ensure that he did not escape. He died in Rome immediately upon swearing what was presumably a false oath. Messengers were sent between England and Rome about his burial.
941	English	4?	Flodoard, D51.7. We do not know whether this party reached Rome, as they turned back in the passes.
a. 951	Theodred	2?	Wills, 1.
956	Messenger	2	Jaffé 3678/9. The message concerned the privileges of St Peter & St Paul, Canterbury. Since these were confirmed, the supposition is that the messenger returned, having, like others, made a round trip.
958	Oscytel Oswald	1 2/4	*Ramsey Chronicle*, pp. 24-5.
959	Ælfsige	1	John of Worcester; GP, ch. 17.
960	Dunstan	1	Gervase; John of Worcester: 'In the third indiction, St Dunstan went to the City of Romulus, and received the Pall from Pope John [XII].'
p. 959	Earl	7	*Stubbs, Memorials,* p. 200. An Earl who had contracted a forbidden marriage went to Rome to appeal against Dunstan's sentence. Although he obtained a ruling in his favour, Dunstan ignored it.
p. 960	Æthelwine	2/4	Stubbs, *Memorials* p. 245. Æthelwine was on his way back from Jerusalem, via Constantinople, and having stopped at Rome to get a Pallium for Dunstan, travelled North through Lombardy. The Emperor's camp followers stole his mule. Æthelwine did not want to lose his mule or its cargo so he prayed to the distant Archbishop. The mule went mad, drove off the robbers and all was well. See also Barlow, *English Church*, p. 22.
962	Æthelmod	4	ASC. Æthelmod 'went to Rome and there passed away on 15 August'.
965	Messenger	2	GP ch. 150. Pope John confirmed the liberties of Glastonbury granted by Edgar.
967	Messenger	2	Dugdale, *Monasticon Anglicanum* I 292 (new ed. 1846). A messenger took letters about the privileges of Westminster, against the Bishop of London. The privileges were confirmed.
971	Messengers	2	There were two sets of messages in 971, both possibly taken by the same group. Jaffé 3571/2 concerned the liberties of Glastonbury. See J. Scott (ed.), William of Malmesbury: De Ant. Glas. Eccles., also GR. The second concerned Winchester.
c. 972	Oswald Germanus	1 2/4	*Ramsey Chronicle*, pp. 24-5. Germanus stayed in Fleury, attracted by the discipline and the beauty of the place, whilst Oswald continued on his way to England.
973	Legation	2	GR, chs. 150-51 According to this, a legation was sent by King Edgar to Pope John asking him to confirm gifts of land to Glastonbury. Henry of Huntington has the same story in Bk 2, ch. 8.

988	Æthelgar	1	Stubbs, *Memorials*, pp. 383-5, 538-9. Later, the newly appointed Archbishop Sigeric was to be invited by Abbot Odbert to visit St Bertin as Æthelgar had done on his way to Rome, in the expectation of giving valuable gifts to the house.
990	Sigeric	1	ASC. Sigeric was consecrated 'and afterwards the same year went to Rome for his Pallium'.
990	Leo	2	Stubbs, *Memorials*, p. 397, trans EHD, 230. Leo arrived and met the King on Christmas Day.
991	Messenger	3	WBB p. 178. Pope John XV wrote a letter about the hostility between Æthelred and Richard I of Normandy. The text is in GR, ch. 149.
995	Two Priests	1/2	ASC(F). Brooks condems this passage in the *Chronicle* as entirely spurious. Barlow is more open: 'ASC(F) in a later insertion which contain some spurious matter; but the story may be true.' I incline to accept it. My reason is that the Papal reason for declining to give the pallium to the two priests was that they were not properly accredited to receive it, not that the only person who could receive it was the Archbishop in person. A totally spurious interpolation would surely have given a more anachronistic reason.
997	Ælfric	1	ASC. Ælfric 'arrived in Rome … where the Pope himself put on him his own Pallium.'
p. 997	Scottish woman	4/9	The Scottish Woman appears in Simeon, *History of the Church of Durham*, ch. 38. She was crippled so that: 'Her feet and thighs were twisted backwards and dragged behind her and she crept on her hands … It so happened that she conveyed herself in this miserable plight to the spot already mentioned, where the most holy body had rested for a few days.' She was cured and 'travelled through many regions and nations performing all her journeys on foot; for she went to Rome to pray and on her return passed into Ireland..' She presumably returned to England for Simeon to have heard the story and may then have gone to Scotland – assuming of course that she existed.
p. 1000	Siflaed	4	Wills pp. 94-5.
Cxi	Venetian	4	A young man from Venice, of consular rank on both his father and his mother's side, and of a most famous family had wandered in expiation of his grievous sin and had come to Ramsey. *Ramsey Chronicle* lxvi.
1002-23	Leofwine	4	Leofwine killed his mother and was advised to go to Rome and consult the Pope. The Pope imposed a penance. We do not know whether he returned, but since we know what happened he may well have done so. See Barlow, p. 272. Liber Eliensis II.6.
1007	Ælfheah	1	According to D text of the *Chronicle*, 'in this year, [Ælfheah] went to Rome for his Pallium'. William of Malmesbury has the story of the village fire which Ælfheah extinguished (GP. II ch 76) The Vita S Elphegus ch. 5 (MPL cxlix, col 379) adds that he was robbed on the way to Rome. The route was Alpine: 'And Elphegus, on his way to Rome to receive the Pallium from the Pope, crossed the Alps.'
p. 1018	Lyfing	1	Lyfing must have gone to Rome for his pallium and brought back letters for Cnut. He described himself only as Bishop until 1018. WBB p. 436; D68.3
1020-25	Bishop	2	The Bishop came not from Rome but from Benevento. He had been warmly welcomed by Cnut and Emma, OEC p. 118; Eadmer *Historia. Novella*, 107-10
1022	Æthelnoth + Leofwine	1 2	Æthelnoth 'went to Rome and was there received with great ceremony by the venerable Pope Benedict who with his own hands put the Pallium on him.' There was an inscription in Coventry: 'Archbishop Æthelnoth bought this arm of St. Augustine with a hundred talents of silver and one of gold, when he was returning from the Pope at Rome'. If we remember that a talent was eighty pounds weight, that was an enormous sum. Abbot Leofwine 'who had been unjustly driven from Ely, was his companion' ASC (E); GP IV. Ch. 175.

1022	Ælfstan	2/3	Ælfstan met the Emperor Henry II in Rome, Ortenberg, OEC, p. 151; Goscelin, HTA 29-31.
1026	Ælfric	1	ASC: 'In this year Bishop Ælfric went to Rome and received the pallium from Pope John on 12 November'.
1027	Cnut + Lyfing	3/4 3	JW; GP II ch. 94.
1040	Eadsige	3/2?	ASC. Brooks, *Canterbury*, p. 299, says that Eadsige's journey to Rome was for the Pallium. However, he had been Archbishop since late 1038 and since he had become a monk between being a Bishop and becoming Archbishop, custom may not have required him to collect his pallium in person. It is as likely that he went to consult the Pope after his difficult relations with Cnut's successors.
1042-66	Dumb Man	9	A dumb man from Canterbury in Edward's reign spent three years in Rome looking for a cure. Cited in Barlow, *Church*, p. 20. There is a strong resemblance to the blind man cured by St Swithun, and one may question whether he actually existed or is another stock figure. *Chron. Evesham* p. 47.
a. 1043	Ælfric Modercope	4?	It is far from certain that Ælfric went on pligrimage to Rome as opposed to anywhere else. Like Siflaed later, it is a matter of probability. Ortenberg lists him as having gone (OEC p.151). I have listed him as a pilgrim, but as he was a man of substance, he may well have been engaged on business as well. He went 'over the sea', which is open to a variety of meanings. Whitelock, *Wills* p. 74-5
1044-65	Leofstan	4?	Quoted in Barlow, *Church*, p. 21, and referred to in OEC p. 104. Leofstan seems to have gone simply as a pilgrim for no other business is indicated. Leofstan's name is entered in the fraternity book at Lucca: Schwarzmaier; *Lucca und das Reich bis zum ende des 11 Jahhunderts*, p. 398, n. 86; BM Add MS 14.847 f21r.
1049	Messengers	2	'Edward, king of England, sent to establish whether Bishop Leofric could transfer his episcopal seat from Crediton to Exeter'. The reply is recorded the following year, H & S, I, 691-2 & WBB 525. I have assumed that it was brought back by the same messengers.
c. 1050	Askyll	4	Askyll was a Danish Nobleman, who, about 1050, gave all his property to Peterborough and retired to Rome. Hart, *Charters Eastern England*, nos. 157-9.
1050	Herman + Aldred + Aelfwine	222	'In this same year was the great Synod in Rome and King Edward sent Bishop Herman and Bishop Aldred and they arrived thither on Easter Eve'. ASC (E); Goscelin; HTA 29-31.
1050	Ulf	2	ASC. 'Afterwards the Pope held a Synod at Vercelli, which Bishop Ulf attended, and it was said that they were very near to breaking his staff if he had not given exceptionally costly gifts, for he did not know how to perform his offices as well as he ought to have done.'
1051	Robert	1	ASC. [D45.13].
1052	Robert	2	ASC. [D45.14].
1052-66	Ketel + Stepdaughter	4 4	Wills, no. 34; [D78]. Ketel and his step-daughter (Ælgifu) went to Rome. He was a thegn of Archbishop Stigand; that being so, there may have been more than simple pilgrimage behind the journey.
1055	Cynsige	1	ASC (D). He 'Fetched his Pallium from Pope Victor'. Cynsige was Archbishop of York.
1055-7	Messengers	2	I have included these messengers although the dating is so wide. The letters (about the privileges of Ely) could have been carried by eg Cynsige or others, or by Harold, at least on his return journey. WBB I. 1-4 & 543-5; *Hist. Eliensis*; Jaffé 4350.

1056	Harold	3	Barlow, *Vita Edwardi*, p. 33.
1058	Messengers	1/2	ASC(D). 'In this same year Pope Stephen passed away, and Benedict was appointed Pope. He sent the pallium to Bishop Stigand.' We must assume that the pallium was brought by an unreported annual 'official' party or by a Papal delegation. It is interesting that the chronicler saw nothing untoward in the sending of the pallium, despite Stigand's being a pluralist.
p. 1058	Goldsmith	4	The goldsmith was at Monte Cassino during the time of Abbot Desiderius, 1058-87. It is possible that his was a post-conquest journey. Cited in OEC p. 104. *Chron. Cassinense*, p. 712.
1061	Aldred Tostig Giso Walter	3 / 4 2 / 4 ? 2 2	VER, p. 35; GP III ch. 115.
1062	Legates	2	GP III ch. 115; *Vita Wulfstani* 17-18. It is clear that the legates followed after, and did not return with the English party. Their purpose was to ensure that Aldred kept his word and also to consecrate Wulstan. William went on to add that no respectable person was consecrated by Stigand. One of the legates was Armefred, Bishop of Sedunum (Sion).
1061-2	Burgheard	4	Burgheard died shortly before he would have completed the round trip. Ortenberg, OEC, p. 236. Sawyer, 1237.
1062	Ælfwine	3	We are told on p 117 that Ælfwine's health was damaged by the rigours of the journey. *Ramsey Chronicle*, p. 176.
1066-8	Ulf + Madselin	4	Wills, p. 95; [D78.3].

APPENDIX 3

THE TIMING OF JOURNEYS

As already noted, there are relatively few hard dates for arrival and departure, and most lie either towards the beginning or the end of our period. What little there is matches the much fuller evidence from Carolingian sources which suggests that travellers moved when they had to and did not wait for the seasons.

Year	Name	Direction	Details
596-7	Augustine	North	Left Rome in May 596 but took the journey slowly.
598	Lawrence Peter	South	Probably set off late in the year, as they waited until Augustine had returned from Arles in June. They must have made an autumn or winter sea or Alpine crossing – probably the former.
601	Lawrence Mellitus	North	Left Rome in June 601, so he had an easy sea or Alpine crossing – probably the former – with a summer continental journey.
601	Messengers	North	Left Rome in June.
609-10	Mellitus	South	Attended a synod in Rome commencing on 27 February 610. Unless he took an inordinate time over the journey he must have made a winter sea or Alpine crossing.
627	Messengers	North	The Papal letters were dated June and presumably the messengers started at once.
653	Biscop Wilfrid	South	Biscop reached Rome by September, which would indicate a summer crossing, assuming that they moved steadily.
668	Theodore Hadrian Biscop	North	They left Rome on 27 May 668 but did not reach Canterbury until a year later. Bede specifically states that they rested on the way, because of the winter and Theodore's exhaustion.
678-9	Wilfrid	South	Wilfrid left England in the early summer, overwintered in Frisia but left there at the first sign of spring. He would have crossed the Alps as soon as the snows cleared for he was in Rome mid-year (Moore p. 25).
678	Winfrid	South	Winfrid probably left England in early spring for he was mistaken for Wilfrid.
678	Envoys	South	(Sent by Wilfrid's enemies). In order to arrive in Rome just before Wilfrid, who left Frisia in early spring, they probably left at about the same time but travelled faster by a more direct route.
678	Biscop Ceolfrid	South	They probably left in early spring, even late winter, for they arrived in Rome after 27 June 678 (Moore p. 20).
679-80	Wilfrid	North	Wilfrid left Rome *plures dies* after the Council ended. It was convened on 27 March 680, so Moore's suggestion of April (p. 26) seems reasonable.
680	Biscop John Ceolfrid	North	They probably left in the early summer for they were in England by September 680. They had however gone via Tours and had stopped there for at least a brief time. That would have lengthened the journey time.
683-4	Messenger of Wilfrid	South	We do not know when the messenger arrived in Rome but he left between July 683 and June 684. Unfortunately we cannot be more precise than that. (Moore p. 29).

688-9	Cadwalla	South	Arrived at Rome and died there on 20 April 689 soon afterwards. He left England no later than May 688 (Bede HE V.7) and was entertained at the Lombard court for an unknown period. He may have crossed the Alps before winter and spent a long time at Pavia but that would conflict with his desire to get to Rome. It is more likely that he set out in May 688 and did not delay too long, taking the Alps in his stride. See Moore, p. 31, n. 3.
716	Ceolfrid	South	Ceolfrid left the Wear on the 4 June and sailed from the Humber a month later. He died at Langres on the 25 September.
718	Boniface	South	Boniface left when the summer was well advanced. Unless he moved extremely quickly he must have had a winter journey. We do not know when he arrived in Rome but he left in May 719.
c. 720	Willibald	South	Willibald also left in late summer. He did not arrive in Rome until November but we do not know how long he stayed in Lucca where his father was ill and eventually died. When he finally left Italy, several years later, he crossed the Alps after Easter, going north.
801	Æthelheard	South	The Archbishop arrived in Rome in January 802 so he must have left England no later than the autumn.
808	Eardwulf	South and Norh	This royal journey has been considered above. If he reached Nijmegen in the spring he must have left Northumberland not long after the beginning of the year. Since he returned the same year, after negotiations in Rome, it is quite possible that both his Alpine crossings were in fair weather in summer and late autumn.
958	Ælfsige	South	We can only speculate that he met his death in the winter. It would be unusual for a traveller to be caught by frostbite in the summer although he may have met freak conditions. Given that Oda died in June and that early decisions had to be made on episcopal appointments, Ælfsige probably attempted a winter crossing late in 958 or early 959.
960	Dunstan	South	Dunstan received his pallium from Pope John XII on 21 September. Assuming that he returned at once, his must have been a summer crossing south and an early winter return.
962	Æthelmod	South	Since he died in Rome on 15 August by implication soom after arrival, we may assume a summer crossing of the mountains and an unhealthy trip across the Po valley.
990	Sigeric	South	We do not know the precise date of his consecration, but if the journey followed shortly afterwards we can put it in the early months of 990. For a discussion, see Ortenberg, in *Anglo Saxon England* 19, 1990.
990	Leo	North	We must assume that he travelled as fast as he reasonably could, since he was on important business. If he arrived at the royal court on Christmas Day, he probably left Rome in the late summer or early autumn.
1022	Æthelnoth	South	Æthelnoth was given his pallium on 7 October 1022. Unless he delayed in Rome, his Alpine crossings must have been in late autumn, south, and the winter, north.
1026	Ælfric	South	According to the *Chronicle*, he received the pallium from Pope John on 12 November. It is unlikely that he stayed in Rome until the spring so he probably made both crossings in the winter.
1050	Herman Aldred	South	These two Bishops attended the Synod in Rome and according to the *Chronicle*, 'arrived thither on Easter Eve.' They must have crossed the Alps in the New Year and probably left England in winter.
1050	Ulf	South	Ulf attended the Council in Vercelli which began in September. Assuming that he did not delay, his was a summer journey south and possibly late autumn north.

1051	Robert	South and North	This rapid journey has already been discussed, but if the record is to be believed, he made the round trip in three to four months, starting from Easter.
1052-3	Robert	South and North	We know that Robert had no choice but to leave hurriedly in September. We do not know when he arrived in Rome nor how long he stayed there but he died in Normandy the next year.
1061	Tostig	North	The party had split, with Tostig's wife going on ahead. The Earl's movements cannot be precisely dated but it is clear that he left Rome in the middle of the year, with a late summer crossing.
1062	Armenfrid	North	The bishop followed Tostig and arrived in England in early Lent, according to GP. See also JW.

Appendix 4

The status of known travellers

People who made the journey more than once are only listed on the first occasion.

I have omitted travellers whose names are unknown, ie 'messenger' or those whose status cannot be guessed. Thus, for example, the 'couriers' of 889 do not appear.

DATE	NAME	CLERIC	LAYMAN
597	Augustine Peter Laurence	Archbishop Monk Priest, later Archbishop	
601	Mellitus Justus Paulinus Rufinianus	Priest, later Archbishop Monk, later Archbishop Priest, later Bishop Priest	
624/7	Romanus	Bishop	
c. 637	Birinus	Bishop	
653	Biscop Wilfrid	Later Abbot Later bishop	
667	Wighard	Archbishop elect	
668	Theodore Hadrian	Archbishop Abbot	
678	Ceolfrid Eddius	Monk, later Abbot Cleric	
679	Coenwald	Monk	
680	John	Abbot	
688	Cadwalla		King
c. 690	Willibrord	Later Archbishop	
c. 692	Oftfor	Monk, later Bishop	
692	Berhtwald	Archbishop	
c. 700	Hwaertbert Monks	Abbot Monks	
c. 700	Æthelwald	'Churchman' (Anderson)	
c. 701	Aldhelm	Abbot	
703	Acca	Priest, later Bishop	
704	Berhtwald's Envoys	Deacon	Laymen
a. 706	Egwin	Bishop	
709	Offa Cenred		King King
a. 713	Northumbrian Abbess + Nuns	Abbess Nuns	

p. 716	Wethburga		Lay woman?
718	Boniface	Later Archbishop	
c. 719	Pega	Anchoress	
721	Willibald Wynnebald Willibald's father	Later Bishop	Layman, later Bishop Layman, later Saint
721	Daniel	Bishop	
722	Bynnan		Layman?
a. 725	Nothelm	Priest	
726	Ine Queen Æthelburga		King Queen
730	Egred		Layman?
a. 733	Egbert	Archbishop	
737	Forthere Frithogytha	Bishop	Queen
738	Marchelm Marcwin		Layman? Layman?*
738	Lullus Father Kinsmen	Monk	Wealthy Layman Laymen?
738	Bugga	Abbess	
p. 740	Cuthbert	Archbishop	
c. 750	Cuthwin	Bishop	
c. 750	Philip	Priest	
751	Bregwin	Archbishop	
757	Forthred	Abbot	
758	Hunuin		Layman?
a. 767	Ælbert Alcuin	Head of School at York, Monk, later Abbot	
a. 785	Pyttel	Deacon	
786	Papal Envoys	Bishops	
790	Beornrad	Bishop	
a. 793	Autbert Sigulf	Priest cleric	
c. 794	Witto	Priest	
795	Odbert Companions	Priest ?	?
797	Wada	Abbot	
798	Sigeric		King
798	Bryne Cildas Ceolbert	Priest	Thegn Thegn

* The brothers' status is uncertain. Although friendly with the (later) Abbot of Utrecht, they were described merely as 'two boys, namely Marchelm and Marcwin, bred of the English race'. See Moore, p. 68, n.1.

801	Æthelheard Cyneberht Torhtmund	Archbishop	Thegn Layman?
804	Æthelric		Layman
808	Eardwulf Ealdwulf	Deacon	King
810	Eadburh		Queen
813/4	Wulfred Wigberht	Archbishop Bishop	
830/57	Helmstan	Bishop	
850	Thegn		Thegn
853	Alfred		Prince, later King
854	Wulfhere	Archbishop	
855	Æthelwulf		
874	Burgred		King
882	Sigehelm Athelstan		Nobleman Chaplain*
887	Æthelhelm		Ealdorman
888	Beocca Æthelswith		Ealdorman Queen
890	Beornhelm	Abbot	
908	Plegmund	Archbishop	
a. 912	Werthyrth		Widow
a. 926	Athelm Oda	Priest, later Archbishop	Thegn
927	Wulfhelm	Archbishop	
c. 935	Ælfred		Noble
a. 951	Theodred	Bishop	
958	Oscytel Oswald	Bishop Priest, later Archbishop	
959	Ælfsige	Archbishop	
960	Dunstan	Archbishop	
p. 959	Earl		Earl
p. 960	Æthelwine	Monk	
962	Æthelmod	Priest	
c. 972	Oswald Germanus	Archbishop Monk	
988	Æthelgar	Archbishop	
990	Sigeric	Archbishop	
990	Leo	Legate	
995	Two Priests	Priests	

* I follow Sturdy's tentative identification, *Alfred the Great*, pp. 165-6.

997	Ælfric	Archbishop	
p. 997	Scottish Woman		Lay woman
p. 1000	Siflaed		Widow
p. 1000	Venetian		Nobleman
p. 1002	Leofwine		Layman
1007	Ælfeah	Archbishop	
c. 1018	Lyfing	Archbishop	
p. 1020	Italian	Bishop	
1022	Æthelnoth Leofwine	Archbishop Abbot	
1022	Ælfstan	Abbot	
1026	Ælfric	Abbot	
1027	Cnut Lyfing	 Archbishop	King
1040	Eadsige	Archbishop	
c. 1043	Ælfric Modercope		Layman
1044/65	Leofstan	Abbot	
c. 1050	Askyll		Nobleman
1050	Ulf	Bishop	
1050	Aldred Herman Ælfwine	Archbishop Bishop Bishop	
1051	Robert	Archbishop	
1052/66	Ketel Stepdaughter		Thegn Lay woman?
1055	Cynsige	Archbishop	
1056	Harold		Earl, later king
p. 1058	Goldsmith		Layman?
1061	Tostig Judith Giso Walter Gyrth Gospatric	 Bishop Bishop	Earl Wife Nobleman Nobleman
1062	Legate	Bishop	
1061/2	Burgheard		Son of Earl
1062	Ælfwine	Abbot	
1066/8	Ulf Madselin		Layman Wife

APPENDIX 5

MISCELLANEOUS REFERENCES, UNDATED OR GENERAL

This appendix contains miscellaneous or unreliable material that has a bearing on travel but has not been included elsewhere in this book.

PEOPLE AND GROUPS

1. *p.* 700
Did Odger, Plechelm, Wiro go to Rome?

Farmer in his *Dictionary of Saints*, gives a full bibliography, mainly under Wiro. See also Levison, pp. 82-3. I have followed Moore in not including them in the list, though they quite possibly did go to Rome. If they did, it is unlikely that they went in a single journey, but more probably from Germany. Levison's footnote reads:

> Wera is one of the seven continental bishops of English origin who about 746 joined Boniface to send a letter of admonition to King Ethelbald of Mercia. (Boniface Epp 73 p. 146). Some scholars belive him to be the bishop of Ultrecht who after 741 was appointed by Boniface. He is commonly associated with St Wiro, whose cult was centred at Odilienberg (formerly St Peter's Berg) near Roermond in Dutch Limburg ... It is evident that later nothing was known about 'Wiro'; he and a second bishop venerated with him, whose name Plechelm (Anglo-Saxon Pleghelm) as it is spelled in a library of Utrecht of the late 10th century (Analectia Bollandiana lv 1937 p. 67) also suggests an English origin ... [His life was composed no earlier than 858.] See also: Raine; Hist Ch York i 380 where he appears as Vira as mentioned by Alcuin.

2. *c.* 780
Birch 293, mentioned by Brooks: *Canterbury*, p. 115.
A Reeve, Ealdhun, gave land to Canterbury when he was about to depart on pilgrimage. But did he go to Rome?

3. *c.* 821
Henry of Huntingdon, bk. II, ch. 13; GP. p.294.
An account of the death of St Kenelm was miraculously carried to Rome by a dove and was translated for the Romans by 'an Englishman (who) was at hand.'

4. 858
Asser, ch. 16.
On his death, Æthelwulf ordered that 'every year a great sum of money, namely 300 mancuses, should be taken to Rome'.

5. *c.* 890
Translated in EHD, no. 223, p. 813.
Flodoard refers to a letter of Fulk, Archbishop of Rheims, to King Alfred 'about the reception of certain Englishmen.' (Were they *en route* to Rome?)

6. CYNEWAERD *c.* 975
According to Douglas Dales: *St Dunstan*, p. 53, Cyneweard, Bisop of Wells, 'may well have made a similar journey (to Rome) at the end of his life in 975.'

7. VOLMARUS. Although probably an invented rather than a real figure, he was given a definite return route, taking an easterly course to Egmond in Holland. We do not khow how he got there from Rome, but it suggests that the Rhine route was still open and used.

8. AN ABORTED JOURNEY *c.* 1050
Quoted in Farmer: Dictionary, citing Nova Legenda Angliae, C. Horstman (ed.).
Bruning, the wealthy and devout priest of St Peter, Northampton, in the mid eleventh century had a simple minded man

servant of Viking family who set out on a pilgrimage for Rome in honour of St Peter whom he called drotinum (ie Lord). But he was repeatedly admonished in visions to return. Once back he saw the same celestial visitor as before, who now told him that the body of a friend of God lay buried under the floor of the Church and that the parish priest should be told where to find him.

They dug, found a tomb with a name on a scroll inside – Ragener, nephew of Edmund of Bury.

COIN AND RELATED EVIDENCE

This evidence is conclusive of neither pilgrimage nor trade for the deposits could arise from either, and in one case, specifically Peter's Pence. Despite this, it indicates a probable presence of English people in one capacity at least.

9. *c.* 944-946
Lunt: *Financial Relations*, p. 28. Lunt argued that this was probably Peter's Pence, stolen or concealed.
'…a hoard of Anglo-Saxon coins ... (was) ... dug up near the house of the VestaL Virgins at the foot of the Palatine Hill, not far from the location of a Papal palace where some of the Papal treasure was kept during the period.'

10. *c.* 990 ONWARDS
Lunt; *Financial Relations*, p. 29. [There were more than 100 coins].
'Another discovery of Anglo-Saxon coins... at the Church of San Paolo fuori le Mura, probably has no relation to Peterr's pence, though the assumption that the money represents a payment of that due has been put forward.'

11. 1045
Lunt; *Financial Relations*, p. 30.
'Shortly before the close of the Anglo-Saxon period, however, we receive glimpses of the receipt of the due by the Papacy. Otto of Friesing, writing a century after the event, related that Benedict IX, when he surrendered the papacy in 1045, reserved for himself the revenues from England.'

DOCUMENTARY APPENDIX

[1] GREGORY OF TOURS; THE HISTORY OF THE FRANKS
Translated by Lewis Thorpe.

[1.1] V. 49. Meanwhile they had begun to cross the river at a point upstream from the bridge which used to be supported on two pontoon boats. The ferry which was carrying Leudast sank and he would have been drowned with his companions, had he not saved himself by swimming. With God's help, the second boat, which was attached to the first and which carried the prisoners, remained afloat.

[1.2] VI. 6. A deacon was about to set out for Rome from this region, to bring back relics of the blessed Apostles and other Saints who watch over that city. When the sick man's parents heard of this, they asked the deacon to be so good as to take their son with him on his journey, for if only he could visit the tombs of the blessed Apostles, he would immediately be cured. The two set off together and came at length to the spot where Saint Hospicius lived. The deacon saluted him and gave him the kiss of peace. He explained the reasons for their journey and said that he was on his way to Rome. He asked the Holy man to give him an introduction to any local sailors whom he might know.

[1.3] VI. 11. [*Guntram*] had the roads blocked so that no one should find the way open to cross his kingdom.

[1.4] VI. 46. When (Chilperic's) time came to die, he died deserted by all. Only Mallulf, Bishop of Senlis, who had been encamped for three days in a tent at Chelles, waiting in vain to have an audience, came forward when he heard that Chilperic had been assassinated...

[1.5] VII. 32. After this, Gundovald once more sent two messengers to King Guntram. They carried consecrated wands, according to the Frankish custom, so that they should not be molested by anybody, but might return with the answer once they had explained the purpose of their mission.

[1.6] VIII. 30. Gundovald then sent two messengers, both of them Churchmen, to his supporters. One of the two, the Abbot of Cahors, carried a letter which he had written under the wax of his hollowed out wooden tablets. He was captured by King Guntram's men and the letter was discovered. He was taken before the king, severely beaten and thrown into prison.

[1.7] VIII. 35. The previous year, when (King Guntram's) army was attacking Septimania, certain ships which were sailing from Gaul to Galicia had been looted on the orders of King Leuvigild...

[1.8] IX. 28. It was announced to King Guntram that Ebregisel had set out, for someone reported to him that Queen Brunhild was sending presents to Gundovald's sons. As soon as he heard it, Guntram had all the roads in his kingdom closely guarded, so that no one could pass through without being searched. Even the clothes and shoes of travellers were examined, and all their possessions too, to see if a letter were hidden in them.

[2] GREGORY OF TOURS; GLORY OF THE MARTYRS
Translated by Raymond van Dam.

[2.1] Ch. 24, p. 43. There was a heretic who did not fear God, did not venerate this holy place, and did not believe in his heart.... The man arrived with a herd of horses. Once the packs had been unloaded, he ordered that stalls be prepared for the horses in the church and that they be stabled there. The wretched man ignored what the local inhabitants told him about the place. Then about midnight he was struck with a fever. Barely able to breathe, he repented (although later than he should have) and commanded the horses to be removed from the building. *He nevertheless went mad and died.*

2.2] Ch. 30, pp. 50-1. During the reign of King Theudebert Mummolus travelled to the Emperor Justinian. As he was journeying by ship, he landed at Patras, where the same apostle [*Andrew*] is buried. [*After being relieved of a gall stone by prayer to the saint*] he returned to his ship a healthy man.

[2.3] Ch. 43, p. 66. Another man collected the public taxes, but while he was travelling he carelessly lost a bag of money. As he approached the city [of Bologna], he realised that he had lost the public funds he was carrying. Then he kneeled before the tombs of the saints and tearfully prayed that by means of their power he might recover what he had lost; otherwise he, his wife, and their children would be reduced to captivity for this loss. As he went outside into the courtyard, he met a man who had found the money lying next to the road. During careful questioning the man said that he had found this sack of money at precisely the hour when the tax collector had requested the assistance of the martyrs.

[2.5] Ch. 44, pp. 67-8. Next (*Apollinaris*) called his servant and ordered his horse to be saddled; he said 'Today we must be freed from the chain of this captivity'. After mounting their horses they crossed the peaks of the Alps that were covered with drifts of snow and reached Clermont. The power of the blessed martyr preceded them, so that no one asked where they were going or whence they had come. It is obvious that they were saved from this tribulation by the assistance of the blessed martyr.

[2.6] Ch. 47, pp. 71-72. As some monks were transporting (St. Saturninus') relics into another region, the path of their journey led them to pass by the boundary of the village of Brioude, which is situated in the territory of Clermont. Since the sun was setting, they turned aside to the cottage of a poor man and requested the lodging they needed. Once the man took them in, they told him what they were delivering …

[2.7] Ch. 68, p. 91-2. Over the Rhone River there is a bridge at the spot where the blessed martyr (Genasius) is said to have (escaped) by swimming. This bridge was placed on top of boats. Once, on the festival of the saint, it broke its anchor chains and began to swing. Because of the great weight of the people the boats broke and submerged the people in the riverbed. Everyone was placed in the same danger, and they shouted with one voice and said: 'Blessed Genasius, save us by the power of your own holiness, lest the people who have faithfully and piously come to celebrate your festival perish'. Soon a wind blew up and the entire crowd of people was brought to the bank. They marvelled that they had been saved by the power of the martyr.

[2.8] Ch. 71, p. 94-5. Once King Sigibert came with an army to Paris…As soon as [*one of his retainers*] discovered that the door [*of the church*] were unlocked and that no custodians were in the church, he rashly and boldly seized the silk shroud that was ornamented with gold and gems and that covered the holy tomb and took it off with himself. As he returned to the camp, it was necessary for him to take a boat. [*With him*] was his servant, whom he had always trusted and who had two hundred gold pieces hanging around his neck. When his servant boarded the boat with him, suddenly, although no one had touched him, he fell from the boat, was crushed by the waters and could not be found again. The man recognised in the loss of the servant and the gold that God had passed judgement on himself. Quickly he returned to the shore from which he had departed, and with great haste he returned the shroud to the tomb.

[2.9] Ch. 72, p. 95. In this city [*Saint-Quintin*] a thief secretly stole a priest's horse. When the priest found him, he was brought to a judge.

[2.10] Ch. 75, pp. 98-9. [*King Guntram*] sent a priest to bring gifts to the brothers who served the saints at Saint Maurice-d'Agaune. He ordered the priest to bring him relics of the saints upon his return. Then, after the priest fulfilled the king's command, while he was returning with these relics, he sought a boat at Lake Leman, through which the Rhone River flows. This lake is about four hundred stades long and one hundred and fifty stades wide. While the priest was returning, as I said, he boarded this boat. Suddenly a storm arose and whipped up the waves. Waves as high as mountains rose to the stars. When the prow sank, the stern of the ship was tossed in the air; when the stern was submerged, in turn the prow was tossed in the air. The sailors were frantic and in such danger wished only for death. The priest then saw that they were being overpowered by these waves and buried beneath the violent foam of the waves. He took from his neck the reliquary that held the relics of the saints and in his faith threw it into the swelling waves. With a loud voice he invoked the protection of the saints and said: 'Glorious martyrs, I request your power so that I may not die in these waves. I ask that you who always offer assistance to those who are dying instead deign to extend your right hand of salvation to me. Calm the waves, and with the strength of your assistance lead us to the shore we hoped for.' As he said this, the wind died down, the waves subsided, and they were brought to shore.

[2.11] Ch.82, pp. 106-7. (*My*) deacon received relics of some martyrs and confessors from Pope Pelagius of Rome. A large chorus of monks who were chanting psalms and a huge crowd of people escorted him to Ostia. After he boarded a ship the sails were unfurled and hoisted over the rigging of a mast that presented the appearance of a cross. As the wind blew, they set out on the high seas. While they were sailing to reach the port of Marseilles, they began to approach a certain place where a mountain of stone rose from the shore of the sea and, sinking a bit, stretched into the sea to the top of the water. As the wind forced them on, the ship was lifted by almighty blast into danger … Suddenly, out of respect for the holy relics, a wind blew from that spot with great force against the other wind. It crushed the waves and repulsed the opposing wind … and by the grace of the Lord and the protection of the saints they arrived at the port they had hoped for.

[3] GREGORY OF TOURS; GLORY OF THE CONFESSORS
Translated by Raymond van Dam
Reproduced by permission of Liverpool University Press.
Ch. 32, pp. 36-37. But after (Abbot Maximus) became conspicuous there (*at Ile-Barbe in the Saone at Lyons*), he decided to return to his homeland. Then when he was intending to cross the Saone river, his boat was swamped and sank, and the priest was covered by the water. Around his neck he had a book of the Gospels and [*the utensils for the celebration of*] the daily liturgy, that is, a paten and a chalice. *(He was saved and brought to the bank by Divine mercy.)*

[4] LETTER OF GREGORY TO CANDIDUS (September 595)
Haddon & Stubbs, III, 5.
Gregory to the priest Candidus, setting out for the patrimony of Gaul:
We ask that, when you start with the help of our Lord Jesus Christ to manage the patrimony in Gaul, you would be so kind as to buy with the money which you will receive, clothing for the poor, and English boys who are seventeen or eighteen years old, who can be given to God and educated in the monasteries; so that the Gaulish money, which cannot be spent in this land, may be usefully spent in the place where it comes from. … But because those [boys] who are available there are pagans, I would like a priest to be sent with them, so that should they fall ill on the way, he may properly baptise those whom he perceives to be dying …

[5] EXTRACT FROM THE LIFE OF ST GREGORY BY A MONK OF WHITBY
From Bertram Colgrave, *The Life of St Gregory by a Whitby monk*. Written 684-714
The faithful relate that before his aforesaid pontificate certain of our nation, beautiful in form and fair haired, came to Rome. When he heard of their coming he was at once eager to see them; and receiving them with the vision of a pure heart, and hesitating over their new and unfamiliar appearance, he asked of what race they were. And when they replied 'Those from whom we are sprung are called Angles' he said 'Angels of God'.

[6] EXTRACT FROM THE LIFE OF COLUMBANUS
Translated by E. Peters, *Monks, Bishops and Pagans* and taken from Jonas' Life of the Saint.
Ch. 42, p. 102. And proceeding on the Loire, they came to the city of Tours. There the holy man begged the guards to stop and permit him to visit the grave of St. Martin. The guards refused, strove to go on quickly, urged the oarsmen to put forth their strength and pass swiftly by the harbour and commanded the helmsman keep the boat in mid-stream. St. Columban seeing this, raised his eyes sadly to Heaven, grieving at being subjected to, great, sorrow, and that he was not permitted to see the graves of the Saints. In spite of all their efforts the boat stopped as if anchored, as soon as it got opposite the harbour, and turned its bow to the landing place. The guards seeing that they could not prevail, unwillingly allowed the boat to go where it would. In a wonderful manner it sped, as if winged, from midstream to the harbour, and entering this accomplished the wish of the man of God.

[7] ST. GALL'S SKILL IN LANGUAGES
G. S. M. Walker, *S. Columbani Opera, p. xxviii-xxix.*
The pagan inhabitants, taking advantage of this change of ruler [*Duke Gunzon*] said that the Irish monks were interfering with the chase, and it now became necessary for Columbanus to leave; he had already thought of preaching to the Veneti, but dissuaded by a vision, he decided to make Lombardy his final home. Gall, worn down by fever, and hoping to continue to preach to a people in whose language he was skilled, refused to follow and Columbanus left in anger, forbidding his truant disciple to say mass as long as he himself should live.

[8] A CHARTER OF PRIVILEGE TO PETERBOROUGH.
From *The Anglo-Saxon Chronicles*, translated by Michael Swanton. This occurs in the E (Peterborough) text only and must be regarded with great suspicion. Swanton commented (p.31, fn. 11) 'this whole account may be largely wishful thinking by the Peterborough source'.
sa 656. I want to free this Minster thus, so that it be subject to Rome only, and I want all of us who cannot go to Rome to seek out St Peter here.

[9] ST BIRINUS
N. E. S. A. Hamilton: *William of Malmesbury: Gesta Pontificum Anglorum*, (1870), Ch. 75.
c. 634. He was ordained bishop by bishop Asterius of Genoa and then went to the sea shore in order to travel to Britain. While he was packing his bits and pieces, the sailors kept urging him to hurry up as the wind was right, and as a result he forgot those cloths known as 'corporal clothes'. He was already out at sea, with the ship happily carving a furrow through the tranquil waters, when he remembered that he had left them behind. He did not know what to do. If he asked the sailors to return, they would simply laugh at him as the voyage had started so easily. But if he kept quiet, he would have to accept that his apostolic service would be faulty. So, waving the weapons of his faith, and gathering all his courage, he clambered down the side of the ship into the water and as fast as he could, made for the shore that he had just left. There he found the 'corporal vestments, picked them up, and once more his courage led to a blessed and fortunate result, for he returned to his companions … Meanwhile, they had been won over by this great miracle, and had cast anchor keeping the ship in one place. They took him back aboard …

[10] ADAMNAN'S ACCOUNT OF ARCULF'S JOURNEY *ante* 700
From Adamnan's *De Locis Sanctis* Denis Meehan (ed.). Meehan suggested that the account was written before Adamnan's visit to King Aldfrith of Northumberland in 686.

Bk. III, 5, p. 119. The matter given above concerning the site and foundation of Constantinople and concerning the round church too in which the salutary wood is stored, and the rest, we diligently learned from the lips of the holy priest Arculf, who stayed in the principal city of the Roman empire from Easter until the Lord's nativity, and subsequently took ship from there for Rome.

Bk III, 6, p. 121. Towards the east from Sicily, at twelve miles distance, there is an island in the great sea, in which day and night Vulcan gives forth a sort of thunder, with such vehemence that one would think the land of Sicily (which is situated a considerable distance away) was being shaken by a terrific earthquake (*terrifico tremore submoveri putetur*). But it seems to thunder more on Friday and Saturday. One notices that at night it is blazing, whereas during the day it smokes. Arculf dictated these things to me about the mountain while I wrote. He beheld it with the sight of his own eyes, fiery by night and smoky by day, and with the hearing of his own ears he heard its thunderous noise when he lodged for some days in Sicily.

[11] BEDE'S ACCOUNT OF ARCULF'S TRAVELS
Bede's *Ecclesiastical History of the English People,* trans. L Sherley-Price.
Bede was less interested in natural features outside Palestine.
Bk V.15, p.294. ... Arculf had travelled to Damascus, Constantinople, Alexandria and many islands; but as he was returning home, his ship was driven by a violent storm onto the western coast of Britain. After many adventures, he visited Christ's servant, Adamnan.
Bede then transcribed much of Adamnan's account of Palestine in Bk. V.16, p295.

[12] EXTRACTS FROM EDDIUS' LIFE OF ST WILFRID
Text and translation by B. Colgrave.
Wilfrid was a great traveller not only to Rome and I make no apology for including so many extracts referring to his journeys. His circumstances, coming at the beginning of English foreign travel, may usefully be compared with those of later travellers.

[12.1] Chapter iii, p. 9. ?652. After the lapse of a few years it came into the heart of this same young man, by the promptings of the Holy Spirit, to pay a visit to the see of theApostle Peter, the chief of the Apostles, and to attempt a road hitherto untrodden by any of our race. [*After waiting a year for a companion, the king of Kent*] found him a guide, a man of high rank and of remarkable understanding named Biscop Baducing, who was bound for the Apostolic See, and prevailed upon him to take the youth in his company… Glad of heart and rejoicing in his journey, he came at last to Lyons, a city of Gaul; there he remained with his companions for a certain time, his stern guide having left him …

[12.2] Chapter iv, p. 11. 653. so, when the bishop had provided him with what he required, he sent him forth to theApostolic See according to his wish,in the peace of Christ, with guides and supplies for the journey.

After a stay in Rome, Wilfrid eventually returned to Lyons where he stayed for three years. He became involved in local politics and was nearly killed. He was finally expelled by Ebroin.

[12.3] Chapter vii, p. 15. ?658. At that time, St. Wilfrid the confessor, after his father the bishop had been buried with due honour, embarked on a vessel with many blessings and with the aid of the holy relics, and when the wind blew as the sailors wished, they made a prosperous voyage towards their own land, to a harbour of safety.

[12.4] Chapter xiii, p. 27. 666. When they were crossing the British sea on their return from Gaul with Bishop Wilfrid of blessed memory, and the priests were praising God with psalms and hymns, giving the time to the oarsmen, a violent storm arose in mid ocean and the winds were contrary … The wind blew hard from the south-east and the foam crested waves hurled them onto the land of the South Saxons which they did not know. Then the sea left ship and men high and dry, fled from the land, and laying the shores bare, withdrew into the depth of the abyss. [*The Saxons then attacked and refused Wilfrid's offer of a ransom. After much fighting*] the great bishop prayed to the Lord his God, who straightway bade the tide return before its usual hour and while the pagans, on the coming of their king, were preparing with all their strength for a fourth battle, the sea came flowing back and covered all the shore, so that the ship was floated and made its way into the deep. They returned thanks to God for the glorious way He had honoured them, and with a south-west wind they prosperously reached a port of safety at Sandwich.

[12.5] Chapter xxv, p. 51. 678. But the enemies of our prelate, mindful of their misdeeds, believed that he would be sailing south to Etaples and making his way by the most direct route (*via rectissima*) to the Holy See, and so they sent ahead their messengers with bribes to Theodoric, King of the Franks, and to Ebroin, a wicked Duke, to persuade them to condemn him to the greater exile, or to slay his comrades and rob him of all his substance. But the Lord freed him from the hands of his enemies, as though from the hands of Herod. For at that time the holy Winfrid, the bishop, who had been driven out of Lichfield, was making his way by the same route and fell into the hands of these same enemies, as though into the jaws of a lion. He was immediately captured and robbed of all his money. Many of his companions were slain and the holy bishop was left naked and in the utmost straits of misery. They thought that he was the holy Bishop Wilfrid, which was not the case, being misled by a fortunate mistake in one syllable.

[12.6] Chapter xxvi, p. 53. 678. On the contrary, however, our holy bishop, with a west wind blowing gently according to his wish, and with the vessels heading eastward, came after a prosperous voyage to Friesland with all his companions.

[12.7] Chapter xviii p. 55. 679. After our bishop the beloved of God had spent the winter among the Frisians winning much people for the Lord, when spring came, he continued the journey he had undertaken with his companions to the Apostolic See. He came to the king of the Franks called Dagobert who received him with great kindness and with all honour for the service which Wilfrid had once rendered him … But when Wilfrid refused [*the See of Strasburg*] he sent him to the Apostolic See with gifts and rich presents making his bishop, Deodatus, the guide.
As the bishops proceeded on their journey under the guidance of God, they came to Perctarit, King of Campania, a humble and peaceful man who feared the word of God. He received the pilgrims kindly … Then in truth the king with thanksgiving sent our holy bishop and his companions to the Apostolic See which they had so long desired to behold, giving him honourable treatment and providing him with guides …

[12.8] Chapter xxix, p. 57. 679. When, therefore Bishop Wilfrid, beloved of God, reached the before mentioned see in safety with all his companions, the cause of his coming had preceded him and had become known there, for at that time Coenwald, a religious monk, had been sent by the holy Archbishop Theodore with letters from him and had reached Rome …

[12.9] Chapter xxxiii, p. 67. 680. [*After the Papal decision*] our holy bishop … spent several days going round the shrines of the saints to pray there; he also obtained from chosen men (*ab electis viris*) a great many holy relics, for the edification of the churches of Britain, writing down what each relic was and to which saint it belonged; and many other possessions he acquired which it is tedious to enumerate now, for the adornment of the house of God, in accordance with his custom. So … he began his journey homewards to his own land with all his train …

So when our holy bishop, triumphantly bearing the decision, had made his way from the Apostolic See through Campania and had crossed the mountains, he came into the land of the Franks [*he ran into a plot to capture him and 'reserve him for the judgement of Ebroin the Duke' but he negotiated his passage*].

[12.10] Chapter xxxiv, p.71. 680. Then, having traversed many lands, and with the help of God having passed over a great tract of sea by ship, he reached his own land unharmed, together with all his companions …

[12.11] Chapter xlvii, p. 95. ?703. [*At the Council of Austerfield, Wilfrid was warned of a trap being laid for him, for*] one of the king's thegns who was greatly devoted to our bishop … stole out of the king's tent; he disguised his appearance … until at last he reached our bishop.

[12.12] Chapter l, p. 103. ?703. [*On his next journey*] the preparations were made and the party embarked with our holy bishop, and, borne oversea by their ship, reached the southern shores, God going before them. Then, making their way together on foot overland, by the help of the holy Apostles, after a long journey, they arrived safely at the Apostolic See. [*On arrival*] they rested several days in a dwelling which had been prepared for them freely (*mansione voluntaria praeparata manserunt*).

[12.13] Chapter lv, p. 121. 704. [*Once more, after the Papal decision*] our holy bishop, in all obedience, visited with his friends the shrines of the saints, and according to his habit, collected from elect men, holy relics authenticated by the names of saints, buying also vestments of purple and silk to ornament the churches. With the blessing of the saints he made his way homewards, over hill and dale, by smooth paths and rough, until after a long journey, he reached the kingdom of Gaul.

[12.14] Chapter lvi, p. 121. 705. Then, as they were journeying, our holy bishop was seized with a very great infirmity of body. At first he was borne on horseback, but at last he was carried on a litter by his friends … until he was brought, scarcely alive, to the town of Meaux … [*he recovered*] and a few days afterwards, when he was healed of this same infirmity, they set out and came to the sea: they crossed its full extent by ship, and by the help of God, they found a safe harbour in the land of Kent.

[13] BEDE COMMENTING UPON THE NUMBER OF PILGRIMS. *c.* 725

Bede's *Ecclesiastical History of the English People*
V. 7. p. 276. Bede commented upon the number of Anglo-Saxon pilgrims: At this time many English people vied with one another in following this custom, both noble and simple, layfolk and clergy, man and women alike.
See also: De Temp. Rat. (Migne, P.L.90,1c, col. 571) apropos Ceolfrid 'At this time (716) many people of English race, nobles and other people, men and women, leaders (*duces*) and ordinary people (*privati*) were accustomed to go to Rome from Divine love, among them my most reverend abbot, Ceolfrid'.

[14] EXTRACTS FROM LAWS RELATING TO TRAVELLERS AND TRADERS
These extracts are grouped together irrespective of date to demonstrate the growing awareness of the presence of foreigners, the need to accommodate them within the social order, and the increasing complexity of the regulations relating to them.

Extracts 14.1 to 14.5 are taken from F. L. Attenborough, *The Laws of the Earliest English Kings* (Cambridge 1922). Reproduced by courtesy of Cambridge University Press.

[14.1] LAWS OF HLOTHERE AND EADRIC, KINGS OF KENT (673-685?)
Clause 15. If a man entertains a stranger (a trader or anyone else who has come over the border) for three days in his own home, and then supplies him with food from his own store, and [if] he [the stranger] then does harm to anyone, the man shall bring the other to justice, or make amends on his behalf.

[14.2] LAWS OF INE (688-694)
Clause 20. If a man from afar, or a stranger, travels through a wood off the highway and neither shouts nor blows a horn, he shall be assumed to be a thief, and as such may be either slain or put to ransom.
Clause 25. If a trader [makes his way into] the interior of the country and [proceeds to] traffic, he shall do so before witnesses.
Clause 33. The wergild of a Welsh horseman, who is in the king's service and can ride on his errands shall be 200 shillings.

[14.3] LAWS OF WIHTRED, KING OF KENT (695)
Clause 26. If anyone catches a freeman in the act of stealing, the king shall decide which of the following three courses shall be adopted – whether he shall be put to death, or sold beyond the sea, or held to ransom for his wergild. (*My underlining*)
Clause 28. If a man from afar, or a stranger, quits the road, and neither shouts, nor blows a horn, he shall be assumed to be a thief [and as such] may be either slain or put to ransom.

[14.4] LAWS OF ALFRED (*c.* 885-99)
Clause 34. Further, with regard to traders, it is decreed: they shall bring before the king's reeve, at a public meeting, the men they are taking with them into the country, and declare how many of them there are; and they shall take with them

[only] such men as they can bring to justice again, at a public meeting. And when they need to have more men with them on their journey, a similar declaration shall always be made to the king's reeve before the assembled company, as often as need arises.

[14.5] THE TREATY BETWEEN ALFRED AND GUTHRUM (886-890)

Clause 5. And we all declared, on the day when the oaths were sworn, that neither slaves nor freemen shall be allowed to pass over to the Danish host without permission, any more than that any of them [should come over] to us. If, however, it happens that any of them, in order to satisfy their wants, wish to trade with us, or we [for the same reason wish to trade] with them, in cattle and in goods, it shall be allowed on condition that hostages are given as security for peaceful behaviour, and as evidence by which it may be known that no treachery is intended.

Extracts 14.6 to 14.8 are taken from A.J. Robertson, *The Laws of the Kings of England from Edmund to Henry I* (Cambridge 1925). Courtesy of Cambridge University Press.

[14.6] EDGAR'S CODE AT ANDOVER (959x963)

Clause 4. And every hearth-penny shall be paid by St. Peter's day.
4.1 And he who has failed to make payment by the appointed time shall take it to Rome and 30 pence in addition thereto, and shall bring back evidence that he has there handed over that amount; and when he comes home, he shall pay 120 shillings to the king.
4.2 And if he again refuses to give it, he shall take it again to Rome, and hand over the same sum as compensation, and when he comes home, he shall pay 120 shillings to the king.
4.3 And on the third occasion, if he still refuses, he shall suffer the loss of all that he possesses.

[14.7] KING ETHELRED'S TREATY WITH THE VIKING ARMY (991 or 994)

Clause 2. And every merchant ship which enters an estuary, even if it belong to a region not included in the truce, shall be afforded protection, provided it is not pursued.
2.1 And even if it is pursued, and reach any town included in the truce, and the men escape into the town, protection is to be afforded to them, and to what they bring with them.
Clause 3. But all of those who are specially included in the truce are to enjoy the protection of the truce, whether on land or on water, whether within an estuary or not.
3.1 If a subject of King Ethelred's who is included in the truce comes to a region to which it does not apply, and the aforesaid fleet arrives there, protection shall be afforded to his ship and to all his goods.
3.2 If he has drawn his ship ashore or built a hut, or pitched a tent, protection shall be afforded to himself and to all his goods.
3.3 If he brings his goods into a house among the goods of men who are not included in the truce, he is to lose his goods, but he shall have peace and his life, if he announces himself.

[14.8] LAWS OF CNUT (1020-23)

Clause 35. If a friendless man or one from afar is so utterly destitute of friends as not to be able to produce a surety, on the first occasion that he is accused he shall go to prison, and wait there until he comes to God's ordeal where he shall experience whatever he can.
Clause 39. If anyone slays a minister of the altar, he shall be both excommunicated and outlawed, unless he make amends to the best of his ability by pilgrimage and likewise by [paying compensation].

[14.9] A REGULATION ON STATUS (1002-1023)

From *EHD*, no. 51.
Paragraph 6. And if a trader prospered, that he crossed thrice the open sea at his own expense, then he was afterwards entitled to the rights of a thegn.

[14.10] LAW OF THE NORTHUMBRIAN PRIESTS (1020-23?)

EHD, no. 52.
Clause 55. Sunday market we forbid everywhere, and every public assembly and all work and all carrying [*of goods*], whether by wagon or by horse or on one's back.
Clause 56. He who does any of these things is to pay the penalty: a freeman 12 ores, a slave with a flogging, except for travellers, who are permitted to carry sustenance for their needs …

Clause 25. If a trader buys among the people in the countryside, he is to do it before witnesses.
If a foreigner is slain, the king has two-thirds of the wergild, his son or kinsman the third part.
Clause. 33. The king's Welsh horseman, who can carry his messages, his wergild is 200 shillings.

[14.11] THE ORDINANCE CONCERNING THE DUNSAETE (Eleventh-Twelfth century)
Corpus Christi 383, Ker, No 65, from D. Hill and M. Worthington, *Offa's Dyke (2003)*, Appendix 2. Reproduced by permission of Dr D. Hill. *This previously unpublished text reveals a network of arrangements for managing frontier relations, of which the following is only a selection.*
2.2. A pledge can be seized from the other bank if justice cannot be obtained in any óther way.
3. If a pledge from one man's cattle is seized on another man's account, let the one on whose account it was taken get the pledge back, or let him satisfy from his own possessions the man whose cattle have been taken.
6. Neither is a Welshman to cross over into English Land, nor an Englishman to Welsh, without the appointed man from that land, who shall meet him at the bank and bring him back there again without any offence.

[15] CADWALLA
There are several versions of his journey.
[15.1] *Anglo Saxon Chronicle. sa 688.* And the same year Cadwalla went to Rome and received baptism from the Pope, and the pope called him Peter, and seven days later he passed away.

[15.2] *Bede's Ecclesiastical History, Bk. V.7, p. 275.*
In the third year of King Alfrid's reign, Cadwalla, King of the West Saxons, who had governed his people most ably for two years, abdicated from his throne for the sake of our Lord and his eternal kingdom, and travelled to Rome. For having learnt that the road to Heaven lies open to mankind only through baptism, he wished to obtain the particular privilege of receiving the cleansing of baptism at the shrine of the blessed Apostles. At the same time, he hoped to die shortly after his baptism, and pass from this world to everlasting happiness. By God's grace, both of these hopes were realised. Arriving in Rome during the pontificate of Sergius, he was baptised on Holy Saturday before Easter in the year of our Lord 689, and he fell ill and while still wearing his white robes departed this life on the twentieth of April and joined the company of the blessed in heaven.

[15.3] *Vita S Vulmari*, AA SS Boll V July
Cadwalla, king of the West Saxons, travelling to Rome, his good works, sanctity and the fame of his great generosity being well known to the royal leaders of the man of God, he arrived and gave thirty *solidi* to decorate the basilica.

[15.4] *Paul the Deacon, Histora Langobardum*, trans. W. D. Foulke (1907), VI. 15, p. 169. *(This was written no later than AD 900).*
Cadwalla, king of the English Saxons, who governed many (*people*) in his beautiful country, hastened to Rome, having been converted to Christ. The king, entering by the Cuninc gate (*Cunincpertem*), was magnificently received by the (*citizens*).

[16] ALDHELM'S JOURNEY TO ROME (*c.* 701)
N. E. S. A. Hamilton*: William of Malmesbury: Gesta Pontificum Anglorum*, (1870), Bk V, Ch. 217.
[16.1] So [Aldhelm] announced his intention to King Ine of the West Saxons, and King Aethelred of the Mercians, whose friendship he enjoyed and through whose generosity he had progressed. Since they had no objection he set out on the road to Rome. But to make it easier to get everything together that he needed for the journey, he went to the estates which he controlled in the county of Dorset. And while he was waiting for the right wind, he built a church there …

[16.2] Bk V, ch. 218. [*For Aldhem's lodging*] There is at Rome a building suitable for gatherings called the Lateran, provided as a palace for the Pontiffs by the Emperor Constantine from a palace of his own. Aldhelm stayed there with the Pope, and had many friendly talks with him.

[16.3] Bk V, ch. 222.
On his return journey Aldhelm brought back a white marble altar. It is said that a camel, (surely no animal of our country could carry such a burden?) carried it safely all the way to the Alps. But there the camel (and it does not matter exactly what animal it was, that carried it) collapsed, injured by the excessive weight or defeated by the steep slopes of the track. The fall crushed the animal and broke the marble into two parts. [*Aldhelm miraculously healed the camel and sealed the crack, which can still be seen*]. … And so with his whole baggage-train intact Aldhelm came to the sea which separates France and England.

[16.4] Bk V, ch. 224.
The saint was walking along the harbour front, and examining the merchandise to see if the sailors had brought anything suitable for church use. In fact, on their voyage to England from France, they had brought a pile of books with them.

Aldhelm spotted a complete Old and New Testament bound together in one volume. He ignored the rest and concentrated on buying this volume, but while he was turning the pages with an expert eye and trying to get the price reduced, the foreign crew laughed at him, making fun as sailors do. Why was he thus rubbishing other peoples' goods and cheapening articles which were not his own? He could run down his own wares if he liked, but he should leave goods which did not belong to him as they were. In reply to their jeers Aldhelm simply smiled. Finally, as he kept arguing about the price of the book, they rudely pushed him away, and with tightened moorings moved further away from the shore.

But it was not long before the wrath of the Lord sharply rewarded the insult done to the saint [*a storm forced the sailors to ask the saint's help and he got his book as a free gift*].

[17] EXTRACTS FROM BEDE'S ECCLESIASTICAL HISTORY
[17.1] The port of London in Bede's time
Bk. II., ch. 3, pp. 107-8. [*The province of the East Saxons*]. Its capital is the city of London, which stands on the banks of the Thames, and is a trading centre for many nations who visit it by land and sea.

[17.2] Mellitus' journey to Rome (610)
Bk. II, ch. 4, p. 110.
At this time Mellitus, Bishop of London, visited Rome to acquaint the Pope with the affairs of the church of the English … Mellitus sat with [bishops from Italy] at this council, which took place on the twenty-seventh of February 610 in the eighth year of the Emperor Phocas. … He also brought back letters from the Pope both to God's beloved Archbishop Laurence and all his clergy, and to King Ethelbert and his people.

[17.3] Bk II, ch. 8, p. 117. Pope Boniface's letter to Justus. 624. Moved by your devotion, my brother, we are sending
you by the bearer of this letter, the *pallium* …

[17.4] Letters to King Edwin and Queen Ethelburga *c.* 625
Bk. II, chs. 10 and 11, pp. 120, 123, 125.
About this time, the king received a letter from Boniface, Bishop of the apostolic Roman see. The Pope also wrote to Queen Ethelberga as follows: 'We have been informed by those who came to report the laudable conversion of our glorious son King Eadbald, that your Majesty … shows a shining example of good works, pleasing to God. … Having mentioned this matter … We beg you to inform us, as soon as a suitable messenger is available, what measure of success …

[17.5]. Bk. II, ch. 16, p. 134. *Refreshments AD 628*. Such was the king's concern for the welfare of his people that in a
number of places where he had noticed clear springs adjacent to the highway he ordered posts to be erected with brass bowls hanging from them, so that travellers could drink and refresh themselves. And so great was the people's affection for him, and so great was the awe in which he was held, that no one wished or ventured to use these bowls for any other purpose.

[17.6] Bk. II, ch. 17, p. 136. *The pope writing to King Edwin, AD 634*. We are glad to accede to your requests on behalf of
your bishops without delay, and in doing so we pay tribute to the sincerity of your own faith, which has often been most highly praised by the bearers of this letter. Accordingly, we have sent two *pallia*, one to each of the Metropolitans …
(The wording makes it clear that the messengers had previously come from England and so were probably English.)

[17.7] Bk. II, ch. 20, p. 141. *Death of Romanus 624/7*
At this time, the church of Rochester was in great need of a pastor, since Romanus its bishop, who had been sent by Archbishop Justus to Pope Honorius as his representative, had been drowned at sea off Italy.

[17.8] Bk. III. Ch. 15, pp. 167-68. 642-651. A priest named Utta … was sent to Kent to bring back Eanfled as a wife for
King Oswy … Intending to make the outward journey by land and to return with the princess by sea, he went to Bishop Aidan and asked him to pray for him and his companions … When Aidan had blessed them and commended them to God, he gave them some holy oil, saying: 'when you set sail you will encounter a storm and contrary winds. Remember then to pour the oil that I am giving you on the sea, and the wind will immediately drop, giving you a pleasant, calm voyage and a safe return home. Everything happened as the bishop foretold. In a rising gale, the sailors dropped anchor, hoping to ride out the storm. This proved impossible; for the roaring seas broke into the ship from every side, and it began to fill. Everyone felt that his last hour had come, when at last the priest remembered the bishop's words. He took out the flask of oil, and poured some of it over the sea, which immediately ceased its raging as Aidan had foretold.

[17.9] Bk. IV. Ch. 1, p. 203-4. *The arrival of Archbishop Theodore and Abbot Hadrian*
The Pope made it a condition that Hadrian himself should accompany him to Britain, since he had already travelled

through Gaul twice on various missions, and had both a better knowledge of the road and sufficient men of his own available. *Archbishop Theodore was then consecrated bishop on the 26th of March 668, and on the 27th of May he set out for Britain.* The travellers crossed by sea to Marseilles, and thence overland to Arles, where they delivered Pope Vitalian's letters of commendation to John, Archbishop of that city, who gave them hospitality until Ebroin, Mayor of the king's palace, gave them a permit to travel wherever they wished. Armed with this Theodore then went on to Agilbert, Bishop of Paris, of whom I have already spoken, who welcomed him kindly and entertained him for a considerable time. Hadrian meanwhile went first to Emme, Bishop of Sens, and then to Faro, Bishop of Meaux, and made lengthy stays with them, since the approach of winter obliged travellers to remain quietly wherever they could. When messengers informed King Egbert that the bishop whom they had requested from the Pope was now in the kingdom of the Franks, he at once sent his High Reeve Raedfrid to escort him; and when the Reeve arrived, he obtained Ebroin's permission to escort Theodore to the port of Quentovic. Here exhaustion compelled Theodore to rest for a while; but as soon as he began to recover, he took ship for Britain. But Hadrian was detained by Ebroin, who suspected that he bore some message from the Emperor to the kings of Britain, which might be to the disadvantage of the kingdom for whose interests he was largely responsible. But when he ascertained that Hadrian had in fact no such mission, he released him and allowed him to follow Theodore.

[17.10] IV. 18. p. 234-35. Bede did not mention John's departure in *The Lives of the Abbots,* below.
Among those who signed the affirmation of the Catholic Faith at this Synod was the venerable John, Arch-cantor of the church of the holy Apostle Peter and Abbot of the monastery of Saint Martin, who had recently come from Rome under instructions from Pope Agatho with the most reverend Abbot Benedict, of whom I have spoken. ... Benedict received Abbot John and conducted him to Britain, where he was to teach his monks the chant for the liturgical year as it was sung at Saint Peter's, Rome. ... After the above-mentioned synod had been summoned for the purpose in Britain, the Catholic Faith was shown to be held untainted by all, and a copy of its decisions was given to John to take back to Rome.
Not long after crossing the sea, on his return journey to his own country, John fell sick and died; and out of devotion to St Martin, of whose monastery he was Abbot, his friends carried his body to Tours, where he was buried with great honour. For on his journey to Britain he had been courteously welcomed there by the brethren who begged him to visit them again on his return to Rome.

[18] BISCOP'S TRAVELS, FROM BEDE'S LIVES OF THE ABBOTS
From D.H. Farmer (ed.), *The Age of Bede*
[18.1] Ch. 2, p. 186. [*Benedict*] therefore left his own country and went to Rome, where, in fulfilment of his long and ardent desire, he made sure he visited the tombs of the apostles and venerated their remains.

[18.2] Ch. 3, p. 187. [*Benedict wished to go to Rome again*]. Not long after a merchant vessel arrived and so he was able to have his wish. At this time, Egbert, king of Kent, has sent a man named Wighard from Britain as bishop-elect to be consecrated in Rome. ... Wighard arrived in Rome but before he could be consecrated he and all his companions fell victims to the plague. [*The Pope therefore appointed Theodore and designated Benedict to serve him*] as guide on the journey home and interpreter when teaching. Benedict did as he was bidden. They returned to Kent where they were very favourably received.

[18.3] Ch. 4, p. 188.
After two years in charge of the monastery he left Britain for Rome, this being the third time, and completed the journey as successfully as before. He brought back a large number of books on all branches of sacred knowledge, some bought at a very favourable price, others the gifs of well-wishers. At Vienne on the journey home he picked up the books he had left there in the care of his friends.

[18.4] Ch. 6, p. 190.
[*Benedict*] was untiring in his efforts to see his monastery well provided for: the ornaments and images he could not find in France he sought in Rome. Once his foundation had settled down to the ordered life of the Rule, he went off on a fourth visit to Rome [679-80], returning with a greater variety of spiritual treasures than ever before. In the first place he returned with a great mass of books of every sort. Secondly, he brought back an abundant supply of relics of the blessed apostles and Christian martyrs which were to prove such a boon for many churches in the land. Thirdly, he introduced in his monastery the order of chanting and singing the psalms and conducting the liturgy according to the practice in force at Rome. To this end, Pope Agatho, at Benedict's request, offered him the services of the chief cantor of St. Peter's and abbot of the monastery of St. Martin, a man called John. [*The text of the fourth benefit, the privilege, is omitted.*] Fifthly, he brought back many holy pictures of the saints to adorn the church of St. Peter he had built ...

[18.5] Ch. 9, p. 194.

Shortly after Benedict had appointed Eosterwine to be abbot of St. Peter's and Ceolfrid of St. Paul's he set off on his fifth journey from Britain to Rome and returned, as always, with a rich store of countless valuable gifts for his churches: a large supply of sacred books and no less a stock of sacred pictures than on previous journeys.

Bede's account of Ceolfrith's last journey is given below, with other accounts.

[19] A MEETING WITH ANGLO-SAXON MERCHANTS, from the Miracula St Bertin

Lib. Miraculorum; Holder-Egger: Mon Bertiniana Minora MG SS XV. I p. 511.

Ante 698. As (St Bertin) was travelling to Rome with a stout heart and having been given permission, he met some English men heading for Rome. And he travelled with them until the city of Langres (Lingonum) where they joined some merchants from Verdun (*Viridunensis negotiatores*), and stayed with them until they took the fork in the road which led to Spain.

Extracts 20, 21, 22 (part), 23 to 27 are from C.H. Talbot, *The Anglo-Saxon Missionaries in Germany* **(1954).**

[20] EXTRACTS FROM THE LIFE OF ST BONIFACE BY WILLIBALD

[20.1] 716 Ch. IV, p. 35 [*Before setting off for Frisia*] So great was the affection of the abbot and brethren, with whom he had lived under the monastic rule, that they willingly provided the money for his needs and continued long afterwards to continue to pray to God on his behalf ... he came to a place where there was a market for the buying and selling of merchandise. This place is called Lundenwich by the Anglo-Saxons even to this day. After a few days, when the sailors were about to embark on their return home, Boniface asked permission of the shipmaster to go on board, and after paying his fare he set sail and came with favourable winds to (*Dorestadt*) ...

[20.2] 718 Ch. V, p. 37-39 *[The journey to Rome]* Now when the winter season was over and the summer was well advanced, he called to mind his intention of the previous year and carefully set about preparing the journey which had been deferred. Provided with letters of introduction from Bishop Daniel, of blessed memory, he tried to set out on his way to the tombs of the Apostles. But for a long time he was detained by the needs of the brethren ... but on the other hand he was anxious not to miss the opportunity of going abroad in the summer season ... Bidding farewell to the brethren, he departed, and after travelling a considerable distance he came at length, in fulfilment of his desire, to the town which is called Lundenwich. He embarked immediately on a small swift ship and began to cross the pathless expanse of the sea. The sailors were in good spirits, the huge sails bellied n the north-west wind, and, helped along by a stiff following breeze, they soon came after an uneventful crossing in sight of the mouth of the river called Cuent. Here, safe from shipwreck, they set foot on dry soil. At Cuentwick [*Quentovic*] they pitched their camp and waited until the remainder of the party came together. When they had all met, they set out straightaway on their journey, for with the passing of the days the threat of winter hung over them. Many a church they visited on their way to pray that by the help of Almighty God they might cross in safety the snowy peaks of the Alps, find greater kindness at the hands of the Lombards and escape with impunity from the savage ferocity of the undisciplined soldiery. [*Having reached Rome*] they went with deep joy to the Church of St. Peter, chief of the Apostles, and many of them offered up gifts, begging absolution of their sins. [*Having gained an audience*] ... the saintly Pope, suddenly turning his gaze upon him, enquired with cheerful countenance and smiling eyes whether he had brought with him any letter of introduction from his bishop. Boniface, coming to himself, drew back his cloak and produced a note, which, conformably to usage, was sealed and folded, and with it the letter of recommendation from his bishop. These he handed over to the Pope ... When the pope had read the letter and examined the note of introduction he discussed the saint's project with him every day until the summer season, in which he was to set out on the return journey, was near. When the end of April had passed and it was already the beginning of May the saint begged and received the apostolic blessing and was sent by the Pope to make a report on the savage peoples of Germany. And so, collecting a number of relics of the saints, [*Boniface*] retraced his steps in the company of his fellows and reached the frontiers of Italy where he met Liudprand, King of the Lombards, to whom he gave gifts and tokens of peace. He was honourably received by the king and rested awhile after the weary labours of the journey. After receiving many presents in return, he crossed the hills and plains and scaled the steep mountain passes of the Alps.

Ch. VI, p. 43 [*On Boniface's recall to Rome*] After he had rested his weary limbs for a brief space of time a message was sent to Blessed Gregory, Bishop of the Apostolic See, saying that a servant of God had arrived; he was then welcomed with great kindness and conducted to the pilgrim's lodge.

[20.3] 731. p. 47. On the death of Gregory the Second ... Once more the saint's messengers journeyed to Rome and spoke with the Bishop of the Apostolic See, presenting to him the pledge of friendship which his predecessor had previously bestowed upon St. Boniface and his people.

p.48. When [Boniface] had spent the better part of a year in these parts, visiting and praying at the shrines of the saints, he took his leave of the venerable Bishop of the Apostolic See and returned home, carrying with him many gifts and sacred relics of the saints.

[20.4] 753 Ch. VIII, pp. 54 -59. [*Boniface's martyrdom*] After a lapse of a few days, he still persevered in his decision to set out on the journey, and so, taking with him a few companions, he went on board a ship and sailed down the Rhine. Eventually he reached the marshy country of Frisia, crossed safely over the stretch of water, which in their tongue is called Aelmere, and made a survey of the lands round about which up till then had borne no fruit. After bravely hazarding the perils of the river, the sea and the wide expanse of the ocean, he passed through dangerous places without fear of danger and visited the heathen Frisians, whose land is divided into many territories and districts by intersecting canals.

A vast number of foes rushed into the camp brandishing their weapons. In the twinkling of an eye the attendants sprang from the camp to meet them and snatched up arms here and there to defend the holy body of martyrs … But the man of God, hearing the shouts and the onrush of the rabble, straightaway called the clergy to his side, and, collecting together the relics of the saints, which he always carried with him, came out of his tent. At once he reproved the attendants and forbade them to continue the conflict, saying 'Sons, cease fighting …' When they had sated their lust for blood on the mortal remains of the just, the heathenish mob seized with exultation upon the spoils of heir victory (in reality the cause of their damnation) and, after laying waste the camp, carried off and shared the booty; they stole the chests in which the books and relics were preserved and, thinking they had acquired a hoard of gold and silver, carried them off, still locked, to the ships. Now the ships were stocked with provisions for the feeding of the clerics and attendants and a great deal of wine still remained. Finding this goodly liquor, the heathens immediately began to slake their sottish appetites and to get drunk. … They broke open the chests containing the books and found, to their dismay, that they held manuscripts instead of gold vessels, pages of sacred texts instead of silver plate. Disappointed in their hope of gold and silver, they littered the fields with the books they found …

The bodies of the holy bishop and of the other martyrs were brought by boat across the water called Aelmere, an uneventful voyage of some days, to the city of Utrecht … From there [*some men from Mainz*] had been sent in a ship by Bishop Lull, the successor of our holy bishop and martyr, to bring the body of the saint to the monastery built by him during his lifetime on the banks of the river Fulda.

[21] BONIFACE'S BODY IN PERIL from the Life of St. Sturm

p. 201. We, his disciples, took the body of the martyr from its tomb in which it had lain for twenty four years and began to leave the monastery with all the servants of God. On the first night we rested at the next cell, where the waters of the Fulda and the Fleden meet. Then early next day we reached Sinner on the far side and there we pitched tent in which we placed the sacred body of the martyr of Christ, whilst the monks encamped around it. After spending three days in tents, messengers came to us on the fourth day … [*to say that it was safe to return*]

[22] LETTERS OF BONIFACE,

From Talbot, *Anglo-Saxon Missionaries*, and *The Letters of Boniface*, edited and translated by E. Emerton.
[22.1] Emerson no. IV, p. 32, *General letter of introduction from Bishop Daniel of Winchester for Wynfred, a priest.*
To all pious and merciful kings and princes, reverend and beloved bishops, holy abbots, priests and spiritual children sealed with the name of Christ, Daniel, servant of the servants of God, greeting.

While all commands of God are to be obeyed with sincere devotion, the witness of Holy Scripture proves how acceptable to Him is the hospitality shown to travellers. The blessed Abraham, on account of his kindly hospitality, was deemed worthy to receive holy angels in person and to enjoy their conversation. Lot also because of the same kindly service was snatched from the flames of Sodom. The grace of hospitality saved him from destruction by fire, because he obeyed the divine commands.

So may it profit your eternal welfare if you will extend to the bearer of these presents Winfred, a holy priest and servant of Almighty God, an affectionate welcome, such as God loves and prescribes. In receiving servants of God you receive Him whose majesty they also serve and Who promises: 'He that receiveth you receiveth me.' Doing this with heartfelt devotion, you will both fulfill the divine command and, trusting in the oracle of God, receive an everlasting reward in His presence.

May Supreme Grace keep Your Eminence safe from harm!

[22.2] Emerton no. VII, p. 40. *Abbess Bugga to Boniface, 720.*
Know also that the *Sufferings of the Martyrs* which you asked me to send you I have not yet been able to get, but as soon as I can I shall send it. And you, my best beloved, comfort my insignificance by sending me, as you promised in your dear letter, some collections of the sacred writings.

I am sending you by this same messenger fifty *solidi* and an altar cloth, the best I can possibly do. Little as it is, it is sent with great affection.

[22.3] Talbot, p. 80. *Pope Gregory II to Boniface, 22 November 726*
Gregory, the servant of the servants of God, to Boniface, our most holy brother and colleague in the episcopate. Your devout messenger Denual has brought us the welcome news that you are well and that, by the help of God, you are making progress in the work for which you were sent. He also delivered to us letters from you reporting that the field of the Lord which had long lain fallow … has now been ploughed up and sown with the truth of the Gospel …

[22.4] Emerton, no. XIX, p. 56. *To the Abbess Bugga, ante 738.*
She [Wiethburga] has written me that she has found at the shrine of St. Peter the kind of quiet life which she has long sought in vain. With regard to your wishes, she sent me word, since I had written to her about you, that you would do better to wait until the rebellious assaults and threats of the Saracens who have recently appeared about Rome should have subsided. God willing she will then send you an invitation.

[22.5] Emerton, XXV, p .63. *To his former pupil Abbot Duddo, possibly in Rome, 735.*
In accord with what my son, the priest Eoban, who brings my letters, may say to you about the marriage of a woman to the godfather of her children …

[22.6] Emerton, XXVI, p. 65.*To the Abbess Eadburga*
I am sending by the priest Eoban the materials for your writing …

[22.7] Emerton, XXXIX, p. 78. *To Abbess Cuniburg, 734-41.*
We beg also that you will send on by the bearer of this letter, two young freedmen, named Begiloc and Man … And if anyone shall unlawfully try to prevent their journey we beg you to protect them. … Some little gifts accompany this letter: frankincense, pepper, and cinnamon – a very small present but given out of heartfelt affection.

[22.8] Talbot, pp. 98 and 102. *Boniface to Pope Zacharias.*
We confess, Father and Lord, that after we had learned through messengers that your predecessor Gregory, of holy memory, had departed tbis life, nothing gave us greater comfort and happiness than the knowledge that God had appointed your Holiness …
Finally, we are sending you some small gifts, a warm rug and a little silver and gold. Though they are too trifling to be offered to your holiness, they come as a token of our affection and our devoted obedience.

[22.9] Emerton, XLVII, p. 98. *An account of the Acts of the Roman Synod, 25 October 745.*
Then Denehard, the pious priest, answered … Wherefore I am sent to present to your Apostolic Holiness this letter of my master which I hold in my hand, that you may cause it to be read before this sacred council.

[22.10] Emerton, L, p. 114. *The Roman Cardinal-Deacon Gemmulus, to Boniface, 745.*
I have received your revered and God-pleasing letter and read it with all due respect and great veneration … We have received also the gift which you sent us – a silver cup and a piece of cloth, a gift doubly precious to us as coming from so honoured a father. Though we cannot repay you in kind, we still send in exchange of loving remembrance four ounces of cinnamon, four ounces of costmary, two ounces of pepper, and one pound of *cozumber*.

[22.11] Emerton, LV, p.123. *To King Æthelbald of Mercia, 745-46.*
We beg Your Gracious Highness to afford my messenger Ceola, bearer of this letter, your aid and protection in my affairs and in his travels and in whatever way his errand may require. May you receive your reward in God's name for the assistance you gave in every way to our messengers a year ago, as they have reported to us.

[22.12] Emerton, LIX, p. 133. *Boniface to Archbishop Egbert of York concerning his letter to King Æthelbald [746-747].*
Meanwhile, as a token of fraternal love, I am sending you a copy of some letters of St. Gregory which I have obtained from the archives of the Roman Church, and which, so far as I know, have not yet reached Britain.
If you so order, I will send more, as I have received many of them. I am sending also a cloak and a towel for drying after washing the feet of the servants of God.

[22.13] Emerton, LXII, p. 140. *To Archbishop Cuthbert of Canterbury, 747.*
Finally, I will not conceal from Your Grace that all the servants of God here who are especially versed in Scripture and strong in the fear of God are agreed that it would be well and favourable for the honour and purity of your church, and

provide a certain shield against vice, if your synod and your princes would forbid matrons and veiled women to make these frequent journeys back and forth to Rome. A great part of them perish and few keep their virtue. There are very few towns in Lombardy or Frankland or Gaul, where there is not a courtesan or a harlot of English stock. It is a scandal and a disgrace to your whole church.

[22.14] *Emerton, LXIV, p. 142 at p. 146. Pope Zacharius to Boniface, I May 748.*
You have asked in another letter, holy brother, that a clergyman may be sent by us to the regions of Gallia and Francia, to hold a synod there. But so long as, by the Grace of God, Your Holiness is there to represent Us and the Apostlic See, it is not necessary to send anyone else.

[22.15] Emerton, LXVIII, p. 155. *From Theophylactus, Archdeacon of the Roman Church to Boniface.*
A little gift of blessing as a souvenir of our friendship: cinnamon, spice, pepper and incense in a sealed packet …

[22.16] Emerton, LXVIV, p. 166-67. *Cardinal-Bishop Benedict to Boniface.*
The venerable priest Lullus, here present as messenger of Your Paternal Holiness, has delivered to us your reverend communication … I am sending you, holy father, a trifling gift, a bath towel (*sabanum*), a face towel (*facitergium*), and a little frankincense, and I beg Your Reverend Paternity to accept it without offence.

[22.17] Emerton, LXXVIII, p. 172. *Boniface to Count Reginbert, 732-54.*
To his dear son Count Reginbert, Boniface, servant of the servants of God, sends greetings without end in the Lord. We beg the favour of your high office, that you may be pleased to allow this bearer of my letters, on his way to Rome to offer prayers and to bring replies in Church matters, to pass safely through your territory and assist him when in need, as you have done by former messengers of ours according to their reports when they have returned. Pray comply with this request that your reward before God may be increased and multiplied.

[22.18] Emerton, LXXXV, p. 177. *King Ethelbert of Kent to Boniface, 748-54.*
Some years ago the venerable abbess Bugga, after a visit to the holy places in the city of Rome for the purpose of offering prayer, returned thence to this, her native land, and to the convent of holy women which she had formerly governed … she called to my special attention that while you were both at Rome and eagerly engaged in making frequent visits to the shrines of the Holy Apostles, you had given her permission to speak familiarly with Your Gracious and Indulgent Holiness … For this I can imagine no more fitting opportunity than just now when we have here certain clerics of Your Excellence who were sent hither into Britain by you as wise and trustworthy agents, and are now anxious, with God's help, to return as soon as possible to your gracious presence. It is, therefore, an especial pleasure to me to send the bearer of this letter, the monk Ethelun, under the protection of the aforementioned men of yours, to deliver into your friendly hands these greetings and requests … By the bearer of this letter I am sending to Your Reverence with my devoted affection, a few little gifts: a silver, gold lined drinking cup (*cancum*) weighing three pounds and a half, and two woollen cloaks (*repte*). [*The king next asked Boniface to obtain for him a pair of falcons for training.*]

[22.19] Emerton LXXXVII, p. 180. *Boniface to King Pippin [753]*
To the most noble lord, Pippin, king of the Franks, Bishop Boniface sends greeting in the Lord.
A certain servant of our church, by name Ansfrid, himself an accomplished liar, craftily ran away from us and now comes to us with an order from you that justice be done him. We have sent him back to you with our messenger and a letter, so that you may know that he has lied to you, and beg you, in your own interest, to protect us against such deceivers and not to believe their falsehoods.

[23] THE LIFE OF ST. LEOBA BY RUDOLF, MONK OF FULDA
p. 214. Likewise, he (*Boniface*) sent messengers with letters to the abbess Tetta, of whom we have already spoken, asking her to send Leoba to accompany him on this journey and to take part in this embassy: for Leoba's reputation for learning and holiness had spread far and wide and her praise was on everyone's lips. The abbess Tetta was exceedingly displeased at her departure, but because she could not gainsay the dispositions of divine providence she agreed to his request and sent Leiba to the blessed man.
p. 216. She was extremely hospitable. She kept open house for all without exception, and even when she was fasting gave banquets and washed the feet of the guests with her own hands.

[24] EXTRACT FROM THE LIFE OF ST WILLIBALD
[24.1] AD 718, p. 156. [*The journey to Rome*] The young servant of Christ, as we have already mentioned, was eager to go on pilgrimage and travel to distant foreign lands and find out all about them.

[24.2] pp. 157-58. At the change of the seasons, towards the end of summer, his father and unmarried brother set out on the journey to which they had agreed. At a suitable time in the summer they were ready and prepared. Taking with them the necessary money for the journey and accompanied by a band of friends, they came to a place, which was known by the ancient name of Hamblemouth, near the port of Hamwih. Shortly afterwards they embarked on a ship. When the captain of the fast-sailing ship had taken their fares, they sailed, with the west wind blowing and a high sea running, amidst the shouting of sailors and the creaking of oars. When they had braved the dangers at sea and the perils of the mountainous waves, a swift course brought them with full sails and following winds safely to dry land. At once they gave thanks and disembarked, and, pitching their tents on the bank of the river Seine, they encamped near the city, which is called Rouen, where there is a market. For some days they rested there and then continued their journey, visiting the shrines of the saints that were on their way and praying there …

[*Immediately after the death of his father in Lucca, Willibald and party*] set out on their way, going steadily on foot through the vast land of Italy, through the deep valleys, over the craggy mountains, across the level plains, climbing upwards towards the peaks of the Apennines. And after they had gazed on the peaks covered with snow and wreathed in banks of cloud with the help of God and the support of his saints, they passed safely through the ambushes of the fierce and arrogant soldiery and came with all their relatives and company to the shrine of St. Peter, Prince of the Apostles. And there they sought his protection and gave many thanks to God, because they had escaped unscathed from the grievous perils of the sea and the manifold difficulties of travel in a foreign land …

[*After a spell of illness, Willibald turned towards Palestine, reaching there via Naples, Sicily and Monemvasia in Greece, landing at Ephesus*]

[24.3] p. 160. [*In Phygela, near Ephesus*] they begged some bread and went to a fountain in the middle of the city, and, sitting on the edge of it, they dipped their bread in the water and so ate.

[24.4] pp. 161-62. Leaving this place (*Arche*) they set out on foot for the town called Emesa, about twelve miles distant … Almost at once they were arrested by the pagan saracens and because they were strangers and without credentials they were taken prisoner and held as captives. *After being questioned* they left (*their interrogator*) and went to the court to ask permission to pass over to Jerusalem. But when they arrived there, the governor said at once that they were spies and ordered them to be thrust into prison.

[24.5] p. 169. Then they came again to Emesa and asked the governor there to give them a letter of safe conduct, and he gave them a letter for every two persons. They could not travel (*to Damascus*) in company but only two by two, because in this way it was easier for them to provide food for themselves.

[24.6] p. 170. When Bishop Willibald was in Jerusalem on the previous occasion he bought himself some balsam and filled a calabash with it; then he took a hollow reed which had a bottom to it and filled it with petroleum and put it inside the calabash. Afterwards he cut the reed equal in length to the calabash so that the surfaces of both were even and then closed the mouth of the calabash. When they reached the city of Tyre the citizens arrested them, put them in chains and examined all their baggage to find out if they had hidden any contraband. … But when they had scrutinised everything and could find nothing but one calabash which Willibald had, they opened it and snuffed at it to find out what was inside. And when they smelt petroleum, which was inside the reed at the top, they did not find the balsam which was inside the calabash underneath the petroleum, and so they let them go.

[25] LIFE OF ST WILLIBRORD

[25.1] pp. 6-7. *The saint was on his way to Francia.* Thus it was that, in fulfilment of the dream which his mother stated she had seen, Willibrord, fully aware of his own purpose but ignorant as yet of Divine pre-ordination, decided to sail for those parts and, if God so willed, to bring the light of the Gospel message to those people who through unbelief had not been stirred by its warmth. So he embarked on a ship, taking with him eleven othrs who shared his enthusiasm for the faith. … So the man of God, accompanied by his brethren, as we have already said, set sail, and after a successful crossing they moored their ships at the mouth of the Rhine. Then, after they had taken some refreshment, they set out for the castle of Utrecht, which lies on the bank of the river, where some years afterwards, when by Divine favour the faith had increased, Willibrord placed the seat of his bishopric.

[25.2] p. 13. On another occasion, when the blessed man was on his way to a cell belonging to him called Susteren, from the name of the stream that flows past it, he took a narrow path running through the cornfields of a certain wealthy landowner. When the keeper of the fields saw this he was furious and began to revile the man of God. Those who accompanied him (Willibrord) wanted to punish the man for insulting him, but the servant of God mildly restrained them, not wishing that anyone should perish on his account, since his whole happiness lay in bringing salvation to all. When he found it impossible to calm the fury of the foolish man, Willibrord did not persist but returned by the way he had come.

Next day, however, the wretch who had not feared to heap insults upon the servant of God was struck down on that very spot with sudden death before a crowd of onlookers.

[25.3] pp. 13-14. Whilst the divinely inspired man in his urgent desire to preach the Gospel was travelling through the coastal regions where the people were suffering from the lack of fresh water he noticed that his companions could hardly bear the pangs of thirst. So he called one of them and bade him dig a small trench inside his tent. *Having found water and* when they had drunk their fill they took with them as much water as they thought would satisfy their needs on the journey that lay before them.

[26] LIFE OF ST STURM

[26.1] p. 184. *Whilst looking for a site for the Abbey of Fulda* As they glided along the river Fulda they kept a sharp lookout for streams and fountains. … At last, on the third day, they came to a spot where the river Luodera flows into the Fulda. But finding nothing that suited their purpose, they turned downstream from there and began to row back to theitr own hermitage, stopping for a short time on the way at a place called Ruohenbach, where it seemed possible that servants of God might be able to live. On the whole they thought that the Archbishop might not approve of it. Then, sailing back along the same river, after a short time they arrived at their own poor huts.

[26.2] p. 186. When he had rested with them for a short time and recovered from his fatigue he saddled his ass and, taking provisions, set out alone, commending his journey to Christ, who is the Way, the Truth and the Life. Alone on his ass, he began his wanderings through the pathless wilderness.
Then the insatiable explorer, scrutinizing with his experienced gaze the hills and the plains, the mountains and valleys, the fountains, the streams and the rivers, went on his way.
Because of the difficulties of translation in relation to the 'pathless wilderness', I give the Latin of the first paragraph.
Cumque parumper penes ipsos fessus respirasset, stravit asinum suum, sumtoque viatico, solus profectus est, iter suum Christo, qui est via et vita, commendans; solus omnino sedens super asinum, per vastissima deserti loca pergere coepit.

[26.3] pp. 186-87 And wherever he spent the night he cut down trees with a tool which he carried in his hand and made a circular fence for the protection of his ass, so that it would not be devoured by the wild beasts which were numerous there. He himself, making a sign of the Cross on his forehead, lay down to rest without fear … One day, whilst he was ambling along, he came to a road (*pervenit ad viam*) leading from Thuringia to Mainz which the merchants use, and in the street which goes over the River Fulda he came upon a great number of Slavs swimming in the river and washing themselves. When the ass on which he was riding saw their naked bodies he began to quiver with fear, and even the man of God could not bear the stench of them. They, on their side, like all heathens, began to jeer at him, and when they tried to do him harm they were held back by divine power, and prevented from carrying out their intention. One of them, who acted as their interpreter, asked him where he was going. *In contrast to that clearly identified trunk road, and after travelling further:* He came at sunset to the path (*ubi semita fuit*) which was called by the old name Ortessveca. There he passed the night after providing protection for his ass against attacks. Whilst he was busy there putting up the fence he heard afar off the sound of water trickling, but he could not make up his mind whether the noise was caused by man or beast. He stood stock still listening intently, and again he heard the trickle of water. Then because the man of God did not wish to shout, and knowing instinctively that a man was astir, he struck a hollow tree with the weapon he was carrying in his hand. The other, hearing the sound of the beaten tree trunk, came running towards him, crying out. When he came near they saw and greeted each other. The man of God asked him who he was and where he came from. The other replied that he was on his way from Wetteran and that the horse he was leading by the halter belonged to his lord Ortis. And so, talking, they passed the night together in that place, for the other man knew the district very well; and when the man of God told him what he had in mind and what he wished to do, the other gave him the names of the various places and explained where the streams and fountains were to be found.

[27] FROM THE LIFE OF ST. LEBUIN

p. 230. [He] therefore, told St. Gregory what the Lord had commanded him and asked to be conducted to the spot in his diocese which the Lord had pointed out and commended to his care. After blessed Gregory had listened to him, congratulated him and welcomed this visitation from the Lord, he directed him to the place he had mentioned and gave him as a companion the servant of god, Marchelmus, who had been one of Willibrord's disciples. Then he was received into the house of a widow named Abarhilda and enjoyed her hospitality for some days.

[28] HISTORY OF THE POPES (EIGHTH CENTURY)

Translated by Raymond Davis, reproduced by kind permission of Liverpool University Press.

[28.1] 753. ch. 15, p. 59. Stephen II ... secretly *sent* through a pilgrim to Pepin King of the Franks, a letter written in the agony that held this province fast. He sent word incessantly to the king of the Franks: the king must dispatch his envoys here to Rome; he must have them summon him to come to him.

[28.2] 753. ch. 17, p. 60. *In order to be able to visit the king of the Lombards, the Pope* at once sent his envoy to that blasphemous king to get a safe conduct for himself and those who were to travel with him.

[28.3] 753. chs. 22-5, p. 61. The envoys of the Franks leaned heavily on Ailstuf to allow the Holy Pope to travel on to France. At this, Ailstuf summoned the blessed man and asked him if it was his intention to make for France. He did not keep quiet about it but openly told him his intention ... Then he gave him leave ... Even after he had given him leave, the evil king of the Lombards still attempted to make him deviate from his journey. But this was perfectly clear to the holy man, so at great speed and with God going before him he came to the mountain barriers (*clusae*) of the Franks ... He continued his journey to the venerable monastery of Christ's Martyr St. Maurice ...

[28.4] 756. ch. 42, p. 70.. So what Aistulf had impiously done loudly resounded in the ears of the King of the Franks; and the blessed Pope arranged for his envoys to be sent on a journey by sea to him in France, along with a certain religious man named Warnehar who had been sent here to Rome by the King of the Franks.

[28.5] 756. Ch. 43, p. 70. Now when the Christian Pepin king of the Franks was approaching these mountain barriers of the Lombards, there came to this city of Rome imperial envoys, George the chief secretary and John the silentiary, who had been sent to the king of the Franks. ... [*The Pope*] attached to them an envoy of the apostolic see, and gave them leave for France. They travelled by sea and reached Marseilles as quickly as they could.

[29] ST CEOLFRITH'S JOURNEY

Extract from the anonymous life of St Ceolfrith: D.S. Boutflower, *Life of Ceolfrid, Abbot of Wearmouth and Jarrow* (Darlington 1912).

[29.1] ch. 26. When his address was ended the antiphon was resumed, and with it the psalm above mentioned, and they pass out to the river, leading forth their father with mournful song as on all but lost to them; and once more he gives to each and all the kiss of peace, their chant again and again interrupted by their tears, and having recited a prayer on the shore he ascends the vessel and sits down at its prow. The Deacons seated themselves beside him, one of them holding a golden cross which he had made, the other lighted candles ...
ch. 27. As the vessel sped across the river, he gazed on the brethren ... Thus he quitted the vessel; bows before the cross, mounts his horse – and departed.

[29.2] ch. 31. Ceolfrid set forth then from his monastery on the fourth day of June, being Thursday, intending to sail down to the sea by the mouth of the river Humber. On the fourth day of July, being a Saturday, he embarked on a vessel, which, before it reached the coast of Gaul, was brought to land in three several provinces, in each of which he was by all persons honourably received and treated with veneration, as one who had determined by the setting of an incomparable example to virtue to crown the grace of his long and holy life.

[29.3] Ch. 32: On the completion of his voyage, he reached the mainland of Gaul on Wednesday the twelfth day of August, and in those parts too he was spendidly honoured by all persons, and especially by King Hilperic himself, who, besides the gifts which he offered him, further gave him letters of commendation through all the provinces of his kingdom, bidding that he should be everywhere received peaceably and that none should presume to hinder him in his journey.. Moreover, he commended him, and with him all his party, to the kindly hospitalities of Liudbrand, king of the Lombards. So he came to Langres, a city of the Burgundians, on Friday, the twenty-fifth day of September; and there, worn out as much by length of days as by sickness – yea, as the Scriptures used to say, failing in a good old age, he was gathered unto his fathers. For he had lived seventy-four years ...

[29.4] Ch. 34 There were in his company about eighty men, drawn from various parts, who all of them followed him in a body and honoured him as their father. For he had given orders to his attendants, that, if they found any of his companions without means of support, they should give him at once either food or money.

[29.5] Ch. 37 So then when their father had been buried, some of the brethren of his escort him returned home, to tell in his own monastery where and when he had departed from the body; and some on the other hand completed their journey to Rome, to deliver the presents which he had sent. Among which presents was of course the Pandect, which we mentioned ...

[29.6] Ch. 38. There were moreover some of Ceolfrid's followers, who, through attachment to their father, chose to remain in this same city of Langres; these, however, afterwards accomplished their intention and desire of reaching Rome. … And for those who were departing whether in this ort hat direction, [Gangwulf] granted both guides and supplies for the way.

[30] CEOLFRID'S LAST JOURNEY, FROM BEDE'S HISTORY OF THE ABBOTS
From D.H. Farmer (ed.), *The Age of Bede.*
[30.1] Ch. 18, p. 204 [As soon as Hwaetberht was elected abbot to succeed Ceolfrid] he set off at once with a few of the monks to find Ceolfrid who was waiting for a ship to take him across the ocean … (*He*) gave him a letter of recommendation to Pope Gregory, some lines of which we think it well to include in this book as a record.

[30.2] Ch. 19, p. 205. *Part of the letter sent for Ceolfrid.*
In the weariness of old age he has devoutedly striven to reach once more the threshold of the blessed apostles which he delighted to remember having visited, seen and venerated in his youth … he has set out again as a pilgrim for the sake of Christ at the end of his days …

[30.3] Ch. 21, p. 207. The following day he [Ceolfrith] was buried with all dignity in the Church of the three Brother Martyrs amidst the tears and lamentation not only of the eighty or more English men who made up his company but also of the local inhabitants who were deeply affected at the thought of so worthy an old man being disappointed of his wish. It was hard for anyone to restrain his tears at the sight of some of Ceolfrid's party starting out to continue their journey without their father, whilst others revoked their intention of going to Rome, preferring to turn back for home to report the news of his burial; and the rest, in their undying love for him, remained to keep watch by his tomb in the midst of a people whose language they could not understand.

[31] THE PAPAL ENVOYS' CROSSING OF THE SEA in 786
English Historical Documents, no. 191.
We indeed set out complying with your orders with a glad countenance, but the Tempter hindered us with a contrary wind; but he who calms the waters ... hearing your prayer, stilled the blue straits, brought us across to a safe haven, and led us to the shores of the English.

[32] AN ENGLISHMAN ABROAD
Cited in F. Ganshof, *Sur les Ports de Provence*, p 31, from *Annales Petaviani*, G.H. Pertz (ed.).
c. 790 There was still one of the English race, whose father, Botto by name, was a merchant in the town of Marseilles.

[33] EARLY FINANCIAL ARRANGEMENTS
[33.1] DUNWALD'S WILL
A.D. 762. Dunwald, minister of the late King Æthelberht, to the church of SS Peter and Paul (St Augustine's), Canterbury; grant of land in Canterbury. Latin with bounds. Sawyer 1182; the text is taken from the 'Kemble' website and the translation from English Historical Documents, no. 72. This document implies a set off between an intended gift of money in Rome and its equivalent value in a property in England. The implications for international credit arrangements bear some thought.
762. I, Dunwald, the thegn of King Ethelbert ... while he lived, now indeed desiring to convey this money for the safety of his soul to the threshold of the Apostles at Rome, along with others, assign after my death ... a residence which is situated in the market place at the Queen's Gate of the city of Canterbury and which Hringwine now holds – the same which the aforesaid king granted with other small lands in his own right for me to possess with his tribute, and to give to whomsoever I should wish – to the Church of the Blessed Peter and Paul, situated nearby, where the body of the same King Æthelbert, my lord, rests, for his soul and my salvation, by an eternal donation, to be possessed with his tribute.

Because of the potential importance of this document, it is worth reproducing the relevant parts in the original Latin.
Ego Dunwald minister dum aduiueret inclite memorie regis Æthelberti, nunc uero pecuniam illius pro anime eius salute ad limina apostolorum Rome cum aliis perferre desiderans, uillam unam post obitum meum, ni forsitan hoc prius me uiuente placeat peragendum, que iam ad Quenegatum urbis Dorouernis in foro posita est, quam nunc Hringuine tenet, quam idem mihi prefatus rex cum aliis terrulis iure proprio cum tributo illius possidendam et cuicumque uoluerim tradendam condonauit. Hanc uidelicet ad ecclesiam propepositam beati Petri et Pauli ubi scilicet corpus eiusdem domini mei regis Æthelberti requiescit pro anime illius et mea salute eterna donatione cum tributo illius possidendam attribuo.

[33.2] ÆTHELRIC'S MORTGAGE TO RAISE MONEY

Birch 313, from. *English Historical Documents*, no. 81.

804. Archbishop Æ thelheard … gave judgment … that I was free to give my land and title-deeds wherever I wished. Afterwards I entrusted them for my friends to keep when for the relief of my soul I sought St Peter and St Paul. And when I came back to my country, I received back my land and repaid the price as we previously agreed, that we might be at peace.

[34] CHARLEMAGNE
[34.1] NOTKER'S LIFE OF CHARLEMAGNE

Translated by Lewis Thorpe.

Bk I, 14. The [*unidentified*] Bishop was greatly upset. He flew hither and thither like a swallow and had not only his Cathedral and the monks' dwellings but even the quadrangles and the courtyards cleaned and swept. Charlemagne ... looked very carefully about him and inspected everything. Then he said to the Bishop: 'My kind host, you always have everything carefully cleaned for my arrival' [*and after a game of formalities, rewarded him.*]

[34.2] EINHARD'S LIFE OF CHARLEMAGNE

From S.E. Turner, *The Life of Charlemagne, by Einhard* (University of Michigan Press 1960), reproduced by kind permission of University of Michigan Press.

pp. 43-44. The king … undertook also very many works calculated to adorn and benefit his kingdom and brought several of them to completion. Among these, the most deserving of mention are the basilica of the Holy mother of God at Aix-la-Chapelle, built in the most admirable manner, and a bridge over the Rhine at Mayence, half a mile long, the breadth of the river at this point. This bridge was destroyed by fire (May 813) the year before Charles died, but, owing to his death so soon after, could not be repaired, although he had intended to rebuild it in stone.

pp. 66-67. *From Charlemagne's will*. It is well known that among his other property and treasures are three silver tables, and one very large and massive golden one. He directs and commands that the square silver table, upon which there is a representation of the city of Constantinople, shall be sent to the Basilica of St. Peter the Apostle at Rome, with the other gifts destined therefor; that the round one, adorned with a delineation of the city of Rome, shall be given to the Episcopal Church at Ravenna; that the third, which far surpasses the other two in weight and in beauty of workmanship, and is made in three circles, showing the plan of the whole universe, drawn with skill and delicacy, shall go, together with the golden table, fourthly above mentioned, to increase that lot which is to be devoted to his heirs and to alms.

[34.3] LETTER FROM CHARLEMAGNE TO KING OFFA

Adapted from G. F. Browne, *Alcuin of York* (1893).

Charles, by the grace of God King of the Franks and Lombards and Patricius of the Romans, to his dearest brother the venerated Offa, King of the Mercians, wishes present prosperity and eternal beatitude in Christ. … We therefore, my most loved brother, mindful of the ancient pact between us, have addressed to your reverence these letters, that our treaty, fixed firm in the root of faith, may flourish in the fruit of love. We have read over the epistles of your brotherliness, which at various times have been brought to us by the hands of your messengers, and we desire to answer adequately the several suggestions of your authority. … With regard to pilgrims, who for the love of God and the salvation of their souls desire to visit the thresholds of the blessed Apostles, as has been the custom, we give leave for them to go on their way peaceably without any disturbance, carrying with them such things as they need. But we have ascertained that traders seeking gain, not serving religion, have fraudulently joined themselves to bands of pilgrims. If any such are found among the pilgrims, they must pay the fixed toll at the proper places; the rest will go in peace, free from toll.

You have written to us also about merchants, and by our mandate we allow that they shall have protection and support in our kingdom, according to the ancient custom of trading. And if in any place they are afflicted by wrongful oppression, they may appeal to us or to our judges, and we will then order true justice to be done. Similarly our men, if they suffer any injustice in your dominion, are to appeal to the judgement of your equity, lest any disturbance should arise anywhere between our men.

You have written to us also about merchants We will and command that they have protection and patronage in our realm, lawfully, according to the ancient custom of trading. And if in any place they suffer from unjust oppression, they may appeal to us or our judges, and we will see that proper justice is done. And likewise for our merchants; if they suffer any injustice in your realm, let them appeal to the judgement of your equity. Thus no disturbance should arise among our merchants.

With regard to the presbyter Odberht, who on his return from Rome desires to live abroad for the love of God, and has not come to us to accuse you, we declare to your love that we have sent him to Rome along with other exiles who in fear of death have fled to the shelter of our protection. We have done this in order that in the presence of the lord apostolic and of your illustrious archbishop – in accordance with their vow, as your notes inform us – their cause may be heard and judged, so that equitable judgement may effect what pious intercession could not do. What could be safer for us than that the investigation of apostolic authority should decide in a case where the opinion of others differs?

With regard to the black stones which your reverence earnestly asked to have sent to you, send a messenger to come and point out what kind they are that you desire. Wherever they may be found we will gladly order them to be given, and their conveyance to be aided. But, as you have set out your wishes about the length of the stones, our people make demand about the length of cloaks, that you will order them to be made to the same pattern as those which used to come to us in earlier times.

Further, we make known to your love that we have forwarded to each of the Episcopal sees in your kingdom, and that of king Ethelred, a gift from our collection of dalmatics and palls, in alms for the lord apostolic Hadrian, our father, your loving friend …

[34.4] EXTRACTS FROM CAPITULARIES AND CHARTERS
From H.R. Loyn and J. Percival (eds), *The reign of Charlemagne.*

THE CAPITULARY OF MANTUA, 781
Article 8. (p. 50). With regard to tolls: let no one presume to levy a toll except in accordance with ancient custom, and let it be levied only in places recognised by law from of old; anyone who levies it unlawfully must make payment according to the law, and in addition must pay our fine to our *missi*.

DOUBLE CAPITULARY OF THIONVILLE FOR THE MISSI, 805
Article 13. (pp. 90-91). Concerning tolls, it is our wish that the old established and lawful tolls should be extracted from trader on bridges, on water crossings and on sales: and that the new and unlawful ones – when ropes are slung across or when people go under bridges in boats or for similar situations, in which no assistance is being provided for the traveller – are not to be exacted.

'DE VILLIS', END OF THE EIGHTH CENTURY
Article 27. (p. 68). And when our *missi* and their retinues are on their way to or from the palace, they shall under no circumstances take lodging in the royal manor houses, except on our express orders or those of the queen. And the count in his district, or the men whose traditional custom it has been to look after our *missi* and their retinues, shall continue, as they have done in the past, to provide them with pack-horses and other necessities, so that they may travel to and from the palace with ease and dignity.

Article 64. (p. 72). That our carts which go to the army as war-carts shall be well constructed; their coverings shall be well made of skins, and sewn together in such a way that, should the necessity arise to cross water, they can get across rivers with the provisions inside and without any water being able to get in – and, as we have said, our belongings can get across safely.

GENERAL CAPITULARY FOR THE *MISSI*, SPRING 802.
Article 27. (p. 76). We ordain that no one in all our kingdom, whether rich or poor, should dare to deny hospitality to pilgrims: that is, no one should refuse a roof, a hearth and water to any pilgrims who are travelling the country in the service of God, or to anyone who is journeying for love of God or for the salvation of his soul. And if anyone should be willing to offer any further benefit to such people, let him know that God will give him the best reward, as he himself said: 'Whoso shall receive one such little child in my name receiveth me'….

CHARTER IN FAVOUR OF ST DENIS, 14 MARCH 775
This charter confirmed the monastery's exemption from virtually all tolls, by land or river. In doing so, it gave us an image of the kind of traffic involved, and perhaps in exaggerated terms the geographical area over which it might trade.
p. 143. … to the effect that throughout the realms of Frankia and Italy which are ours by God's favour, with regard to ships sailing upstream and downstream along the rivers, or carts and their loads, or the monastery's own men or those known to be engaged on the business of the said church of God, wherever and to what region they may travel, in cities, castles, villages, harbours, public bridges and other places of business, or its men who live on its lands, or its estates and lands themselves, or the men who travel outside its estates on business or to purchase wine, no toll nor weir-passage nor tithe nor ship-money nor wheel money nor bridge-toll nor damage nor gratuity nor trading-tax nor post-money shall be exacted; from ships or carts and their loads, or from what men carry on their backs

[35] THE ENGLISH COMMUNITY IN ROME IN THE NINTH CENTURY
[35.1] **816**. *Noted in ASC and JW.*
The English School at Rome was burned.

[35.2] **817-824.** From Raymond Davis (trans.), *The lives of the ninth century Popes* (Liverpool 1995), reproduced by permission of Liverpool University Press.

Ch. 7, p. 8. (under Paschal I).

We think this too should not be passed over in silence, that at that time, with devilish cunning at work, through the carelessness of some men of English race their whole quarter, called *burgus* in their language, was so burnt with an abounding flame of fire, that not even traces of their former dwelling could be found in that place.

[35.3] *c. 846*. *Chronicon Casinense (MG SS III, p. 225)*.

In these days, the Saracens, on leaving Rome, destroyed completely the church of Peter, chief among the blessed apostles and the church of the blessed Paul. In the same place they slew many Saxons, and as many others of all ages and sexes.

[35.4] 864. From J. L. Nelson, *The Annals of St Bertin*, courtesy of Manchester University Press.

There was a wonderful cross, most worthy of honour, which had been very beautifully worked by Helena of holy memory: she had placed in it the wood of the life-giving cross, and handed it over to St Peter as the greatest of gifts. This cross was smashed in all the uproar [over the arrival of Lothar] and thrown into a pool of mud. From there, so they say, the pieces were retrieved by some Englishmen and returned to the cross's custodians.

[35.5] 873-875. *EHD, no. 221*. From a letter of John VIII to the two English Archbishops:

Among other things, all the leading men of England who were then living near the blessed Apostle Peter, having thus been assembled, the opinion ...

[36] DUNGAL'S LETTER (early ninth century)

From Dümmler, MGH Ep. Karol. Aevi., II, Dungal of St. Denis (whichever Dungal it was) wrote a number of letters, in one of which he asks Abbot Adam of Jumièges for a horse, because his has gone lame and blind. He continued in a tone that could have come straight from one of the Colloquies:

[36.1] Letter 4, pp. 579-80. ... For my horse, which was suited to me and convenient and was always steady in his ways, which the lord abbot Sichel, of happy memory, gave me out of charity, is pained and lamed by stiffening and tightening of the sinews so that it is impossible to use it ... *He reminded the Abbot of the spiritual rewards of charity and continued* ...We poor people and pilgrims, may well seem a disagreeable burden to you because of our numbers and our begging and the noise we make.

[36.2] Letter 6, (p. 581). I have sent some money by your aforesaid servant ...

[37] ALCUIN – CARMINA IV

From Alcuin, Carmina IV, E. Duemmler (ed.), MGH Poetae Latini Medii Aevii I, p. 220.

... with strong winds seek the swift flowing estuary of the Rhine abounding with fish

Which enters the sea as it surges about with swift currents

Then your prow has to be pulled with a very long tow rope lest the stern be suddenly dragged backwards by the river.

Further upstream, he recalled reaching the destination. After using sails so far:

After some distance you will cross the river using the oarsmen

Here stop the boat and let the whole ship be stuck firmly in the sand.

[38] EXTRACTS FROM THE LETTERS OF ALCUIN

S. Allott, *Alcuin of York.*

[38.1] Allott, letter 9, p. 14 *Alcuin, in France, to 'his son Joseph', an Irish pupil.* 790.

Write to tell me if our lord the king is travelling or not, if there is peace or war, if you and our people are well, and if there is any news in your part of the world. Also send our supplies to the coast; and let Odwin bring us, as God wills, the five pounds of silver which I sent with you for bartering or selling its equivalent or exchanging. Send another five also of my silver and three-ply garments of goat-hair and wool for the use of my boys [*and other goods*] ... Tell Eanfrith to come to you, that you may know how he is, and he may send me the money he has collected at the monastery – and the goat-hair garment; for I asked him and Frotgoneg for the money he has from Wurmec's township.

[38.2] Allott, letter 31, p. 42. *Alcuin to Colcu, bishop of the monastery in Mayo, 773-786.*

790. But I do not know what will become of us. A quarrel has recently arisen between King Charles and King Offa, and fuel has been devilishly heaped upon the fire, so that on both sides the traders are forbidden to sail. Some think we should be sent there in the interests of peace. Whether I go or not, I ask for the protection of your holy prayers.

[38.3] *See also the extract from the Gesta Abbatum Fontanellensium, trans EHD no 20:*
but as Offa would not agree to this unless Bertha, daughter of Charles the Great, should be given in marriage to his son, the most mighty king being somewhat enraged gave orders that no one from the island of Britain and the English race was to land on the sea coast of Gaul for the sake of commerce. But he was restrained from doing this by ... Father Gervold.

[Alcuin sent sums of money to Colcu for various Irish houses, and also] I have sent you some oil, which is now almost unobtainable in Britain, for you to dispense it where bishops need it for divine worship.

[38.4] Allott, letter 41, p. 53. *Alcuin to King Offa.* **796.**
Be assured that my lord King Charles has often spoken of you to me in a loving and trusting spirit; you certainly have a most loyal friend in him. Hence he is sending envoys to Rome for the jurisdiction of the Pope and Archbishop Æthelheard.

[38.5] Allott, letter 45, p. 57. *Alcuin to Eugenia. c. 796*
It is no great harm that you could not complete the journey you began (to Rome) as God was planning something better for you. Spend on the comfort of the poor what you prepared as travelling money for your long journey. Give what you have, that you may be worthy to receive what you desire ...

[38.6] Allott, letter 65, p. 78. *Alcuin to Arno.* **799.**
The previous letter, which reached us in your name – with some complaints about the behaviour of the Pope and your personal danger there because of the Romans – was brought to me by Baldricus (whom I take to be your priest) with a cloak sewn in Roman style, a garment of linen and wool. I did not want the letter to get into other hands so Candidus was the only one to read it with me, and it was then put in the fire, lest any scandal should arise through the carelessness of the man who keeps my correspondence ... Give my lord David my letter and my gift of the Scriptures on Christmas Day with the greeting of peace.

[38.7] Allott, letter 75, p. 91. *Alcuin to Charlemagne.* **799.**
When I went to Rome as a young man and spent some days in the royal city of Pavia, a certain Jew called Lull had a debate with Master Peter ...

[38.8] Allott, letter 19, p. 27. *Alcuin to Archbishop Eanbald* II. 801.
I have sent your grace that bird of spring, the Cuckoo*, with presents from me – just a little wine for you and the brothers and your friends, also a hundred pounds of tin and four lattices. I feel it right for the belfry to be roofed with tin to give the place distinction.

* Latin *'Cuculus'* – one of Alcuin's pupils.

[38.9] Allott, letter 51, p. 66. *Alcuin to Archbishop Æthelheard.* **801.**
I have sent you, as you asked, the saddle I usually ride on, prepared in the way favoured by churchmen in this district, and also a horse to carry the saddle with you sitting on it, if it please your grace. I have sent my boy to see our people* receive you properly, and bring you back to many happy years of successful preaching...

* at St Judoc's (S. Josse sur Mer).

[38.10] Allott, letter 52, p. 67. *Alcuin to Charlemagne.* 801
I have been told that some friends of your Flaccus, Æthelheard, Metropolitan of the Church of Canterbury and Archbishop of the first see in Britain, Ceolmund of the kingdom of Mercia, once a minister of King Offa, and Torhtmund, a faithful servant of King Ethelred ... wish me to approach your Majesty ... I beg you to receive them with your usual kindness...

[38.11] Allott, letter 20, p. 28. *Alcuin to Eanbald II, Archbishop of York. 801.*
My messenger met your devout fellow-bishop Æthelheard at St Judoc's on his way to Rome. He, with two other bishops*, and our friends Ceolmund and Torhtmund, was well received there with all the kindness he desired – and had previously requested in his letter to me. I wrote to my lord, King David, for their comfort.

* One was Cyneberht, bishop of the West Saxons, according to the *Anglo-Saxon Chronicle*.

[38.12] Allott, letter 120, p. 128. *Alcuin to 'his dear sons in Christ' in Rome.* 801.
My sons, why has no letter sped across the Alps by the hands of the returning Saxons to the chapel in the city of Troyes and thence by the hands of our people to the venerable shrine of Tours?

[38.13] Allott, letter 52, p. 68. *Alcuin to Charlemagne.* 801.
I have been told that some friends of your Flaccus, Æthelheard, Metropolitan of the Church of Canterbury, Ceolmund of the kingdom of Mercia, once a minister of King Offa, and Torhtmund, a faithful servant of King Ethelred … wish me to approach your majesty. They have all been most loyal to me, helping me on my journey and protecting my boys as they travel about. I beg you to receive them with your usual kindness, for each in his place has befriended me.

[38.14] Allott, letter 53, p. 68. *Alcuin to Archbishop Æthelheard.* 802.
Hearing from your letter of your successful journey and your return to our country – and your kind reception by the Pope, I gave heartfelt and joyful thanks to the eternal Lord God.

[38.15] Allott, letter 157, p. 153. *Alcuin to Angilbert.* Undated.
In view of the friendship between us I have ventured to write to you, to ask you to give a kindly reception to the bearer of this letter and beg our lord King Pepin to help him on his pilgrimage. Kings are richly rewarded by God, it is agreed, for helping the poor and especially pilgrims to St Peter's.

[38.16] Allott, letter 158, p. 153. *Alcuin to Bishop Remigius of Chur.* Undated.
I write to commend this merchant of ours, with his goods for Italy, to your protection, that he may go and return safely through the roads of your country and not be held up by toll collectors in your mountain passes but have a clear passage both ways through the generosity of your love …

[39] EXTRACTS FROM THE ROYAL FRANKISH ANNALS
Edited and translated B.W. Scholz, *Carolingian Chronicles* (Michigan 1970), reproduced by permission of University of Michigan Press.

[39.1] 773. The Lord King Charles then went to the villa of Thionville to spend the winter there. To Thionville came an emissary of the Lord Pope Hadrian by the name of Peter, who had travelled by sea to Marseilles and from there by land to the Lord King Charles … The Pope's emissary came by sea because the Lombards had closed the roads to the Romans.

[39.2] 792. A bridge of pontoons was built, connected by anchors and ropes so that it could be put together and taken apart.

[39.3] 798. An envoy of King Alfonso of Galicia and Asturias by the name of Froia came to the king in Saxony and presented a most beautiful tent.

[39.4] 801. In the month of October of the same year, Isaac the Jew returned from Africa with the elephant and arrived at Porto-Venere. Since he could not cross the Alps because of the snow, he spent the winter at Vercelli.

[39.5] 802. On 20 July of this same year Isaac arrived with the elephant and other presents sent by the Persian king, and he delivered them to the emperor at Aachen. The name of the elephant was Abul Abaz.

[39.6] 807. They [the envoys] came to the Emperor and delivered presents which the king of Persia sent to him, that is, a tent and curtains for the canopy of different colours and of unbelievable size and beauty. They were all made of the best linen, the curtains as well as the strings, and dyed in different colours.

Because of the variety of words used to describe tents, it is worth reproducing the original Latin.
ad imperatorem pervenerunt munera deferentes, quae praedictus rex imperatori miserat, id est papilionem et tentoria atrii vario colore facta mirae magnitudinis et pulchritudinis. Erant enim omnia bissina, tam tentoria quam et funes eorum, diversis tincta coloribus.'

[39.7] 808. But Charles, the son of the Emperor, built a bridge across the Elbe, and moved the army under his command as fast as he could across the river against the Linones and Smeldingi. … In the meantime Eardwulf, the king of the Northumbrians from the island of Britain, had been driven from his throne and country. He came to the emperor while the latter was still at Nijmegen and, after saying why he had come, continued to Rome. On his return from Rome he was taken back to his kingdom by the envoys of the Roman Pontiff and the Lord Emperor … As his envoy the deacon Adulf, a Saxon from Britain, was sent to Britain. Two Abbots were dispatched with him by the emperor, the notary Hruotfrid and Nanthar of St Omer.

[39.8] 809. When Eardwulf, king of the Northumbrians, had been taken back to his kingdom and the envoys of the emperor and pontiff were returning, all crossed without mishap except one of them, the deacon Adulf, who was captured by pirates and taken to Britain. But he was ransomed by one of King Cenwulf's men and returned to Rome.

[39.9] 811. In the meantime, the Emperor himself went to the port city of Boulogne in order to inspect the fleet, whose construction he had ordered the year before. There the ships in question had assembled. At Boulogne he restored the lighthouse constructed a long time ago to guide the course of sailors and had a fire lit on its top at night.

[39.10] 826. When the envoys of the Bulgars reported to their king what they had accomplished, he sent his first ambassador again with letters to the Emperor and requested that the borders be determined without further delay, or, if this was not acceptable to the Emperor, that each should guard his frontiers without a peace treaty.

[39.11] 827. The Emperor sent the priest and abbot Helisachar and with him Counts Hildebrand and Donatus to stamp out the revolt in the Spanish march. Before their arrival Aizo, trusting in the assistance of the Saracens, had inflicted much damage on the guards of this border. By constant invasions he had worn them out so thoroughly that some of them deserted the castles which they were to defend and retreated.

[40] THE GIFT OF DONATUS OF FIESOLE

Taken from Gougaud, *Sur les Routes de Rome*, p. 258, quoting C Cippola, *Codice Diplomatico del monastero di San Colombano di Bobbio*. See also A.M. Tommasini, *Irish Saints in Italy,* especially at pp. 248-9.
850. And if some pilgrims of my race should come there, I wish and institute that two or three should live there and be nourished under the protection of the said provost ...

[41] ANNALS OF ST BERTIN

From J.L. Nelson, *The Annals of St-Bertin.*
[41.1] 839 Now after Easter (6 April) when the Emperor was heading back into Francia, the king of the English sent envoys to him to ask the Emperor to grant him permission to travel through Francia on his way to Rome on pilgrimage. *For Æthelwulf's journey to Rome, see below, no. 43.*

The destruction of the Cross in 864 and its salvation by Englishment is in no. 35. 4, above.

[41.2] 864 Charles, as the Pope had ordered, send Rothad to Rome accompanied by Bishop Robert of Le Mans, and the Bishops of his realm also sent representatives to the apostolic see with synodical letters about Rothad's case. But Louis [II] refused all these envoys permission to travel through his lands. The envoys of both the king and the bishops secretly made known to the Pope the reasons why it was impossible for them to come to Rome. Then the rest of them journeyed back to their own fatherland. But Rothad feigned illness and stayed at Besancon, and when the others had gone he made his way via Chur, with the help of his backers Lothar and King Louis of Germany, to Emperor Louis of Italy, intending to reach Rome with his aid. Pope Nicholas requested Louis, through Arsenius the *apocrisiarius*, for permission to send legates to Charles on certain ecclesiastical matters. But Louis refused: he believed that the Pope wished to send those envoys to Francia with hidden designs against himself.

[41.3] 869 While the Pope entered Rome itself, Lothar went to the Church of St Peter. No cleric came to greet him but Lothar went up on his own, with only his personal retinue, to the tomb of St Peter. From there he went to the upper floor of a house near the Church of St Peter to find lodgings, but he found that the place had not even been cleaned out with a brush.

[41.4] 877 Now the Lord Emperor went from Quierzy to Compiegne, and thence by way of Soissons to Rheims. Then he continued is journey by way of Chalons and Ponthion and Langres, and, accompanied by his wife and a huge supply of gold and silver and horses and other movables, he left Frankia and made for Italy. Crossing the Jura he reached Orbe, where he met Bishop Adalgar whom he had dispatched to Rome the previous February to take part in the synod summoned by Pope John. ... Adalgar also informed the emperor, amongst other things, that Pope John would come to Pavia to meet him. ... Charles himself hastened on his way and met the Pope at Vercelli, and having been received with the greatest honour, went on with the Pope to Pavia. ... So they left Pavia and moved to Tortona [*to avoid Karlmann who was preparing to attack them.*]

[42] ANNALS OF FULDA

Translated T. Reuter, *The Annals of Fulda* (Manchester 1992), courtesy of Manchester University Press.
869 King Lothar broke off the negotiations for which he had come to Rome and planned to return to his own kingdom, but he died at Piacenza in July and many others of his magnates were carried off during the same journey.

877 In this year Italian fever and an eye sickness troubled the German people, especially those living around the Rhine; and a terrible malady followed Carloman's army on its return from Italy, so that many coughed up their lives

[43] KING ÆTHELWULF'S JOURNEY TO ROME
As there are three accounts of this they have been brought together for comparison.
[43.1] From the *Annals of St Bertin.*
855 Charles also gave an honourable reception to King Æthelwulf of the Anglo-Saxons who was hastening on his way to Rome. Charles gave him all the supplies a king might need and had him escorted right to the boundary of his realm with all the courtesies due to a king.
856 In July, Æthelwulf, king of the western English, on his way back from Rome, was betrothed to King Charles' daughter Judith. On 1 October, in the palace of Verberie, he received her in marriage.

[43.2] From *The Anglo-Saxon Chronicle.*
855 And the same year King Æthelwulf conveyed by charter the tenth part of his land over all his kingdom to the praise of God and his own eternal salvation. And the same year he travelled to Rome in great state, living there twelve months, and then went towards home. And Charles, king of the Franks, gave him his daughter as queen, and after that he came to his people and they were glad of it.

[43.3] From Alfred P. Smyth, *The Medieval Life of Alfred the Great* (2002), courtesy of Palgrave.
But meanwhile, while King Æthelwulf was lingering beyond the sea for so short a time, a certain infamous thing which was contrary to the practice of all Christians, arose to the west of Selwood. For King Æthelbald [son of King Æthelwulf], and Ealhstan bishop of the church of Sherborne, together with Eanwulf ealdorman of the shire of Somerset, are said to have plotted that King Æthelwulf should not be received again into the kingship when he returned from Rome.

[44] A PAPAL LETTER REFERRING TO ENGLISH RESIDENTS IN ROME, *c.* 873-5.
From Whitelocke, Brett and Brooke, *Councils and Synods.* (1981), p. 2. We can only assume that the messengers brought Pope John's letter to Ethelred, Archbishop of Canterbury. The letter is not precisely dated and it may have been brought with that to Burgred. It testifies to the number and influence of the English residents in Rome. It also hints at a degree of organisation.
Among other things the leaders of all the English men who were then living beside the blessed apostle Peter, having thus been brought together, their opinion …

[45] EXTRACTS FROM THE ANGLO-SAXON CHRONICLES
From *The Anglo-Saxon Chronicles,* translated and edited by Michael Swanton
[45.1] 789 (Text E) And in (King Beorhtric's) days came first three ships of Northmen from Hordaland: and then the reeve rode there and wanted to compel them to go to the king's town, because he did not know what they were; and then they killed him.
Æthelweard has more detail, in Giles' loose but engaging translation (p. 19):
… Suddenly there arrived on the coast a fleet of Danes, not large, but of three ships only: this was their first arrival. When this became known, the king's officer, who was already stopping in the town of Dorchester, leapt on his horse and galloped forward with a few men to the port, thinking that they were merchants rather than enemies, and, commanding them in an authoritative tone, ordered them to be made to go to the royal city; but he was slain on the spot by them, and all who were with him. The name of the officer was Beaduherd.

[45.2] 814. And Archbishop Wulfred and Wigberht, bishop of Wessex, went to Rome.

[45.3] 815. Here Archbishop Wulfred turned back to his own bishopric, with the blessing of the Pope Leo …
855 *For Æthelwulf's journey to Rome, see above.*

[45.4] 873-4. Here the raiding party went … from Lindsey to Repton and took winter quarters there, and [874] drove the king Burhred across the sea 22 years after he had the kingdom; and conquered all that land. And he went to Rome and settled there, and his body lies in St Mary's church in the English quarter.

[45.5] 884. And this same year passed away the good Pope Marinus who freed the English Quarter at the request of Alfred, King of Wessex.

[45.6] 886-7. Here the raiding party went up through the bridge at Paris, and then up along the Seine as far as the Marne as far as Chezy and then settled there and on the Yonne, two winters in those two places ... And in the same year in which the raiding party went out over the bridge at Paris, Ealdorman Aethelhelm took the alms of the West Saxons and of King Alfred to Rome.

[45.8] 888. [Text A] Here Ealdorman Beocca took the alms of the West Saxons and of King Alfred to Rome. And Queen Æthelswith, who was King Alfred's sister, passed away, and her body lies at Pavia. [Text E] Here Ealderman Beocca and Queen Æthelswith, who was King Alfred's sister, took the alms of the West Saxons and of King Alfred to Rome; and she passed away, and her body lies at Pavia.

[45.9] 889. In this year there was none who travelled to Rome except for two runners King Alfred sent with letters.

[45.10] 890. Here Abbot Beornhelm took the alms of the West Saxons and of King Alfred to Rome. ... And in the same year [**889**] the raiding-army went from the Seine to St Lo [dep. Manche] which is between the Bretons and the Franks; and [**890**] the Bretons fought against them and had the victory, and drove them out into a river and drowned many.

[45.11] 962. In this same year, Æthelmod the mass-priest went to Rome, and there passed away on 15 August.

[45.12] 1050. (Text E) And in this same year was the great Synod in Rome, and King Edward sent there Bishop Hereman and Bishop Aldred, and they came there on Easter Eve. And the Pope had a synod again in Vercelli; and Bishop Ulf came to that, and if he had not given very costly gifts they were well near to breaking his staff because he did not know how to do his duties as well as he should.

[45.13] 1051. (Text E) Here in this year in Spring King Edward set Robert in London, as Archbishop for Canterbury; and in the same spring he went to Rome for his pallium ... and the king gave Sparrowhawk, abbot of Abingdon, that bishopric in London ... Then the Archbishop came back from Rome one day before the eve of the Feast of St Peter, and occupied his bishop's seat at Christ Church on the feast of St Peter [29 June].

[45.14] 1052. (Text E) When Archbishop Robert and the French men learnt [*of the settlement with the Godwins*] they seized their horses, and some went west to Pentecost's castle, some north to Robert's castle, and Archbishop Robert and Bishop Ulf and their companions turned out at east gate [*of London*] and killed and otherwise injured many young men, and made their way to Eadulf's Ness [*the Naze*], and there he [*Robert*] got on an unsteady ship and travelled right on across the sea, and abandoned his pallium and all Christendom here in the land, just as God wanted it, because he had earlier obtained the honour just as God did not want it.

[45.15] *Archbishop Robert's flight and death according to William on Malmesbury.*
From Mynors et al, *Gesta Regum Anglorum. Vol 1.*
Bk II, Ch. 199. The archbishop, however, not waiting for force to be exerted, had fled the country while terms of peace were being put together. He made for Rome and appealed to the Apostolic See in his defence. Returning by way of Jumièges, he died and was buried there in St Mary's Church, the noble and sumptuous building which he himself had constructed.

[46] EXTRACTS FROM THE LETTERS OF LUPUS OF FERRIÈRES

Translated by Graydon W. Regenos, *The letters of Lupus of Ferrières.*
[46.1] Letter 5, p. 15. To (faithful father) Einhard. *c.* 836.
Now I have been obliged to postpone slightly the date of my departure for home and a visit to you in the meantime. The reason for this is because the venerable Marcward [*Abbot of Prum 829-853*], whose duty it is to arrange for my return, was being sent on a mission to Italy and had summoned me first to a friendly conference with him ... But the illustrious abbot Hrabanus, returning a little later from the palace could not be certain whether he could be here at that time because of a mission to which he had been appointed. He therefore urged me to delay my return until the fifth day of June because the feast of St. Boniface would not permit his absence at that time unless an Imperial command of some importance should by chance call him away. Accordingly, when Marcward returned he sent someone to ask me when I preferred to leave, and I told him to have the horses brought here for that purpose on the fourth of June so that, Christ being willing, I might be able to set out on the sixth ... Consequently I do not dare to give you a definite date for my arrival, but I do assure you that if God is willing I shall by all means arrive during the week beginning June the fifth.

[46.2] Letter 73, p. 84. To (Bishop) Pardulus.

In accordance with your decision I have sent a messenger to bring back from you a letter covering what you decided concerning my recent letter and those matters which you have thought it necessary for me to know. I therefore ask that you not send him back with empty hands or too slowly.

I hope you are well and happy.

[46.3] Letter 75, p. 85. To Bishop Reginfrid.

On the point of our departure for Rome we learn that we shall pass not far from your city, where we hope to experience in reality your acts of kindness which we anticipate in thought, and particularly in respect to Italian money which we lack completely and which, as we have learned from all those we have asked, is the only currency that will be of use to us there. You will also, if God is willing, give us an opportunity to see you, so as to crown with due graciousness your kind act of service. I am not able, of course, to give you a definite date for our arrival. I suspect, however, that it will be in late summer or early autumn.

[46.4] Letter 76, p. 85. To the venerable V (*unidentified*).

An unexpected yet pleasant opportunity to see you has presented itself to me, for I have learned that a road is open all the way to Rome, whither I am bound, from the city which is under your care and protection. Lay aside, then, all other matters and let us enjoy a real friendly conversation and talk about our present needs and future security. I consider it superfluous, however, to ask your assistance in those things which necessity demands, for I must not underestimate your wisdom but trust implicitly your generosity ... I shall certainly be passing through your city, I imagine, the last of summer or at least the first of autumn.

[46.5] Letter 77, p. 86. To his very dear and beloved father Marcward.

I am setting out to Rome to pray and to take care of certain ecclesiastical matters, which, upon my return, God willing, I shall explain to you dear Father. And since in the accomplishment of my mission I shall need the acquaintance of the Pope [Leo IV], not easily obtainable without the medium of gifts, I fly to you as into the arms of a father, nay a mother, begging that you will be willing to help me in this matter just as you have never failed me before in time of need. Please send me, with these two couriers, if it is at all possible, two blue robes and two linen garments which in German are called *glitza*, of which, I understand, he is very fond. If you find it difficult to send all of these, a mere half will by no means seem little to us. Indeed we are so imbued with secular learning that we ask for more in the hope of getting less. And that you not suspect that we have exhausted our mental resources, we shall consider ourselves well provided, if you will make easier our journey by giving us a horse, a trotter or some other sturdy steed. I shall, of course, bear no hard feelings if I obtain nothing at all, if, after this letter has been shared with our common son, Eigil, you shall both refrain from laughing.

[46.6] Letter 99, p. 118.

To the most venerable bishops of Italy and Gaul and to other esteemed members of the Christian faith, Lupus, abbot of the monastery which is called Bethlehem or Ferrières, situated in the diocese of the city of Sens over which the very reverend Guenilo presides, extends best wishes both for the present and the future.

[*Few people follow the true Godly path*]. I am therefore informing you, Holy Fathers, that two priests, whose names are Aldulf and Acaric, having received my permission and that of the aforementioned bishop, have decided to set out from our monastery for Rome in order to pray and to satisfy their desires. Therefore, I beg that you will kindly assist them both on their way there and back, for they have not been able to take along enough provisions for so long a journey, and we believe that you will share in their reward if they find that you are working with them for the glory of God.

[46.7] Letter 101, p. 120. *Lupus sends greetings in the Lord to his dear friend Reg.*

We are certainly eager, as we should be, to have you come, which your letter has already specifically promised, but we urge you to exercise the greatest caution and choose a road that is safe, especially because revolution has broken out in the country of our king Charles, Plundering is rife, and nothing happens with greater certainty and frequency than wholesale pillaging ... You must therefore seek a cortege large and strong enough to keep off robber gangs or, if it becomes necessary, to drive them out.

Letter 100, p. 119 is addressed to the Pope [Benedict III] in similar terms.

[46.9] Letter 108, p. 126, *to Bishop Hincmar*.

I have been afraid to send you Bede's *Collectanea* on the apostle taken from the works of Augustine, chiefly because the book is so large that it cannot be concealed on one's person nor very easily contained in a bag. And even if one or the other were possible, one would have to fear an attack of robbers who would certainly be attracted by the beauties of the book; and it would therefore probably be lost to both you and me. I intend, therefore, if God wills, to put it safely into your hands myself as soon as we are permitted to meet somewhere in safety.

As for the pine nuts, I have had as many sent to you as the courier could carry, that is to say, ten. Let your rescript, of which

I have been deprived by secretarial delay, as you have written, be received by this courier of mine who has been sent for this purpose and at your suggestion, so that I may be instructed and delighted by reading it.

[46.10] Letter 121, p. 138. *Lupus to his close friend Bishop Odo.*
Best wishes. Having been greatly aided by your many acts of kindness, I now turn to you fully confident that I shall enjoy those further benefits which you have announced through my couriers that you will provide. But, since you have not sent me a horse, and I do not have a good taken me under your care by your own free will and without charge, will you very kindly see that I shall not be shaken to pieces by a hard-riding horse. I have no doubt that you will provide, just as you have kindly indicated, a place in your vicinity where we can pitch our tents and find suitable pasturage for our horses along with yours. Our courier will fill the poor man's place at your monastery until our arrival, which I think will be on June l, God willing, and if he is given permission, he will keep the scraps from being wasted, and will also dry the cups, so that they will not be tarnished by the moisture.

[46.11] Letter 123, p. 139.
To his dear friend Vulfad, Lupus extends all good wishes. The report has spread that the king's plan of arrival has been changed. Will you therefore explain to me by a personal letter why he has made this change, when he will finally come, and where he will be staying in the meantime, so that with God's help I can then decide what I must do. I make this request because messages relayed by couriers are not reliable for they are often noticeably marred by falsehoods.

[46.12] Letter 128, p. 142. *This is an open letter, issued by the bishop of Sens, at Lupus' request.*
To all those who are faithful to Almighty God, Guenilo, metropolitan bishop of Sens extends greetings.
A certain monk of our diocese by the name of Dolivald, a member of the monastery which is called Ferrières, has undertaken, (for he is very religious), a difficult pilgrimage … We commend him to your loving care, requesting that you receive him for the love of God, entertain him, and send him away, both on his way there and on his return, just as a servant of God.

[46.13] No 129, p 143. *This is an accompanying letter, written by Lupus himself to 'his very reverent lords and all Christians'*
A monk of ours whose name is Donivald, a man of high integrity and of commendable devotion, inspired, as we fully believe, by the spirit of God, is setting out to Rome with the blessing of our venerable bishop Guenilo and ourselves that he may pray to God and the holy apostles, Peter and Paul, in his own behalf and ours. … We commend him to Your Holiness, asking that you will not hesitate to bestow upon him whatever is due to all good men in time of need. … We therefore beg that you will kindly entertain him, both going and returning …

[46.14] Letter 130, p. 143, unaddressed.
Since two of our priests, whose names are Ardegarius and Baldric, seem to me to be striving for this goal [righteousness], I have sent to your Reverence one of them, accompanied by a soldier for protection on the way (for the other has been unavoidably detained) so that you might learn from him the desire of them both …

[47] KING ALFRED'S GEOGRAPHY
[47.1] ALFRED'S TRANSLATION OF BOETHIUS' CONSOLATIONS OF PHILOSOPHY (Sedgefield's 1899 edition).
Alfred's interpolations are in italics.
pp. 42-3. But he that is wise and earnest in his quest of good report soon perceiveth how small a thing it (power) is, how fleeting, how frail, and how void of all good. If then thou wilt keenly consider and look into the compass of the whole earth from east to west, and from north to south, as thou mayest read in the book called Astralogium, thou wilt perceive that compared with Heaven all this earth is but as a tiny dot *on a wide board, or as a boss on a shield* according to the judgement of the learned. Dost thou not remember what thou didst read in the works of Ptolemy *who in one of his books has set out the measurements of all this earth?* There thou mayest see that all mankind and beasts take up not nearly one fourth of that part that can be travelled through, for *what with heat and what with cold it is not fit for them to dwell in, and the greater part is taken up by the ocean.* Now subtract from the fourth part, all the tract covered by the sea, and all its encroachments in the form of inlets, and the part taken up by fens, and moors, and all the deserts in any land, and thou wilt perceive that there is left for man to dwell in the merest little plot of ground as it were.

p. 44. Well in one of his (Cicero's) books he mentions that the fame of Rome had not yet crossed the mountains called Caucasus, *nor had the Scythians, who dwell on the other side of those mountains, even heard the name of that city or people.* It had come first to the Parthians, and even to them it was still very new.

p. 73. Though he rule the earth from east to west *that is* from India to *the south east of the earth, even to the island we call* Thule *that is to the north west of this earth, where in summer there is no night, and in winter no day,* yet hath he none the more power if he have no power over his own thoughts, and be not on his guard against those vices we have before spoken of.

[47.2] KING ALFRED'S TRANSLATION OF OROSIUS
From J. Bosworth, *King Alfred's Anglo-Saxon version of ... Orosius* (1858).

Europe begins, as I said before, at the river Don, which runs front the north part of the Rhipean mountains, which are near the ocean, called Sarmatian. The river Don runs thence right south, on the west side of Alexander's altars to the nation of the Roxolani. It forms the fen which is called Maeotis, [Sea of Azov]; and then runs forth, with a great flood, near the city called Theodosia [Kaffa], flowing eastward into the Black Sea and then, in a long strait, south easterly, where the Greek city Constantinople lies, and thence out into the Mediterranean Sea. – The south-west boundary of Europe is the ocean, on the west of Spain, and chiefly at the island Cadiz, where the Mediterranean Sea shoots up from the ocean; where also, the pillars of Hercules stand. *On the west end of the same Mediterranean Sea is Scotland [Ireland].* *

*Bosworth noted that the last sentence was an interpolation by Alfred and followed the common error of his time in placing Ireland much too far to the west.

[48] ASSER'S LIFE OF KING ALFRED
[43.3] From Alfred P. Smyth, *The Medieval Life of Alfred the Great,*

[48.1] Ch. 8. In the same year King Æthelwulf sent his son – the previously mentioned Alfred – honourably to Rome, in the company of a great number of nobles and non-nobles. At that time the lord, Pope Leo, was then ruling the apostolic see. He anointed the same child Alfred fully ordaining him as king, and he confirmed him, receiving him as an adopted son.

[48.2] Ch. 35. *About the Viking army, at Reading.* On the third day after their arrival there, [two] of their counts, with a great part of the (army), rode out to plunder, while the others constructed a defensive earthwork between the two rivers Thames and Kennet, on the right hand [southern] side of the same royal estate.

[48.3] Ch. 79
In those times, I also was summoned by the king and I came to the Saxon land from the western and furthest parts of Britain. When I had resolved to come to him through great expanses of territory, I reached the region of the Right-Hand [southern] Saxons which is called Sussex in the Saxon language, accompanied by guides of that race. And there I first saw the king on the royal estate which is called Dean. When I had been kindly received by him, and during the various exchanges of our opinions, he asked me most firmly to devote myself to his service and to become his *familiaris*, and to relinquish for his sake, all that I had in the left-hand [northern] part and to the west of the Severn, and he promised also to give me back a greater recompense.

[48.4] Ch. 80. *Asser used the same idiom in describing his own native Wales, observing that*
... at that time and for a long time before, all the regions of the right-hand [southern] part of Britain belonged to King Alfred and they belong to him still.

[49] EXTRACTS FROM WILLIAM OF MALMESBURY
Gesta Regum Anglorum, trans. Mynors et al., (1998), Vol. 1. Courtesy of Oxford University Press.
[49.1] Bk. II, Ch. 137, p. 223 He (Alfred) ... wished to put out my [Athelstan's] eyes in the city of Winchester; but on the discovery of their infernal contrivances, he was sent to the church of Rome to defend himself on oath before Pope John. This he did at the altar of St Peter; but at the very instant he had sworn, he fell down before it, and was carried by his servants to the English school, where he died the third night after.

[49.2] Bk. II, Ch. 184, p.331. *[Concerning Æthelnoth]* on his way home, at Pavia, he bought for one hundred talents of silver and a talent of gold an arm of St Augustine, doctor of the Church, and dispatched it to Coventry.

[50] LAND SOLD FOR THE JOURNEY
These details emerge from a later re-grant of the land involved. Birch 537; Finberg *West Midlands, no. 270.*
c. 912. (Athelred) gave this charter to Cuthulf his thegn for that land in Marclive, that is ten *manentes* which land his kinsman Cered acquired from Burgred king of Mercia for 10,000 *siclis*. Then at his death he gave possession to his wife

Werthryth. Then when the aforesaid wife wanted to go to Rome, Cuthulf acquired it from her with a suitable amount of money, in the presence of the Bishop and the nobles of the Hwicce …

[51] EXTRACTS FROM FLODOARD
Annales de Flodoard, P H Lauer (ed.) (Paris 1905).
[51.1] 921. p. 5. Numerous English on the way to Rome were knocked down with stones by the Saracens in the Alpine passes.

[51.2] 923. p. 19. A great number of the English who were travelling to the threshold of St Peter for the sake of prayer were killed by the Saracens in the Alps.

[51.3] 929. pp. 44-45. 929 The Saracens having closed the Alpine roads, by which many people wanted to travel to Rome, they were stopped and had to turn back.

[51.4] 933. p. 57. Hugh, king of Italy, moved to Rome; and the Saracens occupied the region of the Alps and raided the surrounding places.

[51.5] 939. p. 74. A diverse group of men, who were going to Rome, were infiltrated and broken up by the Saracens.

[51.6] 936. p. 65. The Saracens went raiding in Germany, and when returning, killed many (*people*) heading for Rome.

[51.7] 941. p. 74. A group of [*English*] and French who were going to Rome, were turned back by the Saracens, who killed not a few of them, nor was it possible to cross the Alps because of the Saracens who occupied the town attached to the monastery of St. Maurice.

[51.8] 951. p. 132. The Saracens occupying the Alpine regions took tribute from those people travelling to Rome, before allowing them to cross.

Lauer printed several appendices, from which the following are taken
[51.9] *De Introductione Odalrici lv cxxxii. Aquensis Episcopi Remis et Redactione Sub Custodia Karoli Regis.*
p.185. At much the same time, Odalricus, Bishop of Aquitaine, who had fled from his See because of Saracen pressure, was received as Bishop of Rheims by Count Heribert.

[51.10] Extract from the Chronicle of Hugh of Flavigny. Bk. I
917. p. 193. Rudolph was made king, and in the twenty-first year of his reign he was killed by Hungarians (Ungris), that is, Saracens, and Ebbo became ruler (*dux*) of the castle of Dol.
929. p. 199. The Alpine routes were then occupied by the Saracens, by whom many people wishing to go on their way to Rome were stopped and turned back.

Lauer observed that Flodoard himself went to Rome 936x939 for an unknown reason.

[52] DE RARIS FABULIS
Translated by Jane Jordan, from W. H. Stevenson, *Early Scholastic Colloquies.*
[52.1] THE GLOSSES
7. An axe; a bill-hook; a sickle; a wagon-body; a two-edged axe (an adze); a spade; a rasp; stone cutting tools; an awl / auger (a gimlet); a gimlet; a claw (ie an augur / nail); a pick-axe; a piece of metal; an anvil; a mallet; a hammer; a rasor (rasorium) or a mattock (rastrum); sickle; an iron axe; a coulter; a ploughshare; a plough; a harrow; a yoke; a plough beam; a plough handle; iron bands?; a goad; a knife; a razor; tongs; a grid iron; a frying pan; a needle; a cooking pot; a whetstone; a comb; a spur; a wash bowl; a haft and a haft; a spear.

[52.2] THE TRAVEL SECTION
The nature of this jumbled compilation has been considered above. The division of the text into its constituent elements is necessarily subjective; some sections, like the second half of paragraph 24, are not relevant to this study, and have been omitted. Others might belong to a domestic section, but have been included since they illustrate travel and domestic life on the road. I have not rearranged the order, although the context suggests that paragraph 16 should be at the end. Although the value for my purpose is the light that it throws on travel, I have retained the repetitions and alternative wordings that give it value as a grammatical exercise.

5. Where is the abbot of this foundation (or the master of this place)?

He has travelled to a feast, (or a banquet, or a meal, or a dinner), which has been prepared for him in the house of one of the elders of that place.

How many have travelled with him?

That is not difficult; the whole community of the monastery, the elders, the priests and the presbyters and the smallest boys together with all the dependants with the exception of one cook (or baker) together with the doorman and except the herdsmen who look after the flocks of sheep, goats, pigs and horses and all the cattle.

Rejoice now at our arrival; prepare a meal for us to eat and put it on the table and place it before us, and fill the tables with all kinds of dishes, so they may be full in front of us.

What kind of food do you want? Just say the names of what pleases you.

It's not difficult; give us wheaten bread and barley bread, darnel, rye, spelt, millet bread, butter, bacon fat (or lard), and milk and *colomaticus* (?curds), and also onions, whey, meat sausage, froth, leaven (rennet), milk food, cheese, posset, the beestings, soup.

Listen, cellarer! Give us a drink of beer (that is ale), wine, spirit, mead, honey wine or honey drink.

9. Listen, master! give me a sip from the drink in your hand!

Listen, baker (or cook)! Give me food from your kitchen (or from your storeroom)!

Listen, dearest brother! Come next to me and sit quietly!

14. Most distinguished master, listen to us.

I shall listen; say what you need.

Our (or my) need is great, because I am a pilgrim in this province (or in this country) or in this region or in this island.

The master says, 'Where were you before?'

I was previously in Ireland (or in Britain, or else I was nurtured (or brought up) in Frankia/France, and I left (or deserted or abandoned) all my belongings and my family and my assistants, and everything I had, both my father and mother, grandfather and grandmother, my brothers, sisters and my wife, my daughter, my sons and my aunts and all my friends and all my, (or our), kin, and I have become a wretch in this country (or region).

15. Listen now, priests, give us alms for the good of your souls! Give us food, drink, clothing and footwear! And then show us the right way, which leads to another city, (or another town, or to the holy church of St Peter). You, however, after you have shown us the way, return in peace to your own home!

And I beseech you, most beloved brothers, because I ask one thing of you, if you reach the foundation of St Peter, that is Rome, in good health, that you chant your prayer in my memory, and I will do likewise.

16. And they arrived at the church of St Peter. And the leader said 'Master, priest! Open the church in front of me, as I want to pray there'.

And the priest said 'Come, and I shall open the church for you, because it is easy to open it as there is no bar across the door'.

And the leader said to the priest 'Let us make an arrangement, you and I, regarding food and drink'.

What do you want from me?

Give me food, bread and meat, and soup ie broth, if you wish, and I shall give you coins, that is silver and gold and bronze and everything that you require. And the priest said 'God will repay it for you, and this is agreeable to me. And for this reason I shall give you cups ie a drink, ie wine, spirit, water-mead, and oil and milk'.

And the leader said to the priest 'Give me your blessing'.

May God the Father bless you, who has blessed everything.

19. Listen, boy, get up and make and prepare, that is, a bath (or a wash-place) for us. And take an axe, to cut (or chop) wood with. Light a fire (or hearth) for us and make it quickly, because I am worn out (or tired) from the effort of the journey (or from the very long and very dirty route of the walk) and marshes, and dung abound on it, and the journey is very difficult and hard except for one thing, whoever has reached the house of St Peter and lives righteously shall never die. What is it for him to live righteously? It is to pray unceasingly and without a lot of talking, and to give alms. And let each man know, who follows this way, that it is of no benefit at all for him to go there and yet to live badly, but it is as in the Gospel, like a dog returning to his own vomit.

20. Now is the time for refreshment. Get up, distributor, and distribute provisions, that is, food (or rations).

And the distributor says: 'Yes, I shall distribute them, if God so wills, so that no one shall be without them ie without them, that is without a part, but so that each person shall have his portion (or share), that is, part.

Let the waiter get up and serve us some cups, cup, that is drink (or goblet).

I shall do it, if God so wills.

22. And the leader says to his overseer, 'Collect up the bits so that nothing is lost through carelessness; you must keep all the utensils, which have been assigned to you by the servers. Let the young men get up, let them prepare the beds, let them soften the straw and let them put woolly blankets (or bedding) on the beds. For now it is time to sleep'.

23. Get up, wake up, and pray to the Lord God of Heaven, because He himself is our Lord God. Get up, friends, and awaken from your usual sleep! Fasten your belts and let us go out on the road in the morning. For the journey is long and the day is short. Let one of you ask which road we should take.
And someone says 'I am experienced; follow me, as I know the short way. It is not necessary to ask anyone. This is your way; however, ask in case you find a shorter or straighter way.
'Brother! If you are experienced, show us the way, which we should follow'.
And the expert says 'In which area, then, do you want to go?'
We want to go to the king's palace (or to the city or to the foundation of St Martin or the road that leads to Rome).
And the expert says 'Go through this area and take the right road (or the left); it doesn't lead you astray, but will take you as far as the town in peace.
Have you heard if there are any criminals (or robbers) on our road, along which we will go.
And the expert said: 'There aren't any'.
And they proceeded to the foundation in peace.

24. And the master of that 'foundation' says; 'friend, your arrival is welcome!'
Peace to you friend.
And to you likewise (or long may you live).
When did you reach that province (or country or this ancestral land or this region)? What stories have you heard, that we do not know (or what misfortunes do you know about, which are told by those who have heard them related?
And the man said 'We know there will be nothing bad, nor that affects us; we haven't heard any stories today'.

27. It's time for us to go from this place, in which we have been, and visit neighbouring houses, where we have received, or requested, food and clothing. Let us go, friend, and visit neighbouring places to ask for a meal and a rest (or hospitality): look diligently for food for us, knock up the owners.
Boys, have you found any provisions for us?
Then they say 'Yes (or of course), we have found some'.
Then the priest says 'May this community prosper, whom you have gone out to, because it has given us all kinds of good things sufficiently and kindly and generously (that is food and all sorts of help). May the churchmen, that is clerics, the churchman, that is cleric, of this foundation (or monastery or place) prosper so that they may bless us. Servants be obedient and go quickly to your work and do that, that is, it, carefully (or diligently).

[53] DE RARIS FABULIS RETRACTATA
I have reproduced only passages which either do not appear in Fabulis itself or are substantially different from the equivalent in that work
11. Most distinguished Principal, listen to us.
What do you need?
Our need is great because we are pilgrims in this region. We were earlier in Ireland and Britain and France and we were brought up (there) and left all our property and, O Principal, we have no father or mother and brothers and sisters and we have abandoned all our friends and all our kin and now we are made wretched in this land.

12. Listen now, priests, give us alms for the good of your souls and give us bread and drink and clothing and footwear. And afterwards show us the right way which leads to another town or estate or even to the Holy Church of St. Peter.

13. Lord Priest, open the door of the church in front of me because I wish to pray there.
Let me open it for you brother, and let us go in to pray together, you and I. What do you wish to give to me?
I will give you silver and clothing in exchange for wine and bread and olive oil and milk. Give me a blessing.
May God bless you who has blessed all things.

17. It is time tomorrow to go from this place in which we are, and let us leave the neighbouring places or habitations, in which we do not have food and clothing and let us visit other places so that we can ask for rest and shelter in them. Seek food and carefully press the owners so that we have nourishment lest we go short on our road. Have you found food brothers? We have certainly found some.

20. Where have these brothers come from and where is their place of origin?

From Britain or Ireland or Frankia we are or have come.

In what place in particular were you and in what region were you brought up? Or in what Church have you been taught? What is the name of your master or teacher or your abbot?

Our region is called Britain or Ireland or England.

Or is your place called .N.?

The church is thus named .N. Our teacher is this called .N. The Principal is truly thus named .N., and our king thus .N.

For what reason have you come here?

For the cause of pilgrimage and not poverty or penury but we have freely left country and parents for the love of God.

21. By what name are you called?

I am called by such a name .N.

22. O master! Tell the bishop of this city or the abbot of this monastery all that we need. We are visitors and pilgrims in these regions. We shall beg from him lodgings and provisions by which our bodies may be refreshed. We have almost run out of food and clothing and footwear. And we desire to greet him face to face.

I will greet him and I wish to tell him about you. Come now and greet the bishop or the abbot or our elders.

We shall go in the name of the Lord. Bless us, Lord.

May God bless you with a good day and may God keep well he who has led you.

23. Whence have you come?

We have come from western parts.

In what part do you wish to hasten or proceed?

We wish to go to Rome and to visit the relics of St Peter the Apostle and St. Paul if God wills and thus we wish for the strength to travel perpetually in exile and to live there to the day of our death.

May Christ, the son of God, likewise help you in this firmness.

Master, give us charity and care according to your mercy and through almighty God, because without doubt we mean to rest with you in your care until we have recovered our health and our strength. Then we ought to have provisions for the journey if it pleases you, because we need this lest we suffer scarcity, that is want, and we ask for an experienced leader of places who can lead us beyond the bounds of this region and for a sign carved and written with your name (*sigillum cum tuo nomine sculptum et scriptum*) that we may be helped and refreshed by all in your name.

You ought to have my seal (*sigillum*) with a letter and I do not want to deny you. But now go to the lodgings in peace and the peace of Christ be with you always and follow the attendant because I have given orders to him that he should minister to you with good will.

[54] CHRONICLE OF SAN JUAN DE LA PEÑA

Trans. Lyn H. Nelson, *Chronicle of San Juan de la Peña,* (Philadelphia 1991), ch. 12, p. 12.

[Ninth Century] Confiding in the grace of Omnipotent God, he crossed the snow covered mountains with men from Cantabria and others of his realms. Since his men were accustomed to being constantly out of doors, they were slowed neither by heat nor cold. Arriving at dawn [at Pamplona] and committing himself to God, he attacked the Saracens so fiercely that they were completely defeated.

[55] A PARALLEL LANGUAGE PHRASE BOOK
Extract from Vatican M/S 566

15. Where are you going to stay this night, companion?

16. To the Count's house.

17. Where have you come from, brother?

18 From the house of my Lord.

19. From the house of my Superior.

20. From what country (have you come)?

21. I have been in Frankia.

71. I want to drink.

72. Have you food for the horses?

73. I have.

75. Do you want to drink good wine?

76. In faith, I would like (to do) that.

[56] ON THE DEATH OF ARCHBISHOP ÆLFSIGE

The Archbishop died of cold in the Alps on his way to Rome, in 959.

[56.1] From *Chronicon ex chronicis by John of Worcester*, translated by Darlington & McGurk, (1995), courtesy of Oxford University Press.

p. 409. Ælfsige, archbishop of Canterbury, while he was making his way to Rome to receive the pallium, was trapped in the Alps by ice and snow and died.

[56.2] From Stubbs, *Memorials, Vita Sancti Dunstani, auctore Osberno*, p. 107.

But when he set out for Rome, to receive the pallium from the apostolic see, he perished wretchedly, having been seized in the Alps by severe cold, a worthy repayment to him by God's revenge, so that he who cooled in his heart away from love of heavenly things perished in his body through the harshness of cold.

[56.3] From *William of Malmesbury, Gesta Pontificum Anglorum*. Translation by Dr Alex Rumble. In a dream, Ælfsige was warned of his imminent death by the ghost of Archbishop Oda.

Ch. 17. He who thought he was mocked by a flying phantom nevertheless journeyed through the Alps towards Rome to receive the pallium. Chilled there by the snowy cold, he could think of no other remedy than to immerse his feet, by which he had dishonoured the tomb of the saint, in the internal organs of disembowelled but still breathing horses. But not being warmed from the cold in this way, his spirit fleeing, he directed himself towards death.

[57] EXETER STATUTES

The translation is taken from *EHD*, no. 137.

p. 605. … and at a pilgrimage south, each man (is to contribute) fivepence.

[58] DUNSTAN'S JOURNEY 960

John of Worcester, translated by Darlington & McGurk.

p. 415. St Dunstan set out for the city of Romulus in the third indiction, received the pallium from Pope John, and so returned by peaceful stages to his own country.

[59] SIGERIC'S JOURNEY 990

[59.1] Stubbs, *Memorials of St Dunstan*, no. xxii, p. 388.

In a letter to Sigeric, Odbert, Abbot of St Bertins reminded the Archbishop that Æthelgar had called there before:

We wish to hear about and remember your father and predecessor Bishop Æthelgar, whose gratitude and paternal affection we enjoyed, and of the remainder of your community, so that the congregation of the French house of St Bertin might remember it with special affection.

[59.2] The itinerary of Archbishop Sigeric of Canterbury, *c.* 990.

Stubbs, *Memorials of St Dunstan, no. XXIV, pp. 391-95.*

The arrival of our archbishop Sigeric at Rome: first to the shrine (*ad limitem*) of the blessed apostle Peter; then to Santa Maria, the *scola* of the English [now Santo Spirito in Sassia]; to St Laurence *in Craticula* [San Lorenzo *in Piscibus*, or San Lorenzino]; to San Valentino *in ponte Molui* [now disappeared]; to Sant' Agnese; to San Lorenzo fuori le Mura; to San Sebastiano; to Sant' Anastasio [Sancti Vincenzo and Anastasio]; to St Paul [San Paolo alle Tre Fontane]; to San Bonifazio [Santi Bonifazio e Alessio]; to Santa Sabina; to Santa Maria *scola Graeca* [Santa Maria in Cosmedin]; to Santa Cecilia; to San Crisogono; to Santa Maria Trastevere; to San Pancrazio.

Then they returned home. In the morning to Santa Maria Rotonda [the Pantheon]; to Sant Apostoli; to St John Lateran. Then we ate with the lord pope John; then to Jerusalem [Santa Croce in Gerusalemme]; to Santa Maria Maggiore; to San Pietro in Vincoli; to San Lorenzo [in Panisperna] where his body lies.

These are the overnight stops [*submansiones*] from Rome to the sea.

1. The city of Rome. 2. San Giovanni in Nono. 3. Baccano. 4. Sutri 5. Forcassi. 6. 'Sancte Valentine' [near Viterbo]. 7. Montefiascone [Sce Flaviane]. 8. Bolsena [Sce Cristina]. 9. Acquapendente. 10. 'Sancte Peitr in Pail' [disappeared]. 11. Le Briccole [Abricola]. 12. San Quirico in Val d'Orcia. 13. Torrenieri [Turreiner]. 14. Ponte d' Arbia. 15. Siena [Seocine]. 16. Borgo Nuovo. 17. Gracciano d' Elsa [Aelse]. 18. S. Martino Fosci. 19. San Gimignano. 20. S. Maria a Chianni [Sce Maria Glan]. 2l. S. Pietro a Coiano [Sce Petre Currant]. 22. S. Genesio [S Dionisii]. 23. A bridging point on the Upper Arno [Arne Blanca]. 24. The river Usciana? [Aqua Nigra]. 25. Porcari [Forcri]. 26. Lucca. 27. Camaiore. 28. Luni. 29.

S. Stefano. 30. Abbazia di S. Caprasio [Aguilla]. 31. Pontremoli. 32. Montelongo [Sce Benedicte]. 33. Berceto [Sce Moderanne]. 34. Fornovo sul Taro [Philemangenur]. 35. Costa Mezzana [Metane]. 36. Borgo San Donnino [now Fidenza; 'Sce Domnine']. 37. Firenzuola [Floricum]. 38. Piacenza. 39. Corte S. Andrea. 40. S. Cristina. 41. Pavia [Pamphica]. 42. Tromello [Tremel]. 43. Vercelli. 44. Santhia [Sca Agatha]. 45. Ivrea (Everi). 46. Poley [Publei]. 47. Aosta. 48. St Rhémy. 49. Bourg-St-Pierre [Petracastel]. 50. Orsières [Lursiores]. 51. St Maurice. 52. Aigde [Burbulei]. 53. Vevey [Vivaec]. 54. Lausanne 55. Orbe 56. Yverdun [Antifern]. 57. Pontarlier [Punterlin]. 58. Nods. 59. Besancon [Bysiceon]. 60. Cussey-sur-l'Oignon [Cuscei]. 61. Seveux [Sefui]. 62. Grenant. 63. Humes [Oismai]. 64. Blessonville [Blaecuile]. 65. Bar-sur-Aube. 66. Brienne-la-Vieille [Breone]. 67. Donnement [Domaniant]. 68. Fontaine-sur-Coole [Funtaine]. 69. Chalons-sur-Marne [Chateluns]. 70. Reims. 71. Corbeny. 72. Laon [Mundothluin]. 73. Sérancourt-le-Grand [Martinweath]. 74. Doingt [Duin]. 75. Arras [Atherats]. 76. Bruay. 77. Thérouanne [Teranburh]. 78. ?? 79. Guines [Gisne]. 80. Sombre [Sumeran].

[60] A DEAD HORSE

Stubbs, *Memorials of St Dunstan*, no. xxiii, p. 390. Translation by Dr Alex Rumble. This is a difficult text. The detail may be obscure but the general meaning is clear enough.

To the lord N., extremely imbued with the beautifullest most beautiful skill in divine and elegant theorising, a fine but now, if it is allowed to be said, because of misfortune, a somewhat poor person, one who is somewhere in servitude [greeting]. Having departed from you, after I flew with sails on the high seas, [my] pack lacked support [needing] ... a species for bearing burdens. By chance I exchanged 30 *solidi* as the estimated price for the suitable horse of a certain cleric. Then, having ridden on the same to the stables [*lit.* houses of the grooms], it died having been killed before I could snatch away the daggers. I am bound by the torment of [owing] a certain debt, from which I am going to be discharged a whole pound, [which is] only half of what I had received from a cleric at Rheims. For the return of this obligation I seek relief from you, O most blessed Elder. Indeed I must pay it on the day of Pentecost. If you do not wish to help by the present bearer, I will have to come myself. The doleful Muse demands that you be healthy for ever. May he whom every faithful one loves make us live.

[61] EXTRACT FROM RICHER'S JOURNEY FROM RHEIMS TO CHARTRES, AD 991

Richer, in R Latouche (ed.), *Histoire de France* (Paris 1937) p. 225-231. Incompletely quoted in R. Lopez, *The Tenth Century*, p. 42.

Richer had met a servant of Heribrand, a cleric in Chartres, sent with an invitation to visit his master. He set off with the 'Chartrain' and a boy.

To help me, I obtained from my abbot only a beast of burden, and it was without money, a change of clothes and other necessities that I arrived at Orbais, a monastery noted for its hospitality. I received there a warm welcome from the Lord Abbot D., who at the same time was generous in his help, and the next day I left for Meaux. But getting tangled up in the winding paths of the woods, we had many frustrations. After being mistaken at a crossroads we faced a detour of six leagues. After passing Chateau-Thierry, the horse, which until then had appeared like Bucephalus, began to drag along at the speed of a nobody. The sun had left the sky and was about to set; it was beginning to rain and our vigorous Bucephalus, exhausted by its extreme efforts, collapsed between the legs of the servant who was riding it, and died in convulsions six miles from the town. Those who have experienced similar accidents and can make a comparison will understand our feelings and our worries. The servant, who had not adjusted to the difficulties of the journey, was worn out; he just lay on the ground looking as if he had died along with the horse. There was no longer a horse to carry our baggage. The rain was flooding down. The sky was a mass of black clouds. The sun, which was already setting, threatened to plunge us into darkness.

Amongst all these anxieties, God did not withhold his advice from my thoughts. I left the servant there with the luggage; I told him what answers to give to any passers-by who questioned him; warned him to resist the temptation of going to sleep and accompanied only by the horseman from Chartres, I went on to Meaux. In the daylight I could just make out, with difficulty, the bridge by which I was approaching, and as I looked at it more carefully I was struck by fresh concerns. The bridge had so many large holes in it that anybody visiting the townspeople could hardly have been able to cross it during the day. The man from Chartres, who was active and quite accustomed to travel, looked all around for a ferry. Since he found none, he returned to the dangers of the bridge, and by the Grace of Heaven the horses crossed safely. Where there were gaping holes, he placed either his shield or sometimes planks lying on the ground under the horses' hooves, by crouching down and by stretching, shuttling backwards and forwards carefully, he succeeded in bringing me and across with the horses.

The night was frightful and covered the world with horrible shadows until I reached the basilica of S Farond, where the brethren prepared a meal of charity ... They welcomed me like a brother with sweet words and gave me enough to restore me. I sent the 'Chartrain' back with horses for the servant who had been left by the wayside; he had to face for a second time the perils of the bridge which he had escaped before. He crossed it with the same care, and after having gone astray, he found the servant in the second watch of the night. He finally found him by hearing him cry out. He collected him but on arriving at the town, he decided not to risk once more what he knew to be the formidable dangers of the bridge, and took refuge in a cottage with the servant and the horses. Although they had passed the day without anything to eat, they spent the night there without anything to eat either.

What a sleepless night I passed! And during the night, what torments I suffered! What worries about the others forced themselves into my mind! At last, happy day dawned; the others turned up early, dead-beat, but we gave them something to eat and fed the horses.

The rest of the journey, on borrowed horses, was uneventful.

[62] EXTRACTS FROM THE LIVES OF ST ODO OF CLUNY AND ST GERALD OF AURILLAC

F G Sitwell, *St Odo of Cluny: being the Life of St Odo of Cluny by John of Salerno and the Life of St Gerald of Aurillac by St Odo.*

Gerald's *Life* gives many examples of the ordinary things that happened along the way, the second and third of these extracts being perhaps the most human.

St ODO
[62.1] Bk II, ch. 6, p. 48
On that same journey a certain feeble old man crossed the Alps with us. He carried a sack filled with bread, and onions, and garlic, and leeks, the smell of which was more than I could stand. But the holy father, as soon as he saw him, put him on his horse, as his manner was, and took the evil-smelling sack himself. Unable to put up with the smell, I fell back from where I was walking at his side. When we had gone through the narrow pass at the top of the Alps and had begun to descend on the other side, I saw him standing a little way ahead and the poor man urging him to remount his horse. Even then he did not return the sack, but hung it on the pommel of his saddle, I passed those who were in front of me in order to come up to him more quickly, and I went full of shame. As I arrived he said to me, 'Come on, for there are still some psalms that we must recite.' When I replied that I could not stand the smell of the sack, he rebuked me saying, 'Alas, this poor man can eat that which nauseates you. You cannot even stand the smell of it. The poor man can carry what you say you cannot even look at.' It was of himself, the true poor man of Christ, that he said this. With such words he rebuked me, and so cured my sense of smell that after that I never noticed the presence of the sack.

[62.2] Bk. II, ch. 7
At this time we were sent to Italy *[ie the Lombard kingdon]* by Pope Leo on a peacemaking mission between Hugh, the King of the Lombards, and Alberic, the ruler of the city of Rome. Not without risk we came at length to Sienna and found that the city was suffering from famine. We had taken for this dangerous journey nearly thirty silver shillings, of which the greater part had already been spent. But I, remembering how it was his custom to keep nothing for his own and our use, and fearing that we and our horses would perish of hunger, if we had nothing with which to buy food, took what was left of the shillings, and slipping away without his knowing it passed through the city. When he himself came to enter it, he was accosted by beggars asking for the usual alms. Scrutinizing his whole party and seeing that I was not there, he guessed at once what I had done.

Ch. 8
On this same journey, and before our money was quite exhausted, we met one of our brethren, the priest Peter, who was coming to stay in Rome. His supplies were able to meet our needs, and we got from him enough money to complete the journey. All this happened in the months of January and February 2. Our way lay by Monte Amiata [*on the direct road from Rome to Siena*], and there were such snowstorms at the time that, although the road was known to us, we could not find it. We were so covered with snow and our limbs so frozen that we could not speak. When I noticed that Odo's aged limbs were shrivelled with the cold, I quickly made him a coat to protect and warm his vital parts. Our mission being completed, we were urged by the natives to return by the coastal road.

[Later] they met a 'poor half-naked man'. Odo took off his coat and covered the poor man, and told me to give him enough money for him to finish his journey. I stopped a moment and asked the man where he was going, knowing that there was nowhere to stay in that great solitude. But he said that he would be able to reach a shepherd's encampment [*pastorale castrum*] while it was still day.

[62.3] Bk II, ch. 17.
On one occasion when he was crossing the Rhône in a boat, accompanied by the leading men of the district, it happened that one of the horses kicked at another and struck the side of the boat in a place where there was a knot in the planking. As soon as the side of the boat was pierced, so great a torrent of water came in through the hole that the boat was quickly filled, and in this state by the manifest help of God it reached the other bank. Odo remained in it until all had disembarked,

and when last of all he had come out, the boat sank. The merit of this man is manifest, who was able by his prayers to obtain what Peter and Paul, and then our father Benedict had previously merited.

[62.4] Bk II, ch. 18.

At this same time he visited Rome on pilgrimage, and not long after, when he was on his way home, there was such a depth of snow in the Burdonian Alps* that the road became completely blocked, though at no time is the mountain without it. The region is inhabited by a race of men who are called Marrones, taking their name I suppose from the Province of Marronea. Guides hired according to custom from among these people were leading him, for without a guide no one could cross these mountains in winter. Now, the sun had not yet set, but what was left of the day was turned to darkness by a heavy fall of snow. As they were going through this horrible and dangerous place, suddenly the horse on which our father was sitting slipped sideways and they both fell together down the steep slope. Leaving go of the reins Odo raised both his hands to heaven as he fell, and immediately his arms found the branch of a tree from which he hung suspended until those in front turned back at his cries and rescued him. But the branch of the tree was no more seen, because there is no tree to be found in that place, nor does any grow there. The horse was never seen again.

* Sitwell noted that this could be in either the Alps or the Appennines.

[62.5] Bk III, ch. 4

The other [*of two brethren*] coming early one morning to the house of one of his relations immediately asked if they had anything they could give him to eat. When they replied that it was not yet the time for a meal, he burst out, 'I have been riding hard all night on a task that was given me by obedience, and have had no rest, and now do you make me fast? If you have anything, bring it to me.' When they told him that they had some fish, he was still more indignant, and full of disdain and arrogance looked around this way and that. Now there was at his feet a flock of fowls,' and in a fury he snatched up a small stick and struck the first one which came near, declaring in an angry voice, 'This shall be my fish today.' Those who were standing around asked in some confusion, 'Is it lawful for you to eat meat, Father?' 'Fowl,' he said, 'is not flesh, fowl and fish have one origin and are created equal, as our hymn' says.' At these words everyone was silent. Meanwhile the fowl which he had killed was roasted and put before him. He took a piece of it and put it in his mouth, but he could neither spit it out nor swallow it, and it deprived him of life. He received blows and buffets in scorn as a reward of his wickedness before he died.

ST GERALD
[62.6] Bk. I, Ch. 21.
Gerald was returning from Italy by the road that goes to Lyons from Turin. He had crossed the Alps … *when he entered a drought area.*

[62.7] Bk. I, Ch. 22.
On another occasion as he was going along the road a peasant was reaping chick-peas nearby. Some of his retinue who were in front, took some of it and began to eat it. When he saw this, spurring his horse, he came at full speed to the man, asking if his followers had taken the chick-pea. 'I gave it to them freely' he said. 'May God reward you!' Gerald replied.

[62.8] Bk. I, Ch. 23.
An incident of the same kind is that which occurred when his servants were preparing a meal under the shade of some cherry trees. He bought for silver from a peasant who was claiming for some branches which were hanging down loaded with ripe fruit, which the servants had broken off before he came. Perhaps someone will say that these small things are not worth relating: but I am showing the mind of this God-fearing man in small things, that indirectly it may be understood that he who does not despise little things, was not able to be brought low by great ones.

[62.9] Bk. I, Ch. 29.
When he came on one occasion to Piacenza, a certain cleric arrived who was in charge of the port [on the river crossing]. As is usual here, this man was expecting very lucrative passage money from the Roman pilgrims. He was in a foul temper and abusing others, including the Bishop of Rodez [*30 miles north of Aurillac*] but Gerald calmed him down with soft words and gifts. *As a result* he remitted whatever was owed of passage money from all of his company and filled his flasks and bottles and those of his party with wine.

[62.10] Bk. I, Ch. 31.
Again on this same journey, a certain man from the neighbourhood of Bourges had broken his hip not far from Rome. Abandoned by his companions, he remained alone with his wife. One of Gerald's soldiers, a certain Boniface by name,

and hearing of his necessity, brought him to Gerald saying: 'Look, my lord, I have found something after your heart's desire which I present to your pleasure: here is a man needing help'. The man of God joyfully took him into his protection and supplying him all his needs conducted him to Brioude. Then he gave him ten shillings more with which he might get back to his own people. This and similar facts witness to the desire of showing mercy with which he was generously fuelled by divine inspiration.

[62.11] Bk II, ch. 17. He gave generously also to the monasteries that lay on the road, and the fame of his great generosity sounded far and wide, so that monks, as well as pilgrims and the needy who were his guests, used to enquire anxiously, at the time when the pilgrims to Rome are accustomed to pass by, if and when Count Gerald was coming. Even the Marruci,* the fierce inhabitants of the Alps, thought nothing more profitable than to carry Gerald's baggage through the pass of Mont Joux.

* *In a footnote Sitwell explained that the Marruci were the Saracens, based at Fraxinetum (S Tropez), on the south coast of France, whence they had spread into the southern Alps. Compare with Flodoard's account, no. 51.*

[62.12] Bk. II, ch. 18. Once when he was making that journey [to Rome], and came to the city of Asti, a thief made off with two of his pack horses, but coming to a river he was not able to get them across before he was taken by Count Gerald's men. Having got back the pack horses, he took no action against the thief.

[62.13] Bk. II, Ch. 23. … on the other side of Sutri, next to the town, there is a rushy field called St Martin's, where the Roman pilgrims are accustomed to camp. The servants had put up the tents there, and the Count [Gerald] happened to be standing alone … *this led to the miraculous cure of a blind man, which Gerald managed to conceal.*

[63] GOODS PASSING THROUGH PAVIA, *c.* 962
Tyler, p. 151, quoting E. Oehlmann, *Die Alpenpasse im Mittelalter.* Reproduced by permission of Blackwell's.
In Tyler's summary… Amongst the goods actually mentioned are the following; arms, such as swords and lances, shields and armour; reins, spurs and horses; salt; metals, for example, lead, tin and copper; scribes' ink (*atramentum*) hawks and even apes.

[64] EDICT OF PAVIA 973
Nos 64 and 65 are taken from R. S. Lopez and I. W. Raymond, *Medieval Trade in the Mediterranean World.*
pp. 37-38. Concerning the customs houses (*clusae*) which have fallen into disrepair, let them be restored and let guards be stationed there, so that neither our men may pass without authorisation of the king nor similarly may strangers enter into our territory without the authorisation or the order of the king ... (Nobody may pass without authorisation of the king) unless the judge sends his own messenger on service useful to the king or receives (*someone coming*) on the king's affairs.

6. Concerning shipping and business by land: no one is to wander around in order to transact business, or for any reason whatsoever, without a written permit (*epistola*) of the king, or without authorisation of his judge.

[65] REGULATIONS OF THE COURT OF PAVIA, *c.* 1010-1020
pp. 56-60. … Merchants entering the kingdom [*of Italy*] were wont to pay the decima on all merchandise at the customs houses and at [*the beginning of*] the roads appertaining to the king ... All persons coming from beyond the mountains into Lombardy are obligated to pay the *decima* on horses, male and female slaves, woollen, linen and hemp cloth, tin and swords. And here at the gate they are obligated to pay the decima on all merchandise to the delegate of the treasurer. But everything that [*pilgrims*] bound for Rome to St Peter's take with them for expenses is to be passed without payment of the *decima*. No one ought to exact the *decima* from the pilgrims themselves bound for Rome or to hinder them in any way. And if anyone does so, let him be anathema.

3. As for the nation of the Angles and Saxons, they have come and were wont to come with their merchandise and wares. And [*formerly*], when they saw their trunks and sacks being emptied at the gates, they grew angry and started rows with the employees [*ministrales*] of the treasury. The (parties) were wont to hurl abusive words and in addition very often inflicted wounds upon one another. But in order to cut short such great evils and to remove danger [*of conflicts*], the king of the Angles and Saxons and the king of the Lombards agreed as follows: The nation of the Angles and Saxons is no longer to be subject to the decima. And in return for this the king of the Angles and Saxons and their nation are bound and are obligated to send to the [king's] palace in Pavia and to the king's

treasury every third year ... [*there followed a list of valuables*] ... And they are to receive a safe conduct from the master of the treasury that they may not suffer any annoyance as they come and go.

[66] ARCHBISHOP ÆLFEAH'S JOURNEY 1007
N. E. S. A. Hamilton, *William of Malmesbury, Gesta Pontificum Anglorum*, Ch. 76.
Aelfheah travelled to Rome to obtain the pallium from the Pope. While he was crossing the Alps and staying the night in a certain village he was attacked by a crowd of rustics who robbed him of all his belongings. Soon after, a fire caught hold in the houses ... The rough village people, reluctantly realising their crime, chased after Ælfheah, caught up with him just as he was leaving the village and continuing his journey. Reverently and respectfully they asked for his pardon and gave him back his belongings. *Ælfeah then put out the fire with the sign of the Cross.*

[67] ÆTHELNOTH'S JOURNEY TO ROME 1022.
From John of Worcester, translated by Darlington & McGurk.
Æthelnoth, Archbishop of Canterbury, went to Rome; Pope Benedict [VIII] received him with great honour and gave him the pallium.

[68] KING CNUT'S JOURNEY
[68.1] *William of Malmesbury, Gesta Regum*, trans. Mynors et al, Vol. I ch. 182
1027. In the fifteenth year of his reign, Cnut set off for Rome and spent some days there; then, after redeeming his sins, by distributing alms among the churches, returned to England by sea.

[68.2] *John of Worcester*, Darlington & McGurk (eds), sa. 1031.
[1031] Cnut, king of the English, the Danes, and the Norwegians, went from Denmark to Rome with great state and offered to St Peter, prince of the apostles, great gifts of gold and silver and other precious objects, and obtained from Pope John the concession that the English school should be free of all tribute and toll. On both the outward and the return journeys he gave generous alms to the poor, and at great price he abolished the many barriers along the way where tolls were extorted from pilgrims. He also swore to God before the sepulchre of the apostles to amend his life and ways, and from there he sent to England an epistle worth remembering delivered by the hand of that most prudent man Lyfing, then abbot of Tavistock but soon after, in the same year, successor to the episcopacy at Crediton of Eadnoth (who was his travelling companion), and by the hands of other ambassadors. He himself returned from Rome by the route he took out, visiting Denmark before England.

[68.3] CNUT'S PROCLAMATION OF 1020
From A.J. Robertson, *The Laws of the kings of England from Edmund to Henry I* (Cambridge 1925), p. 141, courtesy of Cambridge University Press.

3. I have taken cognisance of the written and verbal injunctions which Archbishop Lyfing brought me from Rome from the Pope, namely that I should everywhere magnify the glory of God and suppress injustice and establish perfect security through the power which God has been pleased to grant me.

[69] EXTRACTS FROM THE LETTER OF CNUT TO THE ENGLISH
From Darlington & McGurk (eds), *John of Worcester*.
Cnut, king of all England and Denmark and the Norwegians and part of the Swedes, to the metropolitan Æthelnoth and Ælfric, archbishop of York, and to all the bishops and leading men and to all the English people, both nobles and ceorls, greetings.
1. I inform you that I have recently gone to Rome, and have prayed for the redemption of my sins, and for the safety of the kingdoms whose people are subject to my rule.
2. I had vowed to God to make this journey long ago now, but I could not accomplish it earlier because of the affairs of the kingdom and other sources of obstruction.
5. Be it known to you that a great crowd of nobles was there at the very Easter celebration with the lord Pope John and the Emperor Conrad, to wit all the princes of the peoples from Mount Garganus to the nearest sea, who all both received me with honour and honoured me with precious gifts. However, I was honoured most by the emperor with various gifts and priceless presents, both in gold and silver vessels and in cloaks and extremely precious garments.
6. Therefore I spoke with the emperor himself and the lord pope and the princes who were there about the needs of all the people of my entire realm, both English and Danes, that a juster law and securer peace might be granted to them on the

road to Rome, and that they should not be straitened by so many barriers along the road, and harassed by unjust tolls; and the emperor agreed, and likewise King Robert who governs most of these same toll-gates. And all the princes confirmed by edicts that my people, both merchants and the others who travel to make their devotions, might go to Rome and return without being afflicted by barriers and toll-collectors, in firm peace and secure in a just law.

7. Again I complained in the lord pope's presence and expressed my grave displeasure that my archbishops were so greatly straitened by the vast sum of money which was required of them when they travelled to the apostolic see according to custom to receive the pallium; and it was decreed that this should not henceforth occur.

8. For everything which I requested from the lord pope and the emperor himself and King Robert and the other princes through whose lands our road to Rome lay, for the advantage of my people …

[70] ARCHBISHOP LYFING'S JOURNEY
William of Malmesbury, Gesta Pontificum Anglorum, Ch. 94.
[70.1] For a long time [Lyfing] was close to Cnut in Denmark and joined his train when he went to Rome. Even when Cnut had finished his business and the King had returned to Denmark overland, Lyfing sailed to England carrying the King's letters and to carry out his other commands.

[70.2] From Darlington & McGurk (eds), *John of Worcester.*
And he sent from [*Rome*] to England a memorable letter by a most prudent man, Lifing, who was at that time abbot of the church of Tavistock … who was his companion on the journey, and by his other messengers…

[71] NOTICES ON SEA TRAVEL
FROM THE ENCOMIUM EMMAE, *c.* 1042, A. Campbell (ed.).
[71.1] Bk II, ch. 1. Accordingly, after he had returned to his father's fleet, and replaced the sailors, he [Cnut] spread out the kingly sails to the winds and the sea, but did not take back with him all the military (*militiam*) which [he had brought].

[71.2] Bk II, ch. 3. [Thorkell] did not dare to come onshore without permission, but after casting (*eiectis*) anchor, sent messengers to ask for permission to enter the port.

[71.3] Bk. II, ch. 5. And so the force, as has been described, as soon as it had unfastened the anchors and ropes from the shore, went on board the tall ships and put to sea, and swept through the waves with such force, that you would have thought that they were flying over the water in ships like birds, for they hardly creaked, even though the sea was rough.

[71.4] Bk III, Ch. 4. Turning [*Alfred*] away from London, [*Godwin*] brought him into the town named Guildford and lodged his soldiers there in separate billets in groups of twenties, twelves and tens, leaving only a few, whose duty was to attend to him, with the young man

[71.5] Bk III, ch. 7. When [her faithful retainers] were assembled [Queen Emma] told them her private thoughts. When they started to execute the plan set out by their Lady, the ships' supplies were prepared for exile. Then, blessed with favourable winds, they crossed the sea and reach a particular port not far from the town of Bruges.

[71.6] Bk. III, ch. 9. When, therefore, they were intent on their fortunate voyage and were not only keenly ploughing through the salt foam with bows like brass, but also raising their topsails to the favourable winds – nevertheless the surface of the sea is never constant, but is always found to be unreliable and treacherous, suddenly a grey tempest of winds and clouds built up from behind, and the surface of the sea was at once whipped up by south winds from behind. And so the anchors were dropped from the bows and caught in the sands at the sea bottom, which is what is usually done in such desperate circumstances.

[71.7] Bk III, ch. 10. Thereupon, when the raging of the sea had subsided, and the storm had eased off [Horthaknutr] spread his bellying sails to the favourable winds; and so, having completed a successful voyage, he came to shore at Bruges. There, having moored his ships with anchors and poles (*anchoris rudibusque*), and having detailed sailors to look after them, he went off straightaway with selected companions to his mother's lodging.

[71.8] From *The Seafarer*, translated by Richard Hamer, *A choice of Anglo-Saxon Verse* (1970) courtesy of Faber and Faber.
I sing my own true story, tell my travels,
How I have often suffered times of hardship
In days of toil, and have experienced

120

Bitter anxiety, my troubled home
On many a ship has been the heaving waves,
Where grim night-watch has often been my lot
At the ship's prow as it beat past the cliffs.
Oppressed by cold my feet were bound by frost
In icy bonds, while worries simmered hot
About my heart, and hunger from within
Tore the sea-weary spirit.

[71.9] From Alcuins' poem in praise of the *'Bishops, Kings, and Saints of York'*, taken from the commemorative handbook to the exhibition on Alcuin in York in 2001 (M. Garrison, J.L. Nelson, D. Tweddle, *Alcuin and Charlemagne*, p. 4.)

A haven for ships coming from the furthest port of the ocean,
Whither the tired sailor speeds, makes fast his ship with its long tow-rope.
The Ouse, filled with fish, flows through [York] with its waters,
Its banks stretching past flowery fields on both sides.

[72] THE CEREMONY OF GIFT GIVING, from the *Encomium Emmae*, A. Campbell (ed.).

The passage is worth quoting, not only for Cnut's journey but as a rare description of the ceremonial attached to formal alms giving. This itself was a significant expense for the wealthy traveller.

Bk. II, chs. 20, 21. ... (*Cnut*) went to Rome through those countries (*Italy and Flanders*) and as is shown by many happenings, he demonstrated such great charitable acts on his journey that if anyone wanted to describe them all, although he might write endless numbers of volumes about them he would eventually have to admit to failure because he had not covered even the smallest ones. For I will not set out what he did in individual places, but simply so that what I say may be more believable, as an example I will just tell you what he did in the city of St Omer, and put it on record that I saw what follows with my own eyes. (Ch 21) After he had entered the monasteries, and had been most honourably received, he came forward humbly, and with total dedication prayed for the intercession of the saints in a totally reverent manner, keeping his eyes on the ground, and as it were pouring out floods of tears. When it was time for him to load the holy altars with royal offerings, as he wanted, how often did he first tearfully press kisses on the ground, how often did he punish himself by raining blows upon his breast, what sighs did he give, how often did he pray that the heavenly mercy might not be displeased with him! *(ut sibi non indignaretur superna clementia.)* At length, when he gave them the sign, his offering was presented to him by his followers. It was not a meagre one, nor such as might be put in any ordinary bag, but a man carried it, large as it was, in the generous fold of his cloak: the king placed it upon the altar with his own hand, a willing donation according to the apostolic exhortation. But why do I say on the altar, when I remember seeing him go round every corner of the monasteries, and pass no altar, however small it might be, without leaving gifts and pressing sweet kisses upon it. Next, poor men came and they were all at once given gifts in turn.

[73] MACBETH'S JOURNEY

1052 Melrose Chronicle, from Haddon & Stubbs, II, p. 152.
Macbeth, King of the Scots, broadcast silver by lavishing it on the poor in Rome.

[74] TOSTIG'S JOURNEY TO ROME

[74.1] F. Barlow, *Vita Edwardi Regis.*

1061 (p. 6). At the same time there had also come to Rome at the King's command two royal priests, Giso and Walter, men most suitably and excellently trained in their office, so that they might be ordained bishop by the Lord Pope. After their business had been successfully completed according to their desire, they all left Rome together, and on the same day fell among thieves; and, robbed and plundered, some even to nakedness, they were compelled to turn back again. On that occasion a young man named Gospatric, a kinsman of King Edward, a knight who accompanied Earl Tostig on his journey, bore himself courageously in his service to his lord. For as he rode clad in garments suited to his noble rank in the very van of the pilgrims, he was asked by the robbers, which of them was Earl Tostig. Realising immediately what was their trade, he said that he was, and signalled the earl with all possible signs to ride away. He was believed because of the luxury of his clothes and his physical appearance, which was indeed distinguished; and so he was taken away, in vain hope indeed, with the rest of the booty ... We forgot to say before that, as the Earl's stay in Rome was protracted owing to Bishop Aldred's case, he had sent his wife and her royal escort on ahead, together with most of his own men; and these had had a successful journey, in total ignorance of what had happened to the party which followed behind.

[74.2] Another account, which includes the aftermath to the robbery is given in the *Vita Wulfstani*, translated by M Swanton in *Three Lives of the last Englishmen*. The wording suggests that the bishop did not make the outward journey with Tostig but only joined him for the return: an unfortunate choice.

p. 103. … So after a lengthy dispute Aldred retraced his steps, together with Earl Tostig, who accompanied him breathing dire threats that for this there should be no further annual payments from England to the lord Pope. They got as far as Sutri when they were attacked and stripped by robbers to the sorrow and pity of those who saw them and made their way back to Rome. This affair so moved the rigidity of the Apostolic See that Aldred acquired the pallium of York, having agreed to resign the Church of Worcester provided he could find a better person in the diocese to take his place.

[74.3] *Bernard 'the Wise', writing about the lack of safety around Rome, contrasting it with the near East.*
From Thomas Wright, *Early Travels in Palestine* (London 1848), pp. 30-31.

In Jerusalem or Egypt, if I should go on a journey, and in the journey my camel or my ass which carries my baggage should die, and I should leave everything there without a guard, and go to the next town to get another, on my return I should find all my property untouched. The law of public safety is there such, that if they find in a city, or on the sea, or on the road, any man journeying by night or by day, without a letter, or some mark of a king, or prince of that land he is immediately thrown into prison, till the time he can give a good account whether he be a spy or not.

[But] in Romania many crimes are committed, and there are bad people there, banditti and thieves, and so people cannot go to Rome to visit St Peter, unless they join together in troops, and go armed.

[74.4] *Although* this passage does not relate specifically to Tostig, its description of the dangers of the journey make it appropriate here. It is adapted from J. Stevenson, *William of Malmesbury, History of the Kings, ch. 201*. William was referring to the time of Pope Gregory VI (AD 1045-6).

p. 191. Pope Gregory the Sixth, first called Gratian, was a man of great piety and austerity. He found the power of the Roman pontificate so wasted by the negligence of his predecessors, that, with the exception of a few neighbouring towns, and the offerings of the faithful, he had hardly anything to live on. The more distant cities and properties, which were the property of the church, had been seized by plunderers; the public roads and highways throughout all Italy were thronged with so many robbers that no pilgrim could pass safely unless strongly guarded. Swarms of thieves threatened every path, and the traveller could not find any way of escaping them: they robbed alike the poor and the rich; pleading and resistance were of no use. The journey to Rome was discontinued by every nation, as every man would much rather contribute his money to the churches in his own country, than feed a set of plunderers with his hard earned money. And what was the state of that city which of old was the only dwelling-place of holiness? Of a truth, assassins, a crafty and abandoned set of men, were roaming even in the Forum. Had any one by good planning eluded the people who lay in wait for him upon the road, anxious, even at the peril of destruction, to see the church of the apostle; even then, encountering these robbers, he was never able to return home without the loss either of property or of life. Even over the very bodies of the holy apostles and martyrs, even on the sacred altars, were swords unsheathed, and the offerings of pilgrims were snatched away, when barely out of their hands, and consumed in drunkenness and fornication. The papacy of Gregory was greeted by this storm of evils. At first he began to deal gently with his subjects and, as became a pontiff, rather by love than by terror: he repressed the delinquents more by words than by blows; he pleaded with the townsmen to abstain from the molestation of pilgrims, and the plunder of sacred offerings. The one, he said, was contrary to nature, and it was wrong that a man who breathed the common air, could not live in common peace; that Christians surely ought to have liberty of going wherever they wanted among Christians, since they were all of the same household, all united by the tie of the same blood, all redeemed by the same price …

[75] THE FUNDING OF WESTMINSTER ABBEY
Translated from Hefele, *Conciles IV*, p. 1056.

Edward the Confessor, King of England, had vowed to attend the Council in Rome. In the event, the situation in his kingdom did not allow him to be away for so long and he sent ambassadors to the Pope, with the plea that he be released from his vow. The Pope agreed, on condition that he gave to the poor the sum that the journey would have cost him and he founded a monastery in honour of St Peter. Such was the origin of the monastery at Westminster.

[76] ADAM OF BREMEN
Translated by J. Tschan, *Adam of Bremen, the history of the bishops of Hamburg and Bremen*

Adam reproduced the foundation charter for the see allegedly given by Charlemagne. It was in fact a forgery, probably made in the second half of the eleventh century. For our purpose, despite being a forgery, it shows an understanding of geographical area, extending the principle of 'charter boundaries' to a whole diocese. It also tells us something about the provision of accommodation for travellers in north Germany.

[76.1] p. 17. These are the bounds, firm and inviolable, by which we have ordered it circumscribed: the ocean sea, the Elbe River, the Lune, the Steinbach, the Harsehla, the Wimarch, the Sneidbach, the Oste, the Alpenshausener Muhlenbach, the

Mede, the marsh called Sigfridsmoor, the Twiste, the Twistermoor, the Ascbroch, the Wissebrocb, the Bever, the Otter, and again the Oste; from the Oste to the place at which one comes to the marsh called Chaltenbach, thence to the marsh itself, to the Wumme River; from the Wumme to the Wieste, the Faristina to the Weser River, thence on the eastern bank of this same river the highway, called the Hessewig, which divides Sturmgau from Largau, the Schipse-Graben, the Alpe, the Ane, the Chaldowa, and, again the Weser; from its western bank the highway called Folwech which divides Derve from Largau, as far as the Hunte River, thence that river and the Haarenbach, the woodland which the inhabitants of the place call the Wildloch, the Vehne, the Hochmoor, the Barkenbusch, the Endiriad marsh dividing Emsgau from Ostergau, the Dobbe-Meer, the Sandwater-See, and again the sea.

[76.2] pp. 17-18. *Note the reference to a seal ring.* And that the charter of this donation and circumscription may with the protection of God endure firm in our own and future times, we have signed it with our own hand and ordered it sealed with the impression of our ring.

[76.3] p. 33. He (Ansgar) provided also in many places hospices for the care of the poor and the reception of strangers. One, the most important indeed, he maintained at Bremen. To it he himself went daily, and he was not ashamed to minister to the infirm, of whom he is said to have healed a very great number by word or touch.

[76.4] pp. 41-42. xliv (46) .The *xenodochium* at Bremen, which Saint Ansgar had established for the support of the poor, he enlarged to an imposing extent, and he provided with all diligence for the maintenance of the needy, not only in his bishopric but wherever he was.

[76.5] p. 61. Although the holy archbishop (Ansgar) exercised, as is evident, paternal solicitude for all his churches, he is said to have had great concern for the *xenodochium* at Bremen. This he enriched with incomes so much greater than had been bestowed by his predecessors that, beside the strangers who were frequently received, twenty-four paupers were daily fed in the hospice. In its administration, Levlzo, whom the archbishop had brought with him from Italy, proved most faithful.

[76.6] p. 91. Disturbed by this twofold blow, Canute then entered into a pact with his brother Olaf, the son of Eric, who reigned in Sweden, and, assured of his aid, decided first of all to subjugate England and after that Norway. Equipped with a thousand large ships, Canute therefore crossed the British Ocean. Over this sea sailors say it is a three-day sail from Denmark to England with a southeast wind blowing. This sea, very large and exceedingly dangerous, has the Orkneys on the left and touches Frisia on the right.

[77] WILL OF ÆTHELNOTH AND GAENBURG.
A.J. Robertson, *Anglo-Saxon Charters*, pp. 5-6, no. III, reproduced by permission of Cambridge University Press.
Undated but made while Wulfred was Archbishop of Canterbury (805-32).
Æthelnoth, the reeve at Eastry and his wife Gaenburg, his wife have disposed of their inheritance before Archbishop Wulfred and Aethelhun, his priest, and, Esne, the king's thegn. Whichever of them lives the longer shall succeed to the estate and to all the property. If, however they do not have a child and Archbishop Wulfred is alive, he shall succeed to the estate and pay for it and distribute the value on behalf of their souls, as charitably and as justly as he himself can devise in his wisdom. ... This estate consists of three ploughlands at Eythorne. And if it happens that one or both of them goes south [on a pilgrimage], the bishop shall buy the estate, as shall then be agreed between them.

[78] SUNDRY WILLS from D. Whitelock, *Anglo-Saxon Wills* (1930, courtesy of Cambridge University Press).
[78.1] THE WILL OF SIFLAED
Late tenth or early eleventh century, no. xxxviii.
Here in this document it is made known how Siflaed granted her possessions when she went across the sea...[various minor bequests] And I grant to St Edmund's all that may happen to be left of my property, that is house and homestead in Marlingford, with wood and open land, meadow and live stock And if I come home, then I wish to occupy that estate for me life; and after my death the will is to take effect.

[78.2] WILL OF KETEL
1052-1066, no. xxxiv. Ketel and his step-daughter (Ælgifu) went to Rome. He is described as a thegn of Archbishop Stigand. That being so, there may be more than simple pilgrimage behind the journey.

[Various grants were made] ... and if I do not come back again, I grant to (Archbishop Stigand) as my heriot a helmet and a coat of mail and a horse with harness and a sword and spear ... and I and my step-daughter Aelgifu have made an agreement about the estate at Onehouse that whichever of us shall live the longer is to have as much land as the two of us have there. And if death befall us both on the way to Rome, the estate is to go to Bury St Edmonds for me and for Siflaed [his wife?]

[78.3] THE WILL OF ULF AND MADSELIN

1066x68, no. xxxix. The will was made between November 1066 and 1068, and is valuable for the detail of the mortgage arrangements.

This is the agreement which Ulf and his wife Madselin made with [God] and with St. Peter when they went to Jerusalem. … (two estates sold and one mortgaged) … and Morton on which the Bishop has a mortgage [*literally*, is owed] of eight marks of gold; and if they return home, the bishop is to be paid his gold; but if neither of them return, the bishop is to supply for their souls' sake as much as the land is worth above that gold.

[79] LEGENDARY LIFE OF KING HAROLD II (GODWINSON)

Translated by M. Swanton, *Three Lives of the last Englishmen.*

The story was that Harold was not killed at Hastings but survived, and travelled widely as a pilgrim. His own journeys are not described in detail but the narrative includes an illuminating story about one of his servants.

p. 11. *… This passage recounted the journey of Saebeorht, a servant of Harold, from Chester to the Holy Land and Rome, who …* because he knew that Harold had done so, he undertook the hardship of a pilgrimage embracing voluntary exile from his native soil in order to merit becoming a Holy Man and a servant of God. Whereupon with naked feet he departed from the confines of the City of Chester, leaving there the treasure which he had hoarded for so many years, taking only a portion for the crown of his Heavenly Kingdom and abandoning the rest dug up on the surface of the ground … And hoping as Harold had done to moisten with his tears the resting places of the Holy Men, to listen to strange languages which he did not understand … (eventually he) … returns to his native land as Harold had done.

[80] FEEDING THE MULTITUDE

From the *Chronicle of Evesham Abbey*, translated by D. C. Cox.

This was written by Prior Dominic, in the first quarter of the twelfth century. The context is a eulogy of Abbot Aethelwig and one may well question whether the provision for the poor is accurately stated or whether it was a monastic ideal and a 'puff' for the Abbot.

p. 14. So it was entrusted once more to the care of Abbot Aethelwig who ruled it for a long time afterwards as his own. He was the holy father of the poor, the protector of widows, orphans and wayfarers, and the comforter of all those in sorrow, and caused liberal alms to be distributed generously to everyone wherever he went. Now, in the first part of his reign, King William caused certain counties in these parts, namely Yorkshire, Cheshire, Shropshire and Derbyshire to be laid waste on account of the exiles and outlaws who were hiding everywhere in the woods and doing great harm to many people. From these areas a great multitude of old men, youths and women with their hungry little children came here, despondently fleeing from the desolation, to all of whom this man, in pity, gave succour to the best of his ability. Many died, nevertheless, consumed as they were with bitter hunger, while they were being given food aplenty. … Many wanderers came from Aquitaine, Ireland and many other counties, often came here in those days, all of whom he received and whose wants he supplied.

[81] CROSSING THE ALPS IN SNOW

This is only a short extract from a longer and dramatic passage, cited by Tyler (p. 30), taken from Holder-Eggar: Lamperti Opera, p 286ff.

1067. The mountain was precipitous and … owing to the icy cold, slippery, apparently forbidding any attempt to make a descent. Thereupon the men tried to the utmost of their ability to avoid the danger, now crawling on their hands and feet, now supporting themselves on the shoulders of those in front; now and again, as their feet slipped, falling and rolling. At last, after the greatest peril they reached level ground. The guides placed the queen and her ladies, who were in the rear of the party, upon ox-skins, and drew them down the slope. Some of the horses were lowered on various contrivances, others were dragged down with their feet tied. Some were killed in the process, many were maimed, only a few surviving the danger whole and sound.

[82] EXTRACTS FROM THE GUIDE TO THE PILGRIM ROUTE TO SANTIAGO

Gerson et al. (eds), vol.II.

[82.1] (Chapter VII), pp. 25-27. Upon leaving this country, the way of St James crosses two rivers which flow near the town of St-Jean de Sorde, one on the right and one on the left, of which one is called *gauer* [a torrent], and the other *flumen* [a river], which can not be crossed without a barque – may their boatmen be utterly damned! For, although the rivers are quite narrow, nevertheless, they are in the habit of getting one *nummus* from every person, poor as well as rich, whom they ferry across, and for a beast four, which they undeservedly extort. Furthermore, their boat is small, made of a single tree trunk, scarcely big enough to accommodate horses; also, when you get in, be careful not to fall into the water by accident. You will have to draw your horse behind you by the bridle, outside the boat, through the water. On account of this, get into the boat with only a few passengers because if the boat is overladen with too many people, it will soon be in peril. Many times also, after receiving the money, the ferrymen take on such a throng of pilgrims that the boat tips over, and the pilgrims are killed in the water. Thereupon the ferrymen rejoice wickedly after seizing the spoils from the dead.

Then, beside the Port de Cize is the Basque country, with its capital Bayonne, beside the coast towards the north. The language of this country is barbarous, [the land] is wooded and mountainous, without any wine, bread or food for the body of any kind, but is blessed instead by apples, cider, and milk. In this area, that is Port de Cize, in the town called Ostabat, at St. Jean and St. Michel-Pied-de-Port, there are wicked toll-collectors, who will certainly end up in Hell. What they do, is advance upon the pilgrim with two or three clubs to extort an unfair toll by force. If anyone refuses to give in to their demands or give them the silver they want, they beat them with the clubs and tear the tax money from them by force, while even searching in their breeches. ... Although, in accordance with the rules they ought not to take tax from anyone except merchants, they wickedly demand it from pilgrims and all other travellers. Even when they are entitled, by custom, to demand four or six sous for a service, they take double, that is eight or twelve.

That is why we plead and pray *precipimus et exoramus* that, not only in the Episcopal seats of their country but also in the basilica of Santiago in full hearing of the pilgrims, a sentence of excommunication should be assiduously read out against these toll-collectors, as well as the King of Aragon and the other rich people who receive tribute from them, and all those collaborating with them ... It should be made known that these toll-collectors ought not, by whatever means, to levy any sort of toll against pilgrims, and the ferrymen ought correctly to ask only one *obol* for the crossing for two persons if they are rich, and, for a horse, only a *nummus*, and nothing at all from the poor. In addition, they ought to provide large enough boats for beasts and men to fit in easily.

[82.2] Ch. VII, p. 29. After this valley [Valcarlos] is found the land of Navarre, which abounds in bread and wine, milk and cattle. [*There follows a description of their dress*] ... These people, in truth, are unpleasantly dressed, and they eat and drink disgustingly. For in fact all those who dwell in the household of a Navarrese [master], servant as well as master, maid as well as mistress, habitually all eat their food mixed together from one pot, not with spoons but with their own hands, and they use only one cup for drinking. If you saw them eat you would think they were dogs or pigs. If you heard them speak, you would be think of the barking of dogs. For their speech is absolutely barbarous. They call God, *Urcia,* the Mother of God, *Andrea Maria,* bread, *orgui,* wine, *ardum,* meat, *aragui,* fish, *arraign,* house, *echea,* the master of a house, *iaona,* the mistress, *andrea,* the church, *elicera,* the priest, *belaterra,* which means 'fair earth', grain, *gari,* water, *uric,* king, *ereguia,* Saint James, *Iaona domne Jacue.*

[82.3] Ch. IX, p. 71. When we French people want to enter the basilica of the apostle, we go in from the north side. In front of this entrance, next to the road, is the hospice for the poor pilgrims of St James ...

[82.4] Ch. IX, p. 73. After the fountain is the parvis, as already stated, completely paved with stone, where the scallop shells, which are the badge of the blessed St James, are sold to pilgrims, and wine flasks, sandals, deerskin scrips, pouches, straps, belts and all sorts of medicinal herbs, and other spices, and lots of other things are for sale. There are money changers, and hotel keepers and ther are other merchants in the Street of the French [Via Francigena]. The parvis really is a stone's throw in length on either side.

[83] ORDERIC VITALIS – THE ECCLESIASTICAL HISTORY
Translated by M. Chibnall, courtesy of Oxford University Press.
Although this passage dates from after our period it is worth quoting to make the parallel with Anglo-Saxon wills which were made before departure and to show how pilgrim status continued to be abused.
Bk. III, p. 99. *Tancred of Hauteville* passed on the whole of his inheritance to his son Geoffrey and advised the others to seek their living by their strength and wits outside their native land. They separated and at various times travelled to Apulia, disguised as pilgrims with scrip and staff for fear of capture by the Romans. All of them prosper in one way or another and became Dukes and Counts in Apulia, or Calabria or Sicily.

[84] PETER OF BLOIS, TWELFTH CENTURY

Taken from W. L. Warren, *King John,* (1961), p. 23. Although later than our period, it portrays a life style on the road that had probably changed little.

When our courtiers had gone ahead almost the whole day's ride, the King would turn aside to some other place where he had, it might be, just a single house with accommodation for himself and no one else. I hardly dare say it, but I believe that in truth he took a delight in seeing what a fix he put us in. After wandering some three of four miles in an unknown wood, and often in the dark, we thought ourselves lucky if we stumbled upon some filthy little hovel. There was often a sharp and bitter argument about a mere hut, and swords were drawn for possession of a lodging that pigs would have shunned.

BIBLIOGRAPHY

I have not attempted to provide a list of all the works that could have a bearing on the subject: the result would be so vast as to be a hindrance. Some texts exist in a number of editions and some have been translated several times. I have confined my list to the works that were used in preparing this book and the reader who wants to go beyond it is referred to Professor Simon Keynes' comprehensive and invaluable *Anglo-Saxon England: a bibliographical handbook for students of Anglo-Saxon history*, periodically updated, the latest edition being issued in 2005. That includes all English and many relevant continental sources.

Adam of Bremen, *The History of the Archbishopric of Hamburg-Bremen*, trans. F.J. Tschan (Columbia U.P. 1959).

Adamnan, *De Locis Sanctis,* D. Meehan (ed.) (Dublin 1958)

Alcuin: the bishops, kings and saints of York, P. Godman (ed.) (1982).

Allott S., *Alcuin of York* (York 1974)

Anderson G.K., *The Literature of the Anglo-Saxons* (Oxford 1991)

Anglo-Saxon Chronicles, trans. M. Swanton (2000).

Archibald M., 'Anglo-Saxon and Norman lead objects with official coin types' in Vince A., *Aspects of Saxo-Norman London, II - Finds and environmental evidence* (1989)

Attenborough F.L., *The Laws of the earliest English kings* (Cambridge 1922).

Barlow F., *Edward the Confessor* (1989).

Barlow F., *The English Church* (1979).

Bede, History of the Abbots, in D.H. Farmer, *The age of Bede* (Penguin Books 1983).

Bede, *The Ecclesiastical History of the English People,* trans. L. Sherley-Price (Penguin Books 1990).

Biddle M., 'Felix Urbs Wintonia: Winchester in the Age of Monastic Reform, in D. Parsons (ed.), *Tenth Century Studies* (1975).

Birch W.G. de Grey, *Cartularium Saxonicum* (1885-99).

Birch W.G. de Grey, *Vita Haroldi, the romance of the life of Harold , king of England* (1885).

Blair John, *Anglo-Saxon Oxfordshire* (Stroud 1994).

Liber Monasterii de Hyda, E. Edwards (ed.) (Rolls 1866) [Book of Hyde].

Boswell J., *The Journal of a Tour to the Hebrides* (Penguin Books 1984).

Bosworth J., *King Alfred's version of the compendious history of the world by Orosius* (1858).

Boutflower D.S., *Life of Ceolfrid, Abbot of Wearmouth and Jarrow* (Darlington 1912).

Brook C., *Europe in the Central Middle Ages 962-1154* (1975).

Brooke Z.N., *The English Church and the Papacy* (Cambridge 1952).

Brooks N., *The early history of the church of Canterbury* (1984).

Brown R. A., *The Norman Conquest of England* (Boydell rpr. 1995).

Browne G.F., *Alcuin of York* (1893).

Cameron K., *English Place Names* (1st ed. 1969).

Campbell, Alistair, *The Chronicle of Æthelweard* (1962).

Casinensis Chronica, W. Wattenbach (ed.) MG. SS. VII (1846).

Clark J.M., *The Abbey of St Gall* (1926).

Coen M., 'Legende et miracles du Roi S. Richard', *Analecta Bollandiana* xlix (1931).

Colgrave B., *The Life of St Gregory the Great by a monk of Whitby* (1968).

Colgrave B., *The Life of St Wilfrid by Eddius Stephanus* (Cambridge 1985).

Cox D.C., *The Chronicle of Evesham Abbey* (Evesham 1964).

Dales D., *St Dunstan, saint and statesman* (Cambridge 1988).

Davis R., *The Lives of the Eighth century Popes* [Liber Pontificalis], (Liverpool 1992).

Davis R., *The Lives of the ninth century Popes* [Liber Pontificalis] (Liverpool 1995).

Dozy R.P.A., *Recherches sur l'histoire et la litterature de l'Espagne* (Leiden 1881).

Duckett E.S., *Alcuin, friend of Charlemagne* (1951)

Duemmler E.L., Alcuini – *Carmina* (MGH Poetae Medii Aevii I)

Duemmler E.L., [Alcuin] *Epistolae Karolini Aevi II* (MGH 1895).

Dugdale W., *Monasticon Anglicanum* (Caley (ed.) 1817).

Eadmer, *a history of recent events in England* [Historia Novella], trans. G. Bosanquet (1964).

Ehrwald R., *Aldhelmi Opera*. MGH Auctorum Antiquissimorum XV, Berlin 1919.

Einhard, *The life of Charlemagne*, trans. S.E. Turner (Ann Arbor, Michigan 1966).

Ellis-Davidson H.R., *The Viking Road to Byzantium* (1976).

Emerton E., *The Letters of Boniface* (Columbia U.P. 1940).

Encomium Emmae, trans. A. Campbell *(Royal Historical Society (1949).*

Farmer D.H., *The Oxford Dictionary of Saints* (Oxford 1979).

Finberg H.P.R., *Early Charters of Wessex* (Leicester 1964).

Finberg H.P.R., *The Early Charters of the West Midlands* (Leicester 1961)

Foulke W. Dudley, *Paul the Deacon* (1974).

Fulford M., 'Byzantium and Britain: post Roman Mediterranean imports' *Medieval Archaeology* 33.

Ganshof F., 'Sur les Portes de Provence du VIII au X siecle', *Revue Historique* clxxxiii. 1.

Garrison M., Nelson J.L., Tweddle D., *Bishops, Alcuin and Charlemagne* (York 2001)

Gelling M., *Early Charters of the Thames Valley* (Leicester 1979).

Gerson P. et. al (eds), *The Pilgrim's Guide to Santiago de Compostella* (1998).

Gervase of Canterbury, *The historical works,* W. Stubbs (ed.) (Rolls Series 1879-80).

Gibson M., *Letters of Lanfranc* (1979).

Goscelin, *Historia translationis S. Augustini episcopi Anglorum Apostoli* (PL 155 13-46).

Gougaud L., 'Sur les routes de Rome et sur le Rhin avec les 'peregrini' insulaires' *Révue d'histoire ecclesiastique* 29 (1933).

Grainge C & G, 'The Pevensey Expedition: brilliantly executed plan or near disaster?', in S. Morillo (ed.), *The Battle of Hastings* (Boydell, 1999).

Gregorii Abbatis Trajecti Vita, auct. Liugero, O. Holder-Eggar (ed.), MG SS. XV. I (1887).

Gregory of Tours, *The Glory of the Confessors* trans. Raymond van Dam (Liverpool 1988).

Gregory of Tours, *The history of the Franks*, trans. Lewis Thorpe (Penguin Books 1974).

Gregory of Tours, *The Glory of the Martyrs,* trans. Raymond van Dam (Liverpool 1988).

Grierson P., 'A visit of Earl Harold to Flanders in 1056', *English Historical Review* XL (1936).

Grierson P., 'Grimbald of St Bertin', *English Historical Review* 55 (1940).

Guide du Pèlerin de Saint-Jacques de Compostelle, J. Vielliard (ed.) (Macon 1978).

Gwynn A, 'Ireland and the Continent in the eleventh century', *Irish Historical Studies* VIII, no. 31, (March 1953).

Haddon A.W. and Stubbs W., *Councils and ecclesiastical documents relating to Great Britain and Ireland* (3 vols 1869-71).

Hamer, Richard, *A choice of Anglo-Saxon verse* (1970).

Hart C., *The Early Charters of Eastern England,* (Leicester 1966).

Hare M, Abbot Leofsige of Mettlach: an English monk in Flanders and upper Lotharingia in the late Cx., (*Anglo-Saxon England* 33), 109-144.

Hart C.R., *Early Charters of Northern England and the north midlands* (1975).

Harvey P.D.A., *The history of topographical maps* (1980).

Hay G., 'Pilgrims and the Hospice', The English Hospice in Rome, (*The Venerabile* May 1962).

Hefele C.J., *Histoire des Conciles* (Paris 1907ff).

Hessels J.H., *A late eighth-century Latin Anglo-Saxon Glossary preserved in the library of Leiden University* (Cambridge 1906).

Higham N.J., *The Kingdom of Northumbria AD 350-1100* (Stroud 1993).

Hill D. and Worthington M., *Offa's Dyke* (Stroud 2003).

Hill D., *An atlas of Anglo-Saxon England* (Oxford 1981).

Holder-Egger O., *Libellus Miraculorum* (Mon. Bertiniana Minora, MG SS XV.I).

Holland L.B., *Traffic Ways through France in the Dark Ages 500-1150* (Allentown 1919).

Jaffé P., *Regesta Pontificum Romanorum* (Leipzig 1885-8).

John of Worcester, *The Chronicle of John of Worcester,* trans. R.R. Darlington and P. McGurk (Oxford 1995).

Jones T., *Brut y Twysogyon or the Chronicle of the Princes* (Cardiff 1952).

Kemble J., *Codex Diplomaticus Aevi Saxonici* (1839-48).

Keynes S, 'Anglo-Saxon entries in the Liber Vitae of Brescia', J. Roberts and J.L. Nelson (eds), *Alfred the Wise* (1997)

Kleinclausz A., *Alcuin* (1948).

Krautheimer R., *St Peter's and Medieval Rome* (Rome 1985).

Krusch B., *Vita Genovefae* (MG SSRM 3).

Lamb J.W., *The Archbishopric of Canterbury* (1971).

Landon L., *The itinerary of Richard I* (Pipe Roll Society, NS 13. 1935.

Lauer P.H., *Annales de Flodoard* (Paris 1905).

Lawson M.K., *Cnut* (1993).

Levillain L., *Correspondence de Loup de Ferrières* (Paris 1927-35).

Levi-Provencal E., *Histoire de l'Espagne Musulmane* (Paris 1950).

Levison W., *England and the continent in the eighth century* (rpr. Oxford 1995).

Lewis A.R., *Naval power and trade in the Mediterranean 500-1100* (1951).

Liber Eliensis, E.O. Blake (ed.) (1962).

Liber Eliensis: a history of the Isle of Ely from the seventh to the twelfth centuries trans. J. Fairweather (2005).

Llewellyn P., *Rome in the Dark Ages* (1993).

Lopez R. and Raymond I.W., *Medieval Trade in the Mediterranean World* (Columbia UP 1990).

Lopez R., *The tenth century* (New York 1959).

Loyn H. and Percival J., *The Reign of Charlemagne* (1975).

Lunt William E., *Financial relation of the Papacy with England to 1327* (Cambridge, Mass. 1939).

Macray W.D., *Chronicon Abbatiae de Evesham* (Rolls series 1863).

Macray W.D., *Chronicon Abbatiae Ramesiensis* (Rolls Series 1886).

Matthews S, 'Archbishop Plegmund and the Court of King Alfred', *Journal of the Chester* Archaeological Society, 7 (1999).

Matthews S., 'From Chester to Rome: an early medieval journey', *Trans. Lancashire and Cheshire Antiquarian Society* 94 (1998).

Matthews J.S., 'Life on the Road in tenth century France', *Medieval Life* 10 (1998).

Matthews S., 'The Construction and content of the Vita Haroldi, Gale R Owen-Crocker, *King Harold II and the Bayeux Tapestry* (Boydell 2005).

McCormick M, *Origins of the European Economy: communications and Commerce, AD 300-900* (Cambridge 2001)

Mellows W.T., *The Peterborough Chronicle of Hugh Candidus* (Oxford 1949)

Middleton N., 'Early Medieval Port Customs, tolls and controls on foreign trade' *Early Medieval Europe* 13 (2005).

Migne J.P., *Patrologia Latina* (1844-1904).

Mitchell R.J., *The Spring Voyage* (1964).

Moore W.J, *The Saxon Pilgrims to Rome and the Schola Saxonum* (Friburg 1937).

Nelson J.L. (ed. and trans.), *The Annals of St Bertin* (Manchester 1991).

Nelson Lyn H., *The Chronicle of S. Juan de la Pena* (Philadelphia UP 1991).

Notker, *The Life of Charlemagne*, trans. Lewis Thorpe (Penguin 1969).

Ohler N., *The medieval traveller* (Boydell 1989).

Orderic Vitalis, *the Ecclesiastical History*, trans. M. Chibnall (Oxford 1969-81).

Ortenberg V, *The English church and the Continent in the tenth and eleventh centuries* (Oxford 1992).

Ortenberg V., 'Archbishop Sigeric's Pilgrimage to Rome in 990', *Anglo-Saxon England* 19 (1990).

Peters E., *Monks Bishops and Pagans* (Philadelphia 1975).

Piper P., *Libri confraternitatum Sancti Galli, Augiensis, Fabariensis*, MGH (Berlin 1984).

Raine J., *Historians of the Church of York* (Rolls Series 1879-94).

Regenos Graydon W., *The Letters of Lupus of Ferrières* (The Hague 1996).

Reinaud J.T., *Invasions des Sarrazins en France et de France en Savoie, en Piemont et en Suisse* (1832).

Renouard Y., *La Papauté à Avignon* (Paris 1954).

Reuter T., The Annals of Fulda (Manchester 1992).

Richer, *Histoire de France,* trans. R. Latouche (Paris 1937).

Robertson A.J., *Select Anglo-Saxon Charters* (Cambridge 1956).

Robertson A.J., *The laws of the kings of England from Edmund to Henry I* (Cambridge 1925).

Rollason D.W, *The Mildreth Legend, a study in early medieval hagiography in England* (Leicester 1982)

Sawyer P.H., *Anglo-Saxon charters, an annotated list and bibliography* (1968).

Scholz B.W., *Carolingian Chronicles* (Michigan UP 1970)

Schopp J.W. (ed.), *The Anglo-Norman Custumal of Exeter* (Oxford 1925).

Schwarzmaier J., *Lucca und das Reich bis zum ende des 11 Jahhunderts* (Tubingen 1972).

Sedgefield W., *King Alfred's version of the Consolation of Boethius* (1899).

Sherwani H.K., *Muslim Colonies in France, northern Italy and Switzerland* (Lahore 1964) [Translation of Reinaud].

Simeon of Durham, *A History of the Kings*, trans. J. Stevenson (Church historians 1853-8).

Simeon of Durham, *The History of the Church of Durham*, trans. J. Stevenson (Church Historians 1853-8).

Sitwell F.G., *St Odo of Cluny, being the life of St Odo of Cluny by John of Salerno and the Life of St Gerald of Aurillac by St Odo* (1958).

Smyth, Alfred P., *The Medieval Life of Alfred the Great* (2002) [Asser's Life].

Springer O., 'Medieval Pilgrim routes from Scandinavia to Rome', *Medieval Studies* 12 (1950)

Stancliff C., 'Kings who opted out', in P. Wormald (ed.), *Ideal and Reality in Frankish* and Anglo-Saxon Society (1983).

Steinmeyer E. and Sievers E., *Die Althocdeutsche Glossen* (Berlin 1922).

Stenton F.M., *The early history of the Abbey of Abingdon* (rpr. Stamford 1989).

Stevenson W.H., *Early Scholastic Colloquies,* (Oxford 1929).

Stubbs W., *Memorials of St Dunstan* (Rolls series 1874).

Sturdy D., *Alfred the Great* (1995).

Swanton M., *Three Lives of the last Englishmen* (1984).

Talbot C.H., *Anglo Saxon Missionaries in Germany* (1954).

Thomas C., *Celtic Britain* (1986).

Thorpe B., *The homilies of the Anglo-Saxon church, II, Ælfric's Catholic Homilies* (1846).

Tommasini A.A., *Irish Saints in Italy* (1937).

Tyler J.E., *The Alpine Passes. The middle ages (962-1250)* (Blackewell, Oxford 1930).

Vasiliev A.A., *The Russian Attack on Constantinople in 860* (Cambridge, Mass 1946).

Vita Edwardi Regis, (The life of King Edward), F. Barlow (ed. and trans.) (1962).

Vita Egwini, Mabillon (ed.), A.A.S. S. O.S.B., saec III 330-8.

Vita S. Vulmari, auct. Anon, AA SS Boll V July.

Waite R.G., Paul the Deacon, *Historia Langobardum*, MGH SS Rerum Langobardum (1883).

Warren W.L., *King John* (1961).

Webb D, *Pilgrims and Pilgrimage in the Medieval West,* (2001).

Whitelock D., *Anglo-Saxon Wills* (Cambridge 1930).

Whitelock D., *English Historical Documents*, vol I, *c.* 500-1042 (2nd ed 1979).

Whitelock, D., Brett M, and Brooke C.N.L., *Councils and Synods with other documents relating to the English Church* I (1981).

William of Malmesbury, *History of the English Kings*, R.A.B. Mynors, R.M. Thompson and M. Winterbottom (Oxford 1998).

William of Malmesbury, *History of the kings of England*, trans. J Stevenson (Church Historians 1853-8).

William of Malmesbury, *The Early History of Glastonbury*, trans. J. Scott (Boydell 1981).

William of Malmesbury, *De gestis Pontificum Anglorum*, ed. N.E.S.A. Hamilton (1870).

William of Malmesbury, *Deeds of the Bishops of England*, trans. D. Preest (Boydell 2002).

Williams G., 'Mercian Coinage and Authority', M. P. Brown and C. A. Farr (eds), *Mercia, an Anglo-Saxon Kingdom in Europe* (2001).

Wright T., *Early Travels in Palestine* (1848).

INDEX OF TRAVELLERS

Both this index and the index of places are selective. I have tried to identify those people and places whose mention is significant for the argument. I have included people who made the journey to Rome or a comparable one, or whose accounts shed light upon conditions, like Gregory of Tours or Lupus of Ferrières. Chroniclers are generally not mentioned as such, so that there is no entry for William of Malmesbury.

Two peculiarities should be noted. There are some variant spellings so that we have both Cnut and the older Canute. When quoting other peoples' translations, I have kept to their spellings. Second, in the index of places, there is no entry for Rome. This is simply because to do so would include virtually every page in the book.

INDEX OF PLACES